Lineberger Memorial

Library

Lutheran Theological Southern Seminary   Columbia, S. C.

"I WATCHED A WILD HOG EAT MY BABY!"

"I WATCHED A WILD HOG EAT MY BABY!"

A Colorful History of
TABLOIDS
and Their Cultural Impact

BILL SLOAN

Prometheus Books

59 John Glenn Drive
Amherst, New York 14228-2197

Published 2001 by Prometheus Books

Inquiries should be addressed to
Prometheus Books
59 John Glenn Drive
Amherst, New York 14228–2197
VOICE: 716–691–0133, ext. 207
FAX: 716–564–2711
WWW.PROMETHEUSBOOKS.COM

04 03 02 01   5 4 3 2

Library of Congress Cataloging-in-Publication Data

Sloan, Bill.
    I watched a wild hog eat my baby! : a colorful history of tabloids and their cultural impact / Bill Sloan.
        p. cm.
    Includes index.
    ISBN 1–57392–902–6 (alk. paper)
    1. Tabloid newspapers—United States. 2. Sensationalism in journalism—United States. I. Title.

PN4888.T3 S57 2001
071'.3—dc21
                                                            00–045878

Printed in the United States of America on acid-free paper

CONTENTS

AUTHOR'S NOTE

In October 1968, after completing a half dozen freelance reporting assignments for a New York company called Worldwide Features, I was shocked to receive an invitation to try out for a staff writing position at the infamous *National Enquirer*. As it turned out, Worldwide Features was merely a cover name used by the *Enquirer* in dealing with "legitimate" journalists like myself, who might otherwise have thought it beneath their dignity to write for the country's most notorious "rag."

At the time, I was an investigative reporter/feature writer for the *Dallas Times Herald*, then one of the largest afternoon dailies in the South, where I had worked for seven years and felt quite comfortable. I had helped cover the assassination of President John Kennedy and other major stories, won several writing and reporting awards, and was well-respected in my secure little corner of the world. I had no desire to leave Dallas, much less relocate to an area of the country that had always seemed alien—even hostile—to me. But when I heard what the *Enquirer* was willing to pay, I decided it would be foolish to turn down their offer of a free, all-expense-paid trip to the Big Apple, plus a hefty paycheck, for a week's tryout.

When I got there, I was pleasantly surprised to find that the *Enquirer* had moved away from the gory crime coverage that had been its stock-in-trade until a year or so earlier. It now specialized in upbeat human interest stories that were very similar to some of the stuff I did at the *Times Herald*. And instead of being a bunch of weirdos, the staff was mostly made up of other former daily editors and writers. To my amazement and that of all my friends and family, I ended up taking the job (tripling my Dallas salary in the process) and moving to Fort Lee, New Jersey, just five or six minutes from the *Enquirer* headquarters in Englewood Cliffs.

I seemed to have a knack for the kind of terse, breezy writing that was the *Enquirer*'s forté. Within a few weeks, I was regularly being handed the biggest and toughest writing assignments and occasionally being called to sit in on meetings with Generoso Pope himself, the owner and publisher of the paper. After just nine months on the job, I was promoted to the newly created position of chief writer, placed in charge of an eight-member writing staff, and given the responsibility of finding and hiring other writers. For the next nine months, I sat in on most of the weekly cover conferences in Pope's private office and had many opportunities to watch him in action and see firsthand how his mind worked. To this day, I believe Pope genuinely liked me, and while some of the things he did appalled me, I learned to respect his peculiar genius.

In August 1970, because of my rapid rise at the *Enquirer*, I was offered the job of editor in chief of Montreal-based Globe Communications, Inc., publishers of *Midnight* (now *Globe*), the *Enquirer*'s main rival in the emerging supermarket tabloid field. After several weeks of weighing my options, I decided to take it.

At the direction of Globe owner Mike Rosenbloom, I hired several other experienced U.S. journalists, and immediately undertook a total editorial makeover of *Midnight* to allow it to gain entry into the major chain stores. I was also in charge of the *National Examiner* and the rest of Globe's stable of publications. *Midnight* cofounder John Vader, whom I had replaced atop the editorial pecking order, worked directly under me, and despite a difficult situation, we became good friends.

Unfortunately, though, I and my hand-picked, high-paid associates did our job too quickly and too well. In less than six months, with the new-look *Midnight* being widely accepted by the supermarkets, Rosenbloom fired the whole lot of us (although a couple of the people I had brought in were eventually hired back, at lower salaries).

In March 1971, I returned to my old job at the *Times Herald*, but a year later, I found myself drawn back into the tabloid business. I was contacted by a professional headhunter who had been retained by Allied News Company in Chicago to find an editor with tabloid experience to give a new look and new direction to Allied's flagship paper, the *National Tattler*. Again, the combination of money and challenge proved too much to resist, and I accepted the offer.

From April 1972 until February 1975, I served as managing editor of the *Tattler*, drastically changed its appearance and content, and assembled what I believe was the most talented editorial staff in North America. It was only when the company changed owners and began sliding inexorably toward bankruptcy that I left and returned once more to daily newspapering.

Over the next twenty years, I maintained close contact with many of my old friends and associates in the tabloid industry, and, in fact, sold numerous freelance articles to the major supermarket papers. During this time, I declined several offers to return to the *Enquirer* staff.

Some of the tabloid journalists with whom I worked in the 1960s and 1970s are still active in the tabloid industry as it exists today, and several of them have helped tremendously in providing information for this book. I wish it were possible to recognize them here by name, but for their own protection, I can't do that. David Pecker, president and CEO of American Media, Inc., which now owns all six of the surviving tabloids, has given strict orders that no one in the company except himself may speak for publication on company matters. Indeed, one top editor has already lost his job for daring to let himself be quoted in the press.

I would never betray the loyalty of old friends, and this is why some of the sources quoted concerning current conditions in the tabloid industry couldn't be identified by name.

Because of the unique positions I occupied with three major tabloid organizations, my own knowledge and experiences have also been primary sources of information for this book. A number of the quotes attributed to Generoso Pope, for example, are either drawn from my own recollections or from recollections repeated to me by acquaintances at the *Enquirer*, many of whom are now dead. The same applies to some of the quotes attributed to Joseph and Robert Sorrentino of Allied News.

In a number of instances, particularly in chapters dealing with the events of the 1960s and 1970s, I have sometimes quoted myself and/or referred to myself in the third person, using a form of license employed by many other writers in the past. My purpose was not to conceal anyone's identity, but merely to avoid interjecting myself personally into the narrative. My only intention in doing this was to make the book more readable.

For more than thirty years, tabloid insiders have been saying, "Somebody ought to write a book that really tells the stories behind this crazy business." Well, with the help of a lot of people, that's exactly what I've tried to do. My thanks goes out to all who played a part in it, both those whose names appear in these pages and those who must remain anonymous.

Bill Sloan
Dallas, Texas
January 2001

PROLOGUE
HOW TABLOIDS ARE WRITTEN
FIRST THE HEADLINE, THEN THE STORY

During the mid-1970s, there was a dingy bowling alley bar at the corner of Diversey Avenue and North Pulaski Road on Chicago's northwest side. The place was called the Charm—a misnomer if there ever was one—but it offered two distinct advantages to the small group of tabloid journalists who came there after work on most weeknights. For one thing, the drinks were cheap. For another, it was only a half-block walk from the faceless gray building at 2717 North Pulaski that housed the editorial offices of Allied News Company, publishers of the *National Tattler*, *National Insider*, and *National News Extra*.

On Wednesday nights, the group usually confronted a minor crisis along with their drinks. For the first three days of each week, the top priority for Allied's thirty-five-member editorial staff was producing enough "socko" copy and photos to fill the *Tattler*, the company's flagship paper with an average circulation of about 600,000 a week. The next priority was finding two or three cover-worthy pieces for the *Insider*, which featured "hotter" and more celebrity-oriented content than the *Tattler* and sold a respectable 120,000 copies a week.

By quitting time on Wednesdays, these tasks had usually been accomplished. But that left *News Extra*, Allied's bottom-of-the-barrel entry in the tabloid market, which had to go to press on Friday morning. Ordinarily, nobody had the time or energy even to think about *Extra* until Wednesday night.

With the deadline looming and ideas scarce, it didn't help that there

11

was also virtually no budget for *Extra*. In the judgment of Allied's owners, the 25,000 copies it sold in a typical week to lunatic-fringe readers and campy college kids didn't justify spending any money on agency pictures or freelance articles. The idea was to stuff *Extra* with file photos (doctored as necessary), bizarre in-house columns, a few knockoffs from other papers, and cover stories concocted out of desperation, alcoholic fantasy, and whole cloth.

On one such Wednesday in the spring of 1974, another "editorial conference" was in full swing in a back booth at the Charm. Six Allied staff writers and editors crowded around a scarred formica table covered with bottles, glasses, and overflowing ashtrays. As the booze flowed, it spawned a brazen, berserk brand of creativity.

"What we need," said the managing editor of the *Tattler*, who was also responsible for *Extra*'s content, "is some kind of ongoing thing. Something we can keep going back to for weeks, maybe even months. One-shot ideas are fine in a pinch, but most of 'em don't have any shelf life. That's why we have to keep going through this same brainstorming shit every week."

"Why don't we just drag out one of the old classics?" suggested somebody who obviously wasn't listening very closely. "You know, like 'I Watched a Wild Hog Eat My Baby!'"

"But we just did that one again about a year ago, I think," somebody else said.

"No, no," another guy interrupted, "it wasn't a hog and a baby the last time. It was 'I Watched a Mad Cat Eat My Father!'"

"Well, so what? It's the same general idea."

"Hey, wait a minute." The managing editor banged his glass down with sudden exuberance. "I just got a great idea. It's the ultimate variation on the 'Wild Hog Ate My Baby' theme. It'll give us our main cover line for this week, plus a whole series of cover stories to come—just like I was talking about."

Silence descended on the booth for a moment. The others looked at him expectantly. "We're listening," somebody said.

"'Girl Raped by Abominable Snowman,'" the editor said. "That's our cover line for this week. Then, three or four issues from now, we can have another cover line that says something like, 'Docs Discover Girl Raped by Abominable Snowman Is Pregnant.'"

"Hey, that's pretty good," said one of the writers. "Then we can have another one in, say, six or seven months announcing the birth of the 'Abominable Snowbaby.'"

"Hell, we won't have to wait that long," the ME said, warming to the subject as he drained his glass. "Our readers won't know the difference. But the best part comes later—after this abominable snowkid gets a couple of months old. See, by then, I figure he'll already weigh seventy-five or eighty pounds and eat his weight in raw meat every day."

The articles editor next to the ME stifled a giggle. "Oh, Jesus," he said, "I think I can see what's coming next."

"Yeah, exactly," said the ME. He lit a cigarette, inhaled deeply, and grinned. Everybody could tell he was really getting into it by now. "I mean, it's the perfect turnaround. This abominable snowbaby runs amok, breaks into a farmer's barnyard and attacks his hogs. He's chewing 'em to bits when the horrified farmer rushes out and sees the carnage."

"That's terrific," the articles editor howled. "I can see the headline now. Every college sophomore in America's gonna want a copy of this one. It'll be a collector's item in frat houses across the country."

One guy who was slightly drunker than the rest looked a little puzzled. "I don't get it," he said. "What's the headline gonna say?"

The articles editor turned to him and smiled blandly. " 'I Watched a Wild Baby Eat My Hog!' of course," he said. "What else *could* it say?"

The whole booth erupted into laughter, and the ME signaled the bartender for another round.

✳   ✳   ✳

Hard as it may be to believe, these same journalists, plus a hundred or so others who gravitated from the mainstream press to the *Tattler* and its main competitors—the *Enquirer* and *Globe* (originally *Midnight*)—between the late 1960s and mid-1970s, were destined to alter the media's whole approach to reporting the news in America. The changes accelerated in 1974, when Australian publishing magnate Rupert Murdoch's *Star* arrived on the scene. In the process, the tabs also redefined our very concept of who and what constitutes news—and how far we're willing to go to get it.

Without the tabloids' influence, for example, the average American would probably have had only a marginal awareness of Princess Diana on the night of her tragic death—and the money-hungry photographers who helped kill her might never have been chasing her in the first place. And the lurid sexual misadventures of a second-tier sportscaster like Marv Albert, whose face and name were virtually unknown outside the New York TV market, certainly wouldn't have made the front pages of daily newspapers from coast to coast. *People Weekly*, a tabloid in slick-magazine disguise, was created by Time-Life, Inc., to capitalize on the appeal of the tabs. And such popular TV shows as *Hard Copy, Inside Edition*, and *Entertainment Tonight* can accurately be described as "electronic tabloids."

"Princess Diana was on *People*'s cover dozens of times before her death," says Carlton Stowers, a longtime correspondent for the magazine who played a major role in its sensational coverage of such stories as the Oklahoma City bombing and the Branch Davidian siege at Waco, Texas. "I doubt that any of the tabloids featured her more often or followed her more relentlessly. Yet the tabloids' coverage was dismissed by most people outside the business as sleazy fabrication, while *People*'s was considered serious and responsible. The only real difference was packaging and public perception."

In fact, the success of the tabs, whose estimated circulation peaked at more than 12 million copies a week in the early 1980s, has forced the bulk of America's print and electronic media to embrace a much more sensational approach to the news. But the major tabs have often continued to do a better job with the more sensational stories. The best illustration of this was coverage of the O. J. Simpson case, in which an *Enquirer* reporting team set the pace for everyone and ended up being quoted as a primary source of information by daily newspapers everywhere.

Amazingly, the Allied News staffers who took part in those Wednesday-night *News Extra* "story conferences" were, without exception, mature, experienced newspeople. A few years or months earlier, most of them had worked for some of the most highly regarded news-gathering organizations in the country—the *Los Angeles Times, Chicago Today, Milwaukee Sentinel, Dallas Times Herald, Fort Worth Press, Indianapolis Times,* and Scripps-Howard News Service, among others.

As representatives of the "establishment" press, they had covered many of the major news events of the mid–twentieth century. Even as tabloid journalists, they spent the bulk of their time writing, editing, and researching serious, no-nonsense articles on medicine, science, government, social issues, unexplained phenomena, and, of course, celebrities. Among them, they had won numerous journalistic awards. At least one *Tattler* writer had been awarded a Pulitzer Prize and a couple of others had been nominated for journalism's most coveted honor.

The majority of these journalists had been lured away from the traditional press by one overriding factor—money. At the time, most Americans pictured tabloids as being thrown together in somebody's garage by a few weirdos and junkies who worked for beer money and cigarette change. When the first national tabloids surfaced in the mid-1950s, this image was fairly accurate, but as time went on, everything changed.

In trying to get their products into the nation's supermarkets, tabloid publishers soon realized they had to improve those products. One obvious way to accomplish this was by hiring at least a few top-notch writers and editors. They also quickly learned that no capable veteran journalist was willing to leave, say, the *Chicago Tribune* for the *Tattler* or the *New York Daily News* for the *National Enquirer* unless it meant a fat pay raise. By the early 1970s, to the dismayed disbelief of the rest of the print media, *Enquirer* salaries were the highest paid by any paper or magazine in the country, and other tabloid publishers were being forced to follow suit.

The men and women who produced the *Tattler, Enquirer, Globe,* and *Star* during this era were among the most talented, imaginative, and hard-working journalists in America—and they were compensated accordingly. Starting salaries at the major tabs were up to twice what journeymen reporters and editors were making at most major dailies, and the chance for rapid advancement into editorial management made the tabs even more financially attractive. (In the space of eighteen months, one veteran feature writer went from an annual salary of less than $9,000 at a daily newspaper to a $35,000-a-year position as a tabloid editor. It took another just eight years to go from subsistence-wage reporter on an obscure Scottish daily to the $400,000-a-year editorship of the *Enquirer.*)

The big bucks help explain why many tabloid journalists were routinely able to shift gears between out-and-out trash and serious reportage. One day they were inventing bogus stories for *News Extra* (or the *Enquirer*'s more successful but equally hoked-up companion paper, *Weekly World News*) or even grinding out soft-core porn for the *National Bulletin*, one of *Globe*'s salacious fellow-travelers. The next day they were interviewing real people, writing legitimate articles, and striving mightily for documentation and credibility.

Another reason they were able to do this was that, despite the ethical questions raised by their gear shifting, these journalists had rediscovered a basic truth about their profession. They recognized early on what William Randolph Hearst had figured out eighty years earlier and what practically every TV news executive and major-daily editor realizes today—what qualifies as "hot news" has only the sketchiest relationship to pure information. For all their lofty pretenses, today's mainstream media are essentially just another branch of show biz. The tabloidists understood this at a time when most journalists either didn't or wouldn't admit it. They also understood that the *Tattler, Enquirer,* and *Globe* represented an entirely different, unrelated genre than *News Extra, Weekly World News,* and *Bulletin*—something much of the public still doesn't comprehend.

Tabloid journalists in the 1960s and 1970s became the first among their profession since World War II—at least in this country—to take a questioning, aggressive, often adversarial approach to government and other major forces that control our society. Long before the downfall of Richard Nixon shook the mainstream media out of its lethargic naïveté, the tabs were telling their readers how secretive, scheming, wasteful, and willful the nation's power brokers could be.

Watergate and subsequent government scandals proved how right they were. The period since Watergate has been called the "Age of Endless Exposure," and this is an apt description. Supermarket tabloids led the way into this age, digging in celebrities' garbage and dogging the heels of the famous and notorious wherever they went. The tabloids hit the zenith of their popularity and profitability between the mid-1970s and the late 1980s, but the time came when the public's mounting thirst for exposé-style journalism outgrew the tabs' ability to satisfy it.

The supermarket papers, after all, only came out once a week, and in a rapidly shrinking world where news could circle the globe in seconds, new scandals and horrors were erupting by the hour, sometimes by the minute. In this supercharged news environment, the mainstream press could deliver doses of sensation and shock every day, and television could supply it instantly or endlessly—or both—as circumstances dictated.

At this point, the mainstream media simply "out-tabloided" the tabloids. By the last years of the twentieth century, most popular magazines and many metropolitan newspapers and major TV news operations had, in essence, become tabloids themselves, leaving the supermarket papers to sift through the leftovers or ballyhoo lesser scandals.

Now there's the Internet, and the lengths to which it may carry shock and sensationalism can scarcely be comprehended, much less accurately predicted. But future historians may recognize the "Age of the Supermarket Tabs" for what it actually was: the strongest influence of the past hundred years on the overall direction and philosophy of America's mass media.

In the following chapters, you'll learn why it happened, how it happened, and who made it happen. In a broader sense, you'll also learn how the supermarket tabloids have affected you—even if you've never so much as picked one up on your way through the checkout line.

ONE
SPICING UP THE NEWS
THE EVOLUTION OF SENSATIONALISM

Ever since the invention of movable type and the printing press five and a half centuries ago, people have been clamoring for "news," and for much of that time, journalists have been arguing among themselves about just what "news" is or isn't—and what it should or shouldn't be.

In the process, an endless conflict has developed between two divergent schools of thought within what we now call the journalistic profession. One school believes in covering the news with scrupulous dignity, weighty seriousness—and a great many dull stories. The other school has often thumbed its nose at convention and civility, and catered shamelessly to baser human instincts. Journalists of this persuasion are seldom averse to tweaking the facts a bit or leaving out a few bothersome details to "liven up" the news and get their readers more emotionally involved.

The *New York Times*, with its lofty credo of "All the News That's Fit to Print" and its insistence on referring to every serial rape-murderer as "Mr." amply typifies the philosophy at one end of the spectrum. Such flagrant fabrications as *National News Extra* and, more recently, *Weekly World News* represent the opposite end. The rest of today's print media fall somewhere in between.

The common folk of the Western world, however, have never had much difficulty deciding what brand of news they prefer. Given the chance, they've invariably chosen shipwrecks over shipping notices, crime and carnage over commodity futures, and whorehouse raids over wholesale price indexes. For them, the more shocking the news, the better.

Some intuitive publishers, editors, reporters, and writers have grasped all this since printing began. For the better part of two centuries, they've learned to structure their papers around a couple of basic, undeniable truths about the news business: (1) In its most socially powerful and financially successful form, journalism is at least as much about playing on the reader's emotions as about disseminating information. (2) The best way to sell lots of papers is by entertaining the masses, not by enlightening them.

These are the same precepts that those *News Extra* staffers in Chicago came to understand so well—and practice so adeptly—in the mid-1970s. But they were far from the first to discover them. No single factor has played a bigger role in the way today's news media gather and display the news than the public's timeless desire to be horrified, outraged, amazed, scandalized, amused, infuriated, and titillated (not necessarily in that order).

This lust for sensation predates by many centuries the appearance of the first newspaper in Germany in 1609. It can be found in the bloodcurdling ballads sung by wandering balladeers in the sixteenth century, the crowds that flocked to public beheadings in the Middle Ages, the gruesome "games" of ancient Rome, and all the way back to prehistoric times.

Clearly, then, sensationalism wasn't invented by the modern press, much less the architects of the supermarket tabloids. What the tabs did do, though, over the almost half century between the mid-1950s and the late 1990s, was add an irresistible new flavor to it—one so delectably irreverent and seductively spicy that a vast segment of the reading public became addicted to it.

Because of this addiction, neither school of American journalism will ever be the same again.

* * *

If today's print and electronic media suddenly reverted to presenting the news in as bland and boring a manner as it was presented in the early 1800s, most people would simply ignore it—just as they did then. It wasn't until the 1830s that the public was first introduced to sensational crime reports and bizarre "human-interest" articles, and ordinary citizens started buying and reading newspapers in significant numbers.

Benjamen Day's *New York Sun* and James Gordon Bennett's *New York Herald* were the first American dailies aimed less at upper-class businessmen and politicians than at an audience of semiliterate, urban working people. Up until that time, newspapers had generally been too expensive for most working-class readers, and circulation was largely confined to the wealthy.

The *Sun* and *Herald* gave birth to what became known as the Penny Press, because they were the nation's first papers to sell for one cent per copy, compared to six cents for most other papers of the period. If that sounds like a negligible difference, consider that in 1830, six cents was roughly half a day's pay for a common laborer. Translated into current economic terms, this is the equivalent of today's six-dollar-an-hour worker paying twenty-four dollars for a copy of his local paper—something that's not likely to happen today or any other time.

On this same scale, of course, an 1830 penny would amount to about four dollars now—still a high price—but the journalists who produced the "penny dreadfuls" gave the masses some thrills and chills for their money that couldn't be found anywhere else. Present-day readers would likely find those penny papers as dull as dirt, but at the time, they were the hottest things going. They introduced the term "sensationalism" to our vocabulary to describe their concept of presenting news, and it's been evolving ever since.

The low price and high-octane content of the Penny Press proved a dynamic combination. In just over a decade, U.S. daily newspaper circulation jumped from about 80,000 to over 300,000—not because the public was suddenly more literate or eager for edification but because of the same morbid curiosity and primitive instincts that draw people to fatal fires, grisly accidents, or carnival freak shows. The gruesome, the grotesque, the forbidden, the depraved—the *unthinkable*—have always had tremendous dark appeal, and devotees of the second school of journalism gradually realized how to capitalize on it.

In 1883, a half century after the advent of the Penny Press, Joseph Pulitzer took the next major step in the evolution of sensationalism when his New York *World* introduced "yellow journalism" to the nation. Essentially, it was the same fare offered earlier by Day and Bennett, except that it was now presented in a far more exciting, provocative, melodramatic way.

The *World* thrived on lurid accounts of murder and mayhem—the bloodier and more heinous the crime, the more space it commanded—and fleshed out its reports with vivid descriptions and crude but colorful dialogue. Consider, for example, a *World* story on the murder of a tenement dweller named Kate Sweeney. The writer first describes a young female courtroom witness as resembling "a hard, blighted peach," then quotes directly from her testimony:

> "What was she [the victim] doing in the cellar?"
> "How the ____ should I know? Mabbee she went down there to git some peace."
> "You're a liar," said another woman who had her front teeth knocked out and whose voice hissed viciously through the apertures.

Pulitzer himself described the *World*'s style of reporting as "original, distinctive, dramatic, romantic, thrilling, unique, curious, quaint, humorous, odd [and] apt to be talked about." In essence, it was precisely the same formula that would sweep the supermarket tabloids to the apex of their popularity and profitability a century later.

But even more than Pulitzer, it was William Randolph Hearst who set a lasting standard for the supermarket tabs to follow. When Hearst moved east from California and bought the struggling *New York Journal* in 1895, he began pouring millions into it in a no-holds-barred campaign to overtake and surpass the *World* in circulation. In his obsessive pursuit of this goal, Hearst pushed sensationalism to new and hitherto unexplored heights—or depths, depending on one's perspective. As a by-product of this campaign, he managed to become the only American newspaper publisher ever to start a major war. He got more than a little help from Pulitzer, but when hostilities with Spain broke out in 1898, it was Hearst's *Journal* that inquired in a self-congratulating front-page headline, "How Do You Like Our War?"

Hearst also perfected the journalistic penchant for blowing one's own horn to a fine science. As adept as the supermarket tabs later became at this game, they never came close to matching his gift for self-praise. In a back-patting editorial on the first anniversary of his purchase of the *Journal*, he exulted:

> What is the explanation of the *Journal*'s amazing and wholly unmatched progress? . . .
> No other journal in the United States includes in its staff a tenth of the number of writers of reputation and talent. It is the *Journal*'s policy to engage brains as well as to get the news, for the public is even more fond of entertainment than it is of information.

When George Arnold, a perceptive Hearst reporter, helped establish the identity of a decapitated murder victim whose head was missing—a revelation that led to the arrests of the man's former girlfriend and her new lover—a *Journal* headline trumpeted:

MURDER MYSTERY SOLVED BY THE JOURNAL

Hearst also capitalized on the perverse pleasure that the "common herd" finds when the wealthy, powerful, and famous get knocked off their pedestals and reduced to the same vulnerable, foolish, all-too-human state as the rest of us. Whether the focal point happens to be the stereotypical pompous rich man slipping on a banana peel or a president of the United States sexually disgracing himself before the world, the mass reaction is roughly the same: "Thinks he's better than the rest of us, huh? Well, by God, that'll show him!"

More than seven decades before Teddy Kennedy's misadventure at Chappaquiddick and Jackie Onassis's transformation from martyr's widow to fallen angel—courtesy of the supermarket tabs—Hearst was proving his aptitude at character assassination. He repeatedly assailed Presidents Grover Cleveland and William McKinley as gutless tools of the superrich and cowards who ignored Spanish atrocities in Cuba.

As Hearst and those who followed in his footsteps well knew, one of the keys to successful sensationalism is to accentuate the negative. To most people, no news may be good news, as the old saying goes, but for the sensationalist, just the opposite is true—good news is no news. A positive story may arouse emotions, but it has no shock value. On the other hand, it's easy to sensationalize negative stories, thanks to a shadowy side of human nature that invariably tends to suspect the worst about any person or situation. Confirming such suspicions is a major element of sensationalizing the news.

After Spain's defeat, for example, the *Journal* launched an all-out round of assaults on Secretary of War Russell Alger, whom it branded a heartless mass-murderer. A few of the headlines on Hearst-concocted stories vilifying Alger included these:

DYING HEROES SHIPPED TO HOSPITAL BY FREIGHT

FOOD ROTS ON TRANSPORTS WHILE SOLDIERS STARVE

STORY OF HORRORS HOURLY GROWS WORSE

Decades later, each of the major supermarket tabloids had an ongoing category of stories loosely styled "government waste/stupidity/corruption/coverup" which they tried to fill in every issue. If a story already had substantial shock value, putting a negative spin on it got the reader even more emotionally involved. "Air Force Knows UFOs Exist" made a fairly arresting headline in itself, but adding the phrase "—And the Gov't Isn't Doing Anything About It!" made it even stronger.

The thought of space aliens watching us from the skies was terrifying to millions of Americans in the 1960s and 1970s, but the idea that the government was refusing to face the problem or concealing information about it was also infuriating to many people who instinctively despise and distrust those in power. Thus, one story could be milked for two basic negative emotions.

When a specific personality, rather than faceless "big government" in general, can be singled out for negative target practice, the effect on readers is often intensified. One of the *Journal's* more outrageous pieces of reportage, for example, concerned Teddy Roosevelt while he was police commissioner of New York City in the 1890s. In a story based on reckless rumors, Hearst accused TR of planning to attend a stag party where Ashea "Little Egypt" Wabe, the notorious exotic dancer of the Chicago World's

Fair, was to perform a totally nude belly dance. It was a charge the future president hotly denied, but as the supermarket tabs would prove repeatedly later, denials can sometimes be just as juicy as accusations.

"Hoist," as he was known among admiring New Yorkers, saved his "woist" for William McKinley, however. Between 1898 and 1901, Hearst aimed a withering, continuous barrage of negative fire at McKinley through the pages of the *Journal*. In editorial cartoons, he pictured presidential advisor Mark Hanna as the grossest imaginable monster, covered with dollar signs and leading McKinley around as a pygmy slave.

Hearst's attacks on McKinley were so unremittingly vicious, in fact, that when the president was mortally wounded by an assassin—who was erroneously reported to have a copy of the *Journal* in his pocket at the time of his arrest—Hearst feared the public would blame him directly.

"Things are going to be very bad," he muttered to one of his editors when he heard that McKinley had been shot.

In his first speech to Congress after assuming the presidency on McKinley's death, Teddy Roosevelt had some special harsh words for "the reckless utterances of those . . . in the public press [who] appeal to the dark and evil spirits of malice and greed, envy and sullen hatred."

There was little doubt about the object of Roosevelt's scorn. But in addition to referring to Hearst's merciless assaults on McKinley, TR may also have been remembering that earlier *Journal* "scoop" about Teddy and "Little Egypt."

✳   ✳   ✳

Along with politicians, Hearst also singled out show business celebrities and other famous figures for special attention, just as the national tabloids did later. One of Hearst's favorite ploys was to hire a well-known personality at an exorbitant fee to write or report on other famous people for the *Journal*. He engaged Mark Twain to cover the sixtieth anniversary of Queen Victoria's coronation. He assigned a former U.S. senator to cover the Corbett-Fitzsimmons heavyweight boxing match in Nevada. He sent celebrated artist Frederick Remington to Cuba to illustrate the massive conflict with the "barbaric Spanish ruffians" that Hearst had worked tirelessly to orchestrate and was now certain would soon begin.

After weeks of doing nothing in Havana, Remington wired Hearst:

> Everything is quiet. There is no trouble here. There will be no war. I wish to return.

Hearst wired back confidently:

Please remain. You furnish the pictures and I'll furnish the war.

When the U.S. battleship *Maine* blew up in Havana harbor of causes that remain a mystery even today, more than a century later, Hearst and the *Journal* got "their war." They got it despite the fact that no legitimate evidence ever linked Spain or its military forces in Cuba to the blast, which most historians now believe was simply an accident. When war was declared, the *Journal* celebrated it with a thundering four-inch-tall headline proclaiming:

NOW TO AVENGE THE MAINE!

In the words of Hearst biographer W. A. Swanberg: "Hearst's coverage of the *Maine* disaster still stands as the orgasmic acme of ruthless, truthless newspaper jingoism"—and even that was probably an understatement.

Yet there could have been no better role model for the founders of the early national tabloids than Hearst at his most outrageous and creative. Hearst taught the American public to accept, enjoy, and even admire blatant, heavy-handed sensationalism. Without his example and influence, the modern tabloids might never have happened at all, much less achieved the level of success they enjoyed for more than forty years. More significantly, the "tabloidization" of today's mainstream media and the subtle changes that have taken place in "responsible journalism" over the past quarter century would have been virtually impossible.

Probably not even Hearst could have predicted that the *New York Times* would one day be quoting the *National Enquirer* as a primary source of exclusive information on the O. J. Simpson murder case.

And if the heyday of the tabloids now appears to be fading away, the most obvious reason is that they've simply been out-sensationalized by their more serious minded, more "respectable" counterparts.

* * *

The word "tabloid" entered the English language innocently enough and with none of the scurrilous connotations that later attached themselves to it. In their original context, tabloids were merely papers whose pages were half the size of traditional "broadsheets." It was an innovation that made the paper easier to handle by commuters on crowded trolleys and subways.

The first tabloids appeared in London in the 1890s, where the concept was pioneered by Alfred C. Harmsworth (later Lord Northcliffe), founder of Britain's venerable and still phenomenally successful *Daily Mirror*. By this time, the trend toward sensationalism had already been accelerating on both sides of the Atlantic for more than sixty years.

The first American tabloid of any consequence was the *Daily Continent*, established in New York in 1891 by Frank A. Munsey. It was no match, however, for the Pulitzer and Hearst giants and soon vanished amid the sound and fury of the circulation war between the *Journal* and the *World*.

In the heat of this battle, Hearst had the gall to condemn Pulitzer as "a journalist who made his money by pandering to the worst tastes of the prurient and horror-loving [and] by dealing in bogus news." If there was ever a case of the pot calling the kettle black, this was it. Pulitzer *was* a sensationalist, but he was also, in many respects, an idealist who crusaded endlessly for the public good.

The man for whom the Pulitzer Prize, the most prestigious award in journalism, is now named was far removed from the day-to-day editorial operation of his newspapers (he also owned the *St. Louis Post-Dispatch*). He dictated the overall tone and sociopolitical posture of the *World* but, by and large, he let the professional editors and reporters who worked for him decide which stories to run and how to display them.

Hearst, on the other hand, was the epitome of the hands-on publisher. He undoubtedly had fewer scruples than Pulitzer, and his ethics were defined by whatever sold papers at the moment. But unlike his rival, he was always in the thick of the news-gathering operation, and his instincts for what working-class readers wanted were even sharper than Pulitzer's. He took a personal interest in every big developing piece of news, and he didn't care what it cost to get it. The *Journal* lost an estimated $8 million before it began to show a profit—so much that Pulitzer firmly expected it to go bankrupt any day. But thanks to Hearst's generous and fabulously wealthy mother, there was always plenty more money in reserve, at least during her lifetime.

Regardless of how he managed to do it, Hearst forever altered the style and course of America's media. Along with his disregard for truth and tradition, he pioneered such innovations as sports pages, comic sections, advice columns, and women's features. No figure in the history of newspapers was more despised by the industry's serious school and the national political establishment than Hearst. (One U.S. senator of the 1920s described Hearst's growing chain of papers as "the sewer system of American journalism.") But because of his influence, politicians from the White House on down feared his wrath.

Hearst's editor at the *Journal*, Arthur McEwen, was probably the first person to coin the term "gee-whiz emotion" to describe what the paper's writers were trying to evoke in their readers. Seventy-five years later, every staffer of every supermarket tabloid would be on constant lookout for these very same "gee-whiz" stories.

But neither Pulitzer nor Hearst was sold on the tabloid format, despite its demonstrated success in London. At Pulitzer's invitation, Harmsworth designed a tabloid version of the *World*, which was published on New Year's Day, 1901, and hailed as "the newspaper of the twentieth century." Circulation for the day jumped by more than 100,000 copies, but New York was generally unimpressed and, after that one issue, the *World* reverted to a broadsheet.

During World War I, Harmsworth met Capt. Joseph Medill Patterson, copublisher of the *Chicago Tribune*, who was on leave from the paper to serve in the U.S. Army. Harmsworth convinced Patterson that New York needed a tabloid daily of its own, and immediately after the war, Patterson and his partner at the *Tribune*, Col. Robert R. McCormick, took the Britisher's advice.

In June 1919, McCormick and Patterson published the first issue of the *Illustrated Daily News*, the first successful tabloid daily in North America, and this time New Yorkers ate it up. Predictably, journalism's serious school dismissed this half-sized upstart as a flash in the pan, but they were soon forced to change their tune. Within two years, the *Daily News* led all New York dailies in circulation with over 400,000. By 1924, it was selling 750,000 copies a day and claimed the nation's largest circulation. Before the end of the decade, the figure had hit an unheard-of 1.3 million at a time when sales of all other New York papers were standing still.

By the mid-1920s, Hearst had seen enough to jump belatedly onto the tabloid bandwagon. After changing the name of the *Journal's* morning edition to the *American*, he watched both its and the evening *Journal's* circulation turn stagnant. In 1924, he introduced New York to his own Americanized version of the *Mirror*, and set out to tear away at the *Daily News's* following in the same way that he'd undermined Pulitzer's *World* in the 1890s.

This time, though, he wasn't nearly as successful. Despite his best efforts, the *Mirror's* circulation stalled at 600,000 while sales and readership of the *Daily News* continued to climb.

Hearst promised at the time that the *Mirror's* aim would be "90 percent entertainment, 10 percent information—and the information without boring you." Despite many publishers' pretenses to the contrary, most working American journalists eventually accepted the basic validity of Hearst's philosophy. Many may still disagree with his percentages, but the vast majority came to realize that, like novelists, movie actors, recording artists, and professional athletes, journalists are part and parcel of the entertainment industry.

As the age of print has given way to an age of electronic media and multimillion-dollar-a-year anchor personalities, this has become truer than ever.

*   *   *

Hearst wasn't the only publisher intent on reaping part of the tabloid bonanza. Bernarr MacFadden, the flamboyant "king of physical culture" in the Roaring Twenties, was also intrigued by the runaway success of the *Daily News*. MacFadden had already discovered a publishing gold mine of his own with *True Story* magazine and other revealing periodicals, and he was eager for more.

In August 1922, MacFadden began testing the waters of the sensation-alism market with an oversexed weekly magazine called *Midnight*. It featured large pictures of almost-naked women and verged so closely on obscenity that its staff expected to be carted off to the police station after its first issue. All photos used to illustrate articles were of curvy models in sensuous poses wearing nothing or next to nothing. Headlines on the cover included: "Sold to the Devil—A Desperate Man's Pact with Satan"; "From the Underworld to Fifth Avenue"; "Daughter of a Murderer"; "Last Call for Thrills"; and "Don't Monkey with the Women." There wasn't a word of truth anywhere in the publication. Every story was a total fabrication.

His worried editors pleaded with MacFadden to tone down *Midnight*'s content, but as the weeks passed, and circulation soared, it grew even steamier. "We're going ahead with *Midnight* exactly as she is," MacFadden said defiantly. "In a couple of months, we'll be up to the *Saturday Evening Post*, and that's a nickel magazine. We're a dime."

Before that could happen, however, an agent for the New York Society for the Suppression of Vice came calling at the *Midnight* offices, armed with summonses for the entire staff. He agreed not to serve them in exchange for MacFadden's pledge to cease publication immediately and destroy all copies of the issue that had just come off the press.

"They wouldn't dare do that to a newspaper because of freedom of the press," MacFadden told his associates a short time later. "Anyhow, we've learned something. *Midnight* was just a rehearsal for a magazine pattern we can apply to the daily field."

Two years later, in 1924, MacFadden proudly unveiled his new magazine-style daily, the *New York Evening Graphic*, with this promise to his readers: "We intend to interest you mightily. We intend to dramatize and sensationalize the news and some stories that are not news."

Even the photos in the *Graphic* were phony—"cosmographs," MacFadden called them. He used them for such purposes as showing the wife in a notorious celebrity divorce case supposedly stripped to the waist in the courtroom, and the king of England scrubbing himself with a brush in the bathtub.

Some of its more diplomatic critics have described the *Graphic* as "the *True Confessions* of the newspaper world," but New Yorkers quickly found a more fitting nickname for MacFadden's blistering-hot creation. They called it the "Porno-Graphic," and with good reason.

Even today, more than seventy-five years later, the *Graphic* still represents the absolute nadir of daily journalism in America. And despite its founder's initial confidence, it proved a massive financial disaster for Mac-Fadden. Advertisers shunned the *Graphic* like the plague, and even tabloid readers eventually reached their limit when it came to the amount of gutter-level make-believe they could stomach. By the time the paper died in 1932, after costing MacFadden millions in losses, it had few mourners. But while it lasted, it constituted the raunchiest daily peep-show the nation had ever seen.

The *Mirror* fared somewhat better, although it never turned a profit for Hearst. He sold it in 1928, was forced to take it back in 1930, then managed to bolster circulation by stealing celebrity columnist Walter Winchell away from the *Graphic* and basically turning the *Mirror* into a daily gossip sheet. (It seems appropriate that, after the *Mirror* folded in 1963, many of its expatriates—including its last managing editor—found a home at the *National Enquirer.*)

Among them, though, the *Daily News, Mirror,* and *Graphic*—along with other daily tabloids that sprang up in Los Angeles, Chicago, and other cities—kept the 1920s roaring with their brazen brand of "jazz journalism." They avidly followed the violent careers of such notorious gangsters as Al Capone, Dutch Schultz, and Legs Diamond, but their most blatantly sensational crime coverage was reserved for ordinary people caught up in lurid murder cases. For example, in November 1926, the *Mirror* claimed to have found "new evidence" in a four-year-old double slaying in which a respected minister, the Rev. Edward Hall, and his church's choir leader, Eleanor Mills, had been found shot to death on an abandoned New Jersey farm.

The deaths were originally ruled suicides, but because of the *Mirror*'s relentless digging into the Hall-Mills case, the minister's grandmotherly widow and her two brothers were indicted for murder. More than two hundred reporters flocked to the small-town trial and filed more than 5 million words of copy from the scene. Unfortunately for the *Mirror*, the defendants were acquitted and later filed a libel suit against the tabloid. Such stories as the death of matinee idol Rudolph Valentino in 1926 and Charles Lindbergh's epic 1927 flight across the Atlantic were also milestones in the march of sensationalism.

These papers' insensitivity was matched only by their ingenuity. Case in point: In the spring of 1927, Mrs. Ruth Snyder and her corset-salesman boyfriend, Judd Gray, were convicted of killing Snyder's husband, and as Snyder's date with the electric chair neared, the rare spectacle of a woman being put to death sent the tabloid press into a feeding frenzy.

"Think of it!" blared the *Graphic* the day before the execution. "A woman's final thoughts just before she is clutched in the deadly snare that sears and burns and FRIES AND KILLS! Her very last words! Exclusively in tomorrow's *Graphic.*"

But the *Daily News* upstaged the *Graphic* and stunned even hardened tabloid readers the next day with a riveting front-page photo, obtained secretly by a staff photographer with a miniature camera strapped to his ankle, of Snyder being electrocuted in the death chamber at Sing Sing

Penitentiary. The picture was made at the instant the current surged through her body.

Not coincidentally, it was during this same period that a former Hearst advertising executive named William Griffin began publishing a new full-sized Sunday newspaper in New York. Although its birth received little fanfare in a city with a dozen other, much larger papers, the newcomer was bankrolled by Hearst, who used it as a sort of testing ground for new ideas. It's been said that the best of these ideas were usually adopted by Hearst's mass-circulation dailies, while the worst ones, unfortunately, often lingered at their point of origin.

The paper was called the *New York Enquirer*, and over the next quarter-century, it was destined to go through a series of less-than-impressive incarnations. In the 1930s, it adopted a pro-Nazi tone and espoused the cause of German-American unity. During World War II, it virtually vanished, then reemerged as a "sports paper" heavy on racing news and betting lines.

By 1952, when it was purchased by a young MIT graduate named Generoso Pope Jr., its circulation had dwindled to less than 17,000 and it had become, in Pope's own words, a "dumping ground for publicity agents and columnists who wrote for free and couldn't get their stuff printed anywhere else."

One of the first major alterations Pope made to his property was to scrap its traditional eight-column format and turn it into a tabloid. Chances are, it seemed like a small step at the time—perhaps just an attempt to give a worn-out perennial loser a bit of a facelift—but it proved to be a momentous change.

At the time, no one other than Pope himself could possibly have imagined that such an obscure little paper would become America's first national tabloid, much less that it would grow into the largest-selling weekly publication in the country. No one would have guessed that it would one day rank among the ten most profitable single items in the nation's supermarkets.

And certainly, no one would have dreamed that this ragtag sheet, along with the flock of imitators it inspired, would permanently change the way Americans relate to their news and newsmakers.

But it did. It did all that and more.

The evolution of sensationalism was about to take yet another major step, and America was about to discover a brand-new descriptive term for the most gut-wrenching brand of shock and horror.

It was, of course, the *National Enquirer*.

TWO
THE KID FROM MIT, AKA "THE GODSON"

Picture the young Al Pacino in the original movie version of *The Godfather*, and you have a fairly accurate image, circa 1950, of Generoso Paul Pope Jr., the father of the modern supermarket tabloid. He was clean-cut, fresh-faced, and twenty-three years old, armed with a recent engineering degree from the prestigious Massachusetts Institute of Technology, an engaging smile, and an abundance of connections—in both high and low places.

Much would later be made of the fact that Pope spent a short time after graduating from MIT in the service of the new Central Intelligence Agency, which had replaced the World War II–era Office of Strategic Services as the federal government's primary vehicle for espionage, black ops, and international intrigue.

It's a well-established fact that during this intense period of the cold war—also a time when a very hot war broke out in Korea—it wasn't unusual for the burgeoning CIA to offer jobs to promising young graduates of highly rated colleges and universities. By all accounts, Pope was only nineteen when he earned his degree, so he certainly qualified as a bright kid. Yet he also had glaringly obvious ties to the underworld, so his selection by the spy agency raises questions in itself.

There are conflicting reports on just how long he worked for the CIA. Some say he stayed with the agency for nearly a year; others say he left after only three or four months. In any case, his brief CIA stint came to represent the first threads in a shroud of mystery that would envelop the man for over three and a half decades. Today, more than a dozen years after his

29

death in 1988, Pope remains a singularly enigmatic figure, and the CIA connection is just one intriguing part of the puzzle surrounding him.

Pope described his work with the CIA as being "something called psychological warfare." He reportedly told some people that he quit the agency because he was simply "fed up with the bureaucracy" and never had any further dealings with it. Beyond these few comments, he never saw fit to elaborate. Maybe the experience taught him subtle secret methods of tapping into the minds of tabloid readers. It's also been suggested that the agency itself played some covert role in the founding and growth of the *National Enquirer* and maintained an ongoing interest in its potential as an organ of public disinformation and "brainwashing." No hard evidence has ever surfaced to support such allegations, however.

✳   ✳   ✳

Like Michael Corleone, Pacino's character in *The Godfather*, Pope was the youngest son of a poor Italian immigrant who came to this country as a teenager and attained great wealth and power while frequently operating on the shady side of the law.

Generoso Pope Sr., who arrived in New York aboard the S.S. *Madonna* in 1906, liked to recall in later years that he came ashore with just four dollars to his name. He found a job as a laborer with a Manhattan construction firm, Colonial Sand and Stone Company, and steadily worked his way up the corporate ladder to a management position. By the mid-1920s, after the company nearly went bankrupt and Pope worked out a plan to save it, he ended up owning it. It was a classic success story, but one with dark undertones.

Soon Generoso Sr. had a virtual monopoly on the city's sand and gravel business, thanks to well-placed friends at City Hall and a willingness to grease the palm of anyone who could help him. He routinely paid off those who awarded municipal contracts, then slipped more money under the table to union bosses to keep the work on schedule. The poor immigrant lad of twenty years earlier had parlayed his four dollars into millions and ranked among the most influential members of the city's Italian community. He and his wife, the former Catherine Richichi, were among the most socially prominent Italian Americans in the whole country. Meanwhile, though, Generoso Sr. was also plunging deeply into the maze of corruption and deal making that characterized New York politics of the period.

The heir to his name, Generoso Pope Jr., was born on January 13, 1927, only a few months after the *New York Enquirer* published its first issue. And from the beginning, he must have been the apple of his father's eye. Not only did the elder Pope wait to bestow his own name on the last of his three sons (the two older siblings were named Fortunato Robert Pope and Anthony John Pope), but he also reserved another special honor for Generoso Jr. He asked his close friend, Frank Costello, later one of the two top bosses of the New York Mafia family (the other being Charles "Lucky" Luciano), to serve as the infant's godfather. Costello graciously agreed.

The following year, Generoso Sr. bolstered his power and influence tremendously by buying *Il Progresso Italo-Americano*, the nation's largest Italian-language newspaper, for $2 million. He used it with ruthless efficiency to promote his own special interests and political allies. By now, Pope Sr. was one of the behind-the-scenes kingmakers in the cutthroat politics of the Big Apple. He wined and dined local judges at swank hotels and treated them to tickets to championship fights at Madison Square Garden. And whenever he needed a favor, he knew exactly who to ask.

In 1929, the elder Pope made a triumphal return trip to the small Italian village of his birth, but while he was in Italy, he committed what turned out to be a huge political blunder. Otherwise, with the money and clout he'd amassed—the power he wielded has been called "unprecedented"—he might have one day been a congressman or even mayor of New York.

His stature was now such that, during the Italian trip, he was granted a private meeting with Benito Mussolini and apparently was totally overwhelmed by the experience. He came back to the States loudly singing the praises of Il Duce and his fascists. Over the next decade, *Il Progresso* rarely missed an editorial opportunity to promote the bully-boy in Rome, and Generoso Sr. personally led a campaign to pressure President Franklin Roosevelt to stay on friendly terms with Mussolini. Even Italy's naked aggression against Ethiopia did nothing to change Pope's tune. It wasn't until 1941, when the United States was on the brink of war with Italy, that *Il Progresso* finally printed an editorial repudiating fascism.

Meanwhile, Generoso Sr.'s ongoing idolization of Mussolini, plus his chumminess with Frank Costello and other known gangsters, caused many respectable Italian Americans to turn against him and his paper, and his political strength gradually eroded. In the late 1930s, at about the same time Generoso Sr. was being photographed sitting between New York Governor Herbert Lehman and Lieutenant Governor Charles Poletti at a Columbus Day blowout, rumors linked Pope to the gangland-style murder of Carlo Tresca, an outspoken antifascist and known political foe of Pope's.

By this time, the elder Pope's relationship with high-ranking Mob figures had caught the attention of the FBI. Bureau investigators began compiling an extensive file on Generoso Sr., one that would eventually lead to federal racketeering charges being filed against him. But for as long as he lived, none of these trials and tribulations would keep the elder Pope from playing the role of munificent "big daddy" to his favorite son.

✳   ✳   ✳

All evidence indicates that Generoso Jr. was an exemplary student with an IQ ranking at or near genius level. He attended the exclusive Horace Mann School for Boys in Manhattan, where a friend and classmate was Roy Cohn, who would win notoriety in the 1950s as the acerbic right-wing counsel for Senator Joseph McCarthy's subcommittee on un-American activities.

When Gene, as he now liked to be called, finished up at MIT in 1946, he was still several months shy of his twentieth birthday, but his proud papa had expansive plans for him. Pope Sr. gave him the title of editor of *Il Progresso*, and also made him vice president of Colonial Sand and Stone, distinctions that irritated his older brothers, who had worked faithfully in the family businesses while Junior was off at college. Fortunato Pope (who preferred to be called "Fortune") had special reasons to feel aggrieved, since he'd been functioning as editor of the newspaper for quite some time and was now rudely displaced by his father in favor of his baby brother.

Young Gene looked to be on top of the world. In addition to being the boss at *Il Progresso*, he was also director of radio station WHOM, another family holding; honorary deputy police commissioner of the City of New York; and a member of the New York City Board of Higher Education. He owed those last two titles to his and his father's close friendship with Acting Mayor Vincent R. Impellitteri.

But at that point, the elder Pope died, and his death almost immediately spelled trouble for his annointed son. It thrust Gene into one of the most trying episodes of his life and cast a permanent shadow over his relations with his family. It also marked the beginning of a lifelong tightrope-walking act in which Pope cultivated and capitalized on his connections to the Mob while struggling not to alienate the strong anti-Mob faction within the Italian community.

The trouble apparently started because of Gene's connections to both Impellitteri and Costello at a time when the two were lined up on opposite sides of the political fence. Impellitteri wanted to be more than merely acting mayor of New York; he wanted to be officially elected to the city's most powerful job. He called young Pope to city hall and asked for *Il Progresso*'s support in the upcoming race, but Pope knew that Costello was backing Impellitteri's main opponent, State Supreme Court Justice Ferdinand Pecora, and Gene refused to cross his own godfather. (Some reports indicate that Costello had originally backed Impellitteri for mayor, but had a change of heart and threw his endorsement to Pecora.)

When Pope told Impellitteri that he and his paper would be backing "Frank C's" candidate, the future mayor was understandably upset. He publicly accused Pope of being a tool of the Mafia, and in October 1950, after winning the election, Impellitteri stripped Pope of his honorary police commissioner's title. (Gene hung onto his seat on the board of education until 1954, when he resigned under pressure from another incoming mayor, Robert F. Wagner, during a campaign to rid the city's newsstands of salacious publications emphasizing sex and horror.)

In the meantime, Pope's family was also relieving him of some titles. With Generoso Sr. out of the picture and Gene in political hot water, they reclaimed control of *Il Progresso* by removing Pope as editor and taking his name off the paper's masthead. He also lost his vice presidency at the sand and gravel company. (When the provisions of Generoso Sr.'s will were carried out, however, Gene may have had the last laugh. According to a 1988 *New York Times* report, the will gave Junior sole ownership of *Il Progresso* "along with other businesses," and he continued to own the paper until 1980, when he sold it. If this is true, it's something that Gene never acknowledged publicly in his lifetime. In his occasional media interviews, he often mentioned his father's ownership of *Il Progresso*, but never any personal connection of his own. And during the 1960s and 1970s, Fortune Pope was frequently identified as editor and publisher of *Il Progresso*.)

Gene was so furious over the slights inflicted on him by his family that he virtually renounced his membership in it and vowed to pursue a totally independent course from that day forward. He moved out of the family's luxurious apartment on Fifth Avenue, widening a rift between himself and his brothers that would last as long as he lived. (Fortune and Anthony ended up with control of Colonial Sand and Stone and several other companies. In the late 1950s, they pleaded guilty to illegal stock manipulations, and each was fined $25,000 and given a one-year suspended jail sentence by a federal judge.)

It was apparently at this juncture that Gene hired on with the CIA. At the same time, he drew closer than ever to Costello, who was now widely recognized as the "boss of bosses" of the New York–New Jersey–Connecticut branch of the Mafia.

Also during this period, an audacious plan began to take shape in Pope's agile mind. As the plan grew clearer, he could see how to use Costello's personal wealth and influence—plus the powerful tentacles of the organization that Costello controlled—to ensure its success. Let his brothers keep the businesses they'd stolen out from under him, Gene must have thought. Now he had his sights set on something much bigger and bolder—something that would reach far beyond New York's Italian-American community and beyond New York itself.

Something that would make the whole country sit up and take notice.

*　　*　　*

On the surface, Pope could hardly have found a more unlikely vehicle for setting his grand plan into motion. When he bought the *New York Enquirer* in 1952, it was comatose, moribund, and all but forgotten by the newspaper-reading public of the nation's largest city. It still showed up on news-stands each Sunday afternoon, as it had every week since 1926, but it scarcely merited a yawn from passersby.

As a matter of coincidental interest, William Randolph Hearst, the man responsible for establishing the *Enquirer* in the first place, had died the previous year. But by then, the paper had passed through a succession of owners, and any ties it had to Hearst had long since been severed. Many of Hearst's high-profile dailies across the country were themselves drifting in a sea of red ink in early 1952, but when it came to leading a tenuous existence, the *New York Enquirer* was in a class by itself.

At various points during his rise to publishing prominence, Pope enjoyed telling about how he bought the *Enquirer* and adding occasional embellishments to the story. He particularly liked portraying himself as flat broke at the time—something that clearly wasn't true. He may, indeed, have been hard pressed for liquid assets, but he was certainly no pauper.

"It puzzled me at first," he said during a 1969 interview with Newton Fulbright, a writer for *Editor & Publisher*, "to know why anybody would sell a newspaper to a kid of 25 . . . I had no money. I borrowed a lucky silver dollar from my lawyer to pay for cab fare down to the contract signing. Next day when I went down to the *Enquirer* office, I discovered nobody had been paid in months and I was a week away from bankruptcy."

Various sources have set the purchase price paid by Pope at $75,000, with a down payment of $20,000 or $25,000, which seems utterly exorbitant, given the paper's condition. But despite Pope's claims of poverty, he probably could have paid considerably more if necessary, because, according to one of his closest associates, the money came—directly and interest-free—from none other than Frank Costello.

Dino Gallo, who had been Pope's assistant at *Il Progresso* and later served for thirty-five years as secretary of the *Enquirer*'s parent company, talked freely about Costello's long string of financial contributions in an interview published in the January 2000 issue of *Talk* magazine.

According to Gallo, the original down payment was only the beginning. It was followed by a succession of $10,000-a-week subsidies that kept the paper afloat for the first year or so after Pope bought it. "Gene always needed more money," Gallo told the magazine. "So even though we were paying back, Frank Costello was always helping him pay the bills."

When money was collected from newsstand sales the week following a loan, Gallo would deliver a cash-stuffed envelope to one of Costello's henchmen at the Waldorf-Astoria Hotel. And when some of the mom-and-pop stores that sold the *Enquirer* complained about its lurid content and wanted to stop carrying the paper, they received a "courtesy call" from another friend of Gene's, a Mob enforcer named Mickey Zupa. They almost always changed their minds.

Costello himself—"Uncle Frank," as he was known to employees of the era—was a frequent visitor to the *Enquirer* office. As Barney Giambalvo, who was hired by Dino Gallo in 1960 and remained an *Enquirer* employee until 1995, recalled in a February 2000 interview:

> "Uncle Frank" was still a regular visitor after I came to work there. When they found out he was coming, word would spread around the office, and everybody would be careful not to do or say anything to offend him. I remember one guy who had a bumper sticker on the back of his desk that said something like "No Parking—Mafia Staff Cars Only." At the last minute, somebody ripped it off, so "Uncle Frank" didn't see it.

All told, Costello is believed by some sources to have poured $250,000 or more into the pump-priming operation at the *Enquirer*. Whether it was all in the form of interest-free loans that were eventually repaid or whether some of it was an outright gift to a godson, the point is the same: Pope's publishing venture was financed from the outset by a steady stream of cash contributions from the most notorious mobster of the era.

With this in mind, it's interesting to consider one of Pope's few—extremely few—public utterances on the subject.

In 1976, Pope was asked by CBS reporter Mike Wallace during a nationally televised segment of *60 Minutes* if Mafia money had ever been used to subsidize or support the *Enquirer*'s operation.

This was Pope's response: "I think it's pretty obvious to anyone who understands or reads or knows anything about this organization—whatever it is—that if there were [Mafia money backing the *Enquirer*], there still would be. Because they never let go once they get their hooks into you, and that obviously hasn't happened."

For whatever reason, Wallace seemed completely satisfied with the answer. He let the matter drop with no further questions.

$$* \quad * \quad *$$

It took Pope about five years to stabilize his floundering brainchild and drag the paper back to solvency.

The office, according to Gallo, who worked there and should know, was "literally a dump," littered with broken furniture and typewriters that didn't work. To New York's journalistic fraternity, the paper had long been a laughingstock, so even if Pope had had the money, it would've been next to impossible to hire experienced, first-class professional help.

None of this kept Pope from including a bold, idealistic mission statement in his first issue as publisher. "In an age darkened by the menace of totalitarian tyranny and war," he wrote, "the *New York Enquirer* will fight for the rights of man, the rights of the individual, and will champion human decency and dignity, freedom and peace."

The period from 1952 to 1955 was especially difficult as the young publisher struggled to find a formula and approach that would appeal to perpetually jaded New York readers. Early on, he maintained the traditional eight-column format and tried to capitalize on late-breaking developments in major hard-news stories that occurred late on Saturday nights or early Sunday mornings after the dailies had gone to press.

Once in a while, since the *Enquirer* was the only paper in the city that came out on Sunday afternoon, it scored a scoop that translated into a sharp increase in sales. Years later, after the paper had evolved into a national tabloid selling up to two million copies per week, Pope still kept a memento of just such a scoop on the wall of his private office. It was a framed matrix of a 1952 front page of the old broadsheet that headlined a major turning point in the Korean War. The *Enquirer* may well have been the first paper in the country to report the event.

But its readership—what there was of it—showed little interest in most international news. The weekend that Soviet troops invaded Hungary and crushed its freedom fighters under the treads of their tanks, Gene thought the story merited printing ten thousand extra copies, but nobody bought them.

For more than a decade after buying the paper, Pope also continued giving heavy play to sports events—late Saturday game scores, fight results, and especially racing results and betting lines. Winning numbers in the Italian lottery were another standard feature, although they had to be disguised so that only the players—and not the authorities—would recognize them.

Beginning in 1955, the *Enquirer* actually published a weekly "sports edition" that was distributed separately from the regular paper—and substantially outsold it for several years. "For a while, the sports edition was outselling the feature edition by three or four to one," said Barney Giambalvo. "But the feature edition gradually caught up in sales, and the sports edition was dropped in 1963."

The *Enquirer*'s sports coverage had always been slanted so heavily toward gambling and oddsmaking that Pope decided to disassociate himself from sports coverage entirely, according to Giambalvo. Thus, when the *Enquirer* finally hit the big time, it almost never carried a sports-related article. (Of course, if the O. J. Simpson story had broken during Pope's lifetime, he doubtless would've made an exception.)

As Gene would sometimes remind his editorial staffers in later years, he happened on the basic formula that transformed the *Enquirer* into a phenomenal newsstand success quite literally by accident. One day as he was driving home, he encountered one of those horrendous traffic jams for which New York is notorious. The tie-up was caused by hundreds of gawking motorists intent on getting a look at the mangled victims of a fatal car crash. For Gene, the tragic scene was an inspiration.

"I noticed how auto accidents drew crowds, and I decided that if it was blood that interested people, I'd give it to them," Pope unabashedly told a *Time* reporter in 1972.

And give it to them, he did—in spades.

Although Pope had lost his honorary police commissioner's title, he still had lots of solid contacts within the NYPD—including homicide cops who were more than willing to provide the most stomach-churning kind of crime scene photos for a sawbuck or two.

Pope took maximum advantage of these contacts, and the word gradually spread to other cops in other departments: "Hey, there's this newspaper guy who'll pay fifty bucks apiece for gory pictures—the gorier the better!"

Since the days of Hearst, Pulitzer, and Bernarr MacFadden, New Yorkers had been treated to a steady diet of journalistic shock and sensationalism. But during the 1940s and 1950s, even the daily tabloids adhered for the most part to an unwritten rule against out-and-out gore. Many editors felt that the public had witnessed enough violence and horror during World War II to last a lifetime, and they now shied away from the type of gruesome photos that their predecessors might have run eagerly in the 1920s or 1930s. The conservative school of journalism was firmly in control, and in comparison to today's print media, the average big-city paper was drab, droning, colorless, and predictable.

Pope was determined that the *Enquirer* would be none of these things. He subscribed to no stodgy rules or limitations, nor did he share those other editors' reticence about wallowing in blood and guts. His high-toned pledge about "decency and dignity" was quickly forgotten as the *Enquirer's* circulation increased by leaps and bounds—to seventy-five thousand, then one hundred thousand—fueled by readers who got a kick out of seeing mutilated corpses and hacked-off heads.

But Gene was astute enough to know that gore alone wasn't enough to sustain the kind of mass following he was after. It could serve as the catalyst for the rest, but there had to be more. In deciding what that "more" should consist of, he religiously studied the content and tactics of other ultrasensational publications, both in this country and overseas.

He was particularly intrigued with the British national newspapers. As the patriarch of English-language tabloids, the *Daily Mirror* still set a standard in the reporting and presentation of news that many others tried to copy. But, ironically, it was the flamboyant weekly broadsheet *News of the World*, owned by Rupert Murdoch, that left the deepest impression on Pope.

At the time, few people in the United States—even professional journalists—had ever heard of Murdoch, whose *National Star* would later become the *Enquirer's* most formidable rival for supremacy at the supermarket checkout. Murdoch was already a fabulously successful publisher in Australia, where he owned Sydney's largest daily, but *News of the World* was his first major venture outside Down Under. After Murdoch bought it in the late 1960s, it hit the U.K. like a bombshell, and quickly surged ahead of the more conservative *Sunday Mirror* to claim the largest circulation of any paper in the English-speaking world.

Murdoch's paper ran its share of graphic crime coverage, but it was also a showcase for celebrity scandal and anything freakish, grotesque, or bizarre—the identical "gee-whiz" stories that Hearst's editors had sought seventy years earlier.

From the first time he saw *News of the World*, Pope was outspokenly admiring—and envious. In conferences with his editorial minions, he cited Murdoch's paper dozens of times as an example of what he wanted to achieve in America. By the end of the 1960s, Murdoch's sheet was selling close to 7 million copies a week in a country with only a fraction the population of the United States.

"If *News of the World* can sell that many papers in Britain, we should be able to sell at least three times as many in this country," Pope told his staff time and again. "That's the goal we should be shooting for."

Another publication that undoubtedly helped Pope refine his formula was *Confidential* magazine, an early forerunner of the national tabs, which appeared in 1952, the same year that Pope bought the *Enquirer. Confidential's* creator, Robert Harrison, introduced a whole new style of outrageous, sexually charged celebrity stories that made the magazine an explosive success.

Harrison's reporters were utterly ruthless in digging through the dirty linen of Hollywood's biggest names. Some of their stories were ludicrous (Frank Sinatra crediting Wheaties cereal with making him an inexhaustible lover, for example), but some of them struck with sledgehammer force.

The term "paparazzi" was unknown in those days, but *Confidential* routinely used hidden cameras, long-range lenses, and sheer strong-arm tactics to get photos and information that no other periodicals had—and wouldn't have dared print if they did. By 1958, Harrison was so deluged with celebrity lawsuits that he was forced to give up the magazine. Under different ownership, a milder version of *Confidential* continued in publication up until the 1970s, but it was a mere shadow of its former self.

At any rate, *Confidential's* initial impact and wildfire newsstand sales helped convince Pope that "hot" celebrity material had to be part of his total package, and he began emphasizing scandalous show biz coverage early on, primarily in several toughly written gossip columns. ("Charles Laughton was so drunk in a London pub the other night that he passed out . . . Charlie had his face on the barroom floor for almost seven hours before they came to get him out.")

Early in 1957, the *Enquirer* turned the corner to profitability, and the following year, a labor dispute that shut down New York's dailies gave it an added circulation boost. By late 1958, sales were consistently reaching the 250,000 mark, and the paper had become a significant money maker. Although distribution was still confined mainly to the New York metropolitan area, Pope had already changed the name to *National Enquirer*, and his vision for his paper was steadily expanding.

Ready or not, America was about to get its first nationally circulated tabloid. And in the truest sense of the term, it was going to be a bloody shame.

✳   ✳   ✳

Although 1957 marked the arrival of stability and relatively smooth sailing at the *Enquirer*, the same can't be said for its owner and publisher. A violent incident that spring landed Pope on the front pages of the New York dailies and brought him under the scrutiny of police and FBI investigators. In the minds of many, the incident confirmed rumors that Pope was a Mafia fellow-traveler, and its aftermath would keep the stigma of direct Mob involvement hanging over his head for the rest of his life.

Pope no longer needed continuous infusions of cash from Frank Costello to keep his business afloat, but he saw Costello often and usually had dinner with him a couple of times a week. On the evening of May 2, 1957, Pope and Costello dined together at the L'Aiglon, an elegant French restaurant on East Fifty-fifth Street in Manhattan, along with a group that included Costello's wife, Loretta; Phillip Kennedy, the head of a New York modeling agency; *Enquirer* columnist John J. Miller; and Miller's wife, Cindy.

After a sumptuous meal, at Costello's suggestion they went down the street to the Monsignore, an Italian restaurant that featured strolling violinists, for after-dinner drinks. At about 10:45 P.M., Costello excused himself from the others and said he needed to get home. Kennedy said he had to go, too, and he and Costello left in the same taxi. Moments later, Miller made a phone call from the Monsignore to one Vinnie Mauro, a longtime acquaintance of Costello's who'd talked of meeting the group that evening, then claimed he'd been detained. Miller told Mauro that Costello had just left.

It was 10:55 P.M. when the taxi pulled up in front of the Majestic apartment building on Central Park West where Costello had lived for many years. Costello paid no attention to the black limousine that pulled up just behind the taxi or to the man who darted into the Majestic just ahead of him.

As Costello hurried toward the elevator, the man whirled toward him, and Costello saw a gun in the man's right hand. "This is for you, Frank," the man yelled.

The assailant fired one shot directly at Costello's face from a distance of about ten feet, then ran from the building, jumped into the waiting limousine and sped away.

Although it bled profusely, the wound itself wasn't serious—the bullet merely grazed Costello's skull—but its implications were sinister and far-reaching. If someone was trying to knock off the "boss of bosses" for the whole Northeast, it meant a power struggle was going on in the uppermost echelons of organized crime.

Gene Pope had been among the last people to see "Mr. C." before the gunman struck—and the phone call placed by Pope's employee, Miller, could have helped set Costello up for the hit. Could Pope have somehow been involved in the plot? To this day, no one knows for sure.

Costello and Kennedy both denied seeing anything suspicious that night. They said they had no idea who the hitman might have been. Questioned by police, Pope and Miller said the same thing.

Pope had also been well acquainted with Albert Anastasia, another Mafia boss who was riddled with bullets as he sat in a barber's chair not long after the attempt on Costello. Was Pope somehow connected with this murder, too?

After the failed attempt on his life, Costello's star rapidly declined in the Mob. Although he was practically unscathed physically, his power was effectively broken by the incident. In exchange for his life, Costello gave up all his Mafia holdings and positions, and retired. Within a few months, Uncle Frank was sent back to prison to serve out the rest of a five-year sentence for income tax evasion that had been interrupted by some clever legal maneuvering. When he was released in 1961, Costello resumed his habit of dining regularly with Pope, Kennedy, and the Millers. But it's interesting to note that, according to Costello biographer Leonard Katz, Pope soon dropped out of this close-knit little group, claiming that he was "too busy" with the fast-growing *Enquirer* to continue such socializing.

Vito Genovese—later tabbed by Mafia soldier-turned-informer Joe Valachi as the mastermind behind the hits on Costello and Anastasia—rose to claim most of the power once held by Uncle Frank. Joseph Bonanno, Carlo Gambino, and Joseph Colombo also shared in the spoils and soared in prominence within the Mob. Since all these members of the Mafia's new "power elite" would later be visitors at Pope's office, did Uncle Frank's godson gain directly from this changing of the guard? Or was he merely protecting his own backside?

No one will ever know for sure, of course. Today, as they did during his lifetime, these unanswered questions remain a part of the lingering mystery surrounding Generoso Pope Jr.

*   *   *

Numerous other questions remain about the formative years of Pope's *Enquirer*. Unfortunately, no amount of present-day research is likely to turn up complete answers.

Early files of the *Enquirer* and all the other supermarket tabs that followed it were sketchy and haphazardly kept at best, and only a few scattered copies of the earliest issues have survived to the present. Libraries had scant interest in compiling permanent collections or preserving them on microfilm (although reports persist that the New York Public Library still has copies of 1950s-vintage *Enquirers* stashed away somewhere in its archives), and their owners weren't particularly concerned about posterity, either.

In the case of the *Enquirer*, in particular, many file copies from the "gore era" were probably destroyed intentionally when the paper was trying to tidy up its image and get into the supermarkets in the late 1960s. Staffers from the "squeaky-clean" period that started in 1967–1968 used to leaf through bound volumes of the old issues and alternately gasp and chuckle at the difference, but these volumes were never available to outsiders. In recent years, the paper's management has become even more protective of older files, and, in fact, has denied that any file copies exist prior to 1968.

For all these reasons, the exact dates of certain important events in the *Enquirer*'s evolution can't be pinpointed today. Among these is the date of the changeover from broadsheet to tabloid format. By all accounts, it happened soon after Pope bought the paper, probably in 1952, but if a copy of the first tabloid edition exists, it must be locked away in someone's private collection.

Likewise, the precise date of the first issue bearing the name *National Enquirer* also isn't known. Some sources place the changeover at the beginning of 1960, but Barney Giambalvo and other early staff members say it actually happened in the mid- or late 1950s. (In a report on the Frank Costello shooting in May 1957, the *New York Herald Tribune* still referred to Pope as "publisher of the *New York Enquirer*.") More than likely, early 1960 was, instead, when the paper first began to be distributed on a truly nationwide basis. Prior to that, it was "national" in name only, but during the last years of the fifties, it gradually spread out from the New York area to cover more and more territory.

"For a while, it was only in New York, New Jersey, and Connecticut," Giambalvo recalled. "But then it moved into Massachusetts, Pennsylvania, Ohio, and so on, and by 1960 it was pretty much all over the country."

Within a year or two, it was available at newsstands in virtually every American city. By mid-decade, it had become something of a household word from coast to coast—although not one often repeated at the family dinner table.

Pope's grand vision was becoming a reality. Some weeks, sales were starting to flirt with the 1-million mark. Even at a cover price of just fifteen cents a copy, the *Enquirer* was making its publisher a very wealthy man.

But deep down inside, Gene knew there had to be a whole lot more where this largesse was coming from. He grew more convinced every day that this was only the beginning.

THREE
POPE GENE I
AMERICA'S SULTAN OF SLIME

As the 1960s unfolded and the *Enquirer* mushroomed into a national publishing phenomenon, Gene Pope's evolving personality continued its striking parallels with Mario Puzo's Michael Corleone.

Like the maturing Pacino character of *Godfather II*, Pope's demeanor was also changing and coarsening. The boyish enthusiasm of the early 1950s was giving way to a cynical, obsessive drive for wealth and power. The engaging smile was still there and the voice was still soft and shy, but behind them lurked the uncompromising mannerisms of a budding tyrant whose eyes could turn cold and vicious without warning.

The *Enquirer* had become virtually Pope's whole life. He'd married Patricia McManus, the first of his three wives, when he was in his early twenties, but she died not long after; his second marriage, to Edith Moore, had ended in divorce. (Unsubstantiated rumors circulated in the office for years that foul play had been involved in the first Mrs. Pope's death and that Pope had had his second wife committed to a mental institution prior to the divorce.) Although he had three young children by this time, he apparently spent little time with them, because he was devoting almost every waking moment to perfecting his creation.

He was now in the habit of issuing sweeping editorial policy pronouncements—referred to behind his back as "papal decrees"—and he was already demonstrating his willingness to fire writers and editors in wholesale lots if they failed to carry out his orders to the letter.

And when the *Enquirer*'s circulation hit a plateau near the midpoint of

43

the decade and resisted Pope's best efforts to keep it climbing, it did nothing to improve the boss's mood or make him easier to work for.

By late 1965, when Pope married his third wife, Lois Berrodin, a blonde nightclub singer with Grace Kelly looks, the paper had been selling in the neighborhood of one million copies a week for a year or two. But it was no longer enjoying the rapid month-to-month growth that had characterized the early 1960s. Sales still inched upward from time to time, but then dipped back to the same level despite wider distribution and a higher nationwide profile. And Pope spent countless hours analyzing sales reports and studying the marketplace trying to figure out why.

One reason for the slowdown seemed fairly obvious: For a while, Pope had had the gore-and-sleaze market all to himself, but as the *Enquirer*'s success caught the attention of other publishing entrepreneurs across the continent, competition was popping up here and there.

First and most notable among the new entries in the national tabloid field was *Midnight*, a Montreal-based publication that had appropriated the name of Bernarr MacFadden's shameless weekly of the 1920s—along with certain of its editorial mannerisms. Founded in 1954 on the flimsiest of shoestrings, *Midnight* had remained unnoticed outside Montreal for several years, but it gradually picked up distributors in other Canadian cities, and in the early 1960s it began showing up here and there in the northern United States. Not long afterward, the *National Insider*, *National Tattler*, and *National Informer* published their first issues in Chicago. Various other lurid tabs appeared and then vanished, often after only a brief life span.

On an issue-to-issue basis, none of these newcomers came close to matching the *Enquirer* for unadulterated shock and gross-out horror, although each scored a coup occasionally. But the competing tabs supplemented their bloody crime coverage with blatant sex, an element that was glaringly absent from Pope's paper.

To this day, the mistaken perception remains that the *Enquirer* of the early and mid-sixties specialized more or less equally in "sex and gore." Even *Editor & Publisher*, the newspaper industry's most respected trade journal, helped perpetuate that notion in August 1969, when it ran a largely favorable article on Pope and his paper under a headline that read:

Sex on shelf, *National Enquirer*
goes after supermarket shoppers.

The fact is, though, there was no sex *to* shelve. Plenty of bloodstains to eradicate, yes, but virtually no sex. For almost a decade and a half, the *Enquirer* consistently reveled in the slimiest details of the most disgusting depravities conceivable to the human mind. Yet, for reasons best known to

Pope himself, he shied strictly away from explicit sexual themes. His celebrity columns contained scattered references to flings, affairs, and various hanky-panky, but they were never played up in cover headlines and usually cloaked with a tone of moral disapproval, even outrage:

> Barbara Hutton . . . caused quite a stir in a Tangiers bar when she imbibed far too much and wanted to do a strip for her youngish date. The lad decided Barbara had had enough and half dragged her out of the place.

At this time, a typical issue of the *Enquirer* contained no less than five celebrity gossip columns, each devoted almost entirely to the alleged antics of Hollywood stars. Together, they accounted for close to 100 percent of the paper's total celebrity coverage, since feature articles on big-name personalities were extremely rare. Yet items as "racy" as the one above were very much out of the ordinary. More often than not, as former *Enquirer* staffer Reginald Potterton put it in an April 1969 *Playboy* article, the paper turned a "blind eye to . . . boudoir debaucheries."

According to *Enquirer* columnists, Potterton wrote, "it's not broads that make star life what it is, it's bashing and booze. In fact, they say, all movie and television celebrities spend their waking hours either stupefyingly drunk or pummeling one another—and innocent passersby—into insensibility." He cited such examples as: "Pint-sized actor C. charged muscle man D. and walloped him with punch after punch," and "E. kicked his screen wife in the throat."

Pope had apparently decided that, even when the biggest names in show biz were involved, violence and mayhem was simply a bigger turn-on to his audience than sex. He'd surmised that his regular readership was as self-righteous as it was bloodthirsty, and that trying to titillate them with sex would be counterproductive. Besides, sexual taboos were still strong in American society during the sixties. Violating them meant incurring the wrath of forces ranging from the church to the PTA to the U.S. Congress, but the reaction was less severe to the stuff Pope was peddling.

Someone had already coined the term "the other pornography" to describe the *Enquirer*'s stock-in-trade, but even at its goriest and most loathsome, Pope's paper was never censored or condemned by the National Office for Decent Literature. Many sexually oriented publications, on the other hand, felt the NODL's wrath on a regular basis.

All these factors may have figured into Pope's avoidance of Hollywood bed hopping and other sexual themes as fodder for feature articles. But whatever the rationale, shunning sex gave the competition an opening, and they quickly capitalized on it. By 1965, the *Enquirer*'s four largest rivals had a combined average weekly circulation estimated at 350,000 to 400,000.

*　*　*

At this juncture, however, Pope enjoyed two tremendous advantages over his upstart rivals. For one thing, he'd established alliances with some of the nation's most powerful periodical wholesalers and distributors, many of them Mob connected, and he was willing to make it worth their while to give his paper preferential treatment.

For another thing, most of his competitors were operating on hand-to-mouth financing, just as he'd been forced to do at the beginning. But now those hard times were in the distant past for the *Enquirer*. The money was rolling in, and it gave Pope the resources he needed not only to keep key cogs in the distribution network well oiled with payoffs, but to offer top dollar for the best—or worst—stories and photos.

In every phase of the "war of the bizarre" that would rage for years among the national tabloids, Pope almost always set the trends for his rivals to follow. He often did it with total disregard for ethics and good taste, but also with ingenuity, free spending, determination, and a seemingly uncanny knack for knowing what would make the *Enquirer* irresistible to certain people. And he never did it more effectively than during the bloodiest days of the "gore era."

If anyone ever compiles a list of the sickest, most offensive headlines ever printed, these entries from the *Enquirer* of the early to mid-1960s are bound to rank somewhere near the top:

Kills Son and Feeds Corpse to Pigs

400-Lb. Baby Sitter Punches Infant to Death

Commits Suicide With a Machine Gun

Digs Up Wife's Rotting Corpse and Rips It Apart

Kills Pal & Eats Pieces of His Flesh

Man, 23, Beats Woman, 102, to Death in Self-Defense

In the opinion of most veterans of those tabloid wars, however, a headline from the September 8, 1963, issue of the *Enquirer* qualifies hands-down for the all-time gross-out grand prize. It described the mutilation-slaying of Olympic skier Sonja McCaskie in the words of the man who admitted murdering and dismembering her:

"I Cut Out Her Heart and Stomped on It!"

Appearing on the same cover with the headline were photographs of the dead woman's heart, headless torso, and severed foot.

William Bates, who joined the *Enquirer* as a photo editor in 1963, recalled it as no place in those days for anybody with a queasy stomach. On one occasion, while working with a particularly gruesome set of pictures, Bates didn't have time to take a lunch break, so he asked a more fortunate coworker to bring him back a sandwich when he returned.

"Unfortunately, I neglected to specify what kind of sandwich," Bates said. "When this guy came back with rare roast beef au jus, I had to run out of the room to keep from throwing up."

As gut-wrenching as the photos and headlines were, there was also a distinctive tone to the stories accompanying them that often smacked of the most sadistic, coldhearted kind of satire. Part of it undoubtedly resulted from a psychological defense mechanism on the part of those responsible. As one writer of the period put it: "Christ, the stuff made me sick, too, but sometimes you had to force yourself to laugh at what you were doing. Otherwise, you'd have a screaming fit or jump out the window."

But part of this dark undertone was so calculated that it became a sort of signature style. Like a grinning skull, it cropped up again and again, and made many *Enquirer* articles read like tongue-in-cheek "cruelty jokes." Potterton called it "black humor at its blackest."

Under the headline "Murders His Dad for $8," for example, the July 28, 1963, issue carried the story of thirty-eight-year-old James Lignos, who beat his aged father to death with a board after the father awoke to find the son going through his pockets in search of money for booze.

"The father was still alive in his blood-soaked bed," the story continued, "when James took $8 from his pockets and went to a saloon to drink it up.

"But the father died later and James was cold sober when he went on trial. And he cried as he told the judge: 'Send me to the electric chair!'"

Enquirer writers—those who survived more than a few issues—learned to write terse, blunt, black-humor introductory paragraphs that were almost an extension of the headlines above them. A few examples:

- Eva Fedorchuk battered her husband's face to a bloody pulp with a pop bottle. Then she told police he'd cut himself while shaving.
- Salvador Jiminez took his girlfriend at her word when she told him to drop dead. He walked out of her house and blew his brains out.
- The two policemen rushed to the bank in answer to an alarm. When they saw Santa Claus coming out the door with his bag they started to chuckle. The laugh died in their throats—because Santa Claus had a special present for them. He lifted a tommy gun and shot them full of holes.

Likewise, many headlines incorporated a twist of bitter irony that some readers found darkly humorous:

After 25 Years of Trick Shooting—I Missed and Killed My Daughter

She'll Marry the Man Who Cut Her Throat

He Crashes Head on into Another Car And Kills Driver—His Brother

Family Eats Barbecued Meat—Finds It Was Their Dog

George Bernard, who claimed to have been an undercover reporter for the *Enquirer* from 1964 to 1968, while also fronting as a representative of a group of British radio stations, told of "raiding morgues in the middle of the night" to obtain photos of dead bodies for Pope's paper.

"Imagine the anguish, the despair and the hatred generated towards the *Enquirer* by the family and friends of the deceased when they saw their loved ones plastered through the pages of what was then the most terrifying tabloid in the country," Bernard wrote in a self-congratulatory book published nearly a decade after his alleged exploits.

"When you 'raid a morgue,' you pull the corpse out of a special drawer, photograph the deceased, then return the body to where you found it," Bernard added. "Not a very pleasant business. Yet again, who ever said covering stories for the *Enquirer* was utopian?"

Mutilated animal photos also enjoyed a high priority, according to Bernard. In particular, he recalled one picture spread of a stallion's severed head lying in a pool of its own blood. The horse had been decapitated when it stuck its head out of its trailer and struck the wall of a tunnel. (Could that have been where the moviemakers got the idea for the bloody horse's head in the bed of a man who was stubborn enough to cross Vito Coreleone in *The Godfather*?)

"Only God could help me if my cover was ever exposed," confided Bernard, who also provided considerable fodder for the *Enquirer's* Hollywood gossip columns. " . . . to succeed as an effective *Enquirer* reporter, it was necessary to establish at least one dependable front, or cover. If you had two covers going for you, you were way ahead of the game. For the mere mention the *National Enquirer* sent shivers down one's spine and became the instant kiss of death. . . . "

＊　　＊　　＊

Even when the focus shifted from mutilation murders, cannibalism, and grave robbing to such relatively staid subjects as consumerism and social conscience, the treatment wasn't for the weak-stomached or fainthearted. One of the most memorable examples of how gross a "consumer" story can get was an issue that appeared on newsstands during Thanksgiving week of 1965.

The entire front cover was devoted to a large photo of a plump roast turkey on a garnished platter. The picture was surrounded by a sort of halo of headlines set at angles above the festive bird, each indicating some noxious substance with which turkeys in general were supposedly contaminated—"Fecal Smears," "Yellow Pus," "Deadly Chemicals," "Cancer Spores," and the like. In bold, inch-and-a-half-high capital letters, a banner headline screamed a dire warning:

ONE BITE CAN KILL YOU!

Five or six years later, when the *Enquirer* had turned "squeaky clean" and was courting the likes of Kroger, Safeway, A&P, and Jewel for high-profile space at their checkout counters, veteran staffers used to show newcomers that Thanksgiving cover and laugh as the rookies turned a little green.

"What do you think the supermarket guys would say if they could see this?" the old-timers would chortle. "Hell, they wouldn't let us within a block of their stores."

Under the guise of social conscience, one front-page photo showed the torn-apart face of a male driver killed in an auto accident. A four-page spread inside included pictures of the man's severed arm, the charred bodies of his wife and infant sons, and the mangled driver on the morgue table after his face had been stuck back together. The copy contained a brief admonition to use seatbelts, and a bold headline added sanctimoniously:

The Enquirer joins with the National Safety Council in the plea: DON'T LET THIS HAPPEN TO YOU!

Public service articles? Yes, indeedy, Pope was very big on those, especially the ones that gave the paper an opportunity for self-glorification. At the height of the "gore era," Pope paid a ten-year-old French girl's expenses to come to the United States for reconstructive plastic surgery on her pitifully deformed face. The operation was less than a success, and afterward, the child's features remained as grotesque as ever. But this didn't keep Pope from running "before" and "after" pictures of the girl under the headline:

ENQUIRER FIXES HER FACE

* * *

Where the rest of American journalism was concerned, the *Enquirer* of the first half of the 1960s could hardly have been a worse disgrace or bigger pariah. Its million-copy-a-week sales notwithstanding, most members of the mainstream press couldn't have regarded it with greater contempt if it had been printed on used toilet paper. The idea that any journalist with talent or ability—much less a trace of professional principle—would ever actually work for such a malodorous rag seemed too absurd even to think about.

But Pope—GP, as he now liked to be called by associates—was counting on two proverbial, time-tested truths to alter the situation in his favor. Great Truth No. 1: Times change. Great Truth No. 2: Money talks.

He eventually proved accurate on both counts, but in the meantime, he struggled against heavy odds to upgrade the caliber of his staff. The problem, however, wasn't related to subsistence-level wages or shabby working conditions.

The *Enquirer*'s original hole-in-the-wall office was now only a distant memory. For several years, its staff had been housed in anonymous but decidedly upscale quarters at 655 Madison Avenue in the heart of Manhattan's tony publishing district.

The sign on the outer door identified the tenant in the lofty high-rise merely as "Best Medium Publishing Co.," but the suite of offices beyond the door easily outclassed most of the newsrooms of New York dailies. *Enquirer* writers and articles editors worked in private cubicles with state-of-the art equipment, free coffee, paid vacations, a pension plan, and other fringe benefits. And *Enquirer* editorial salaries —which would take off within a few years like a rocket bound for the stratosphere—already compared favorably to what major dailies were paying reporters and copy editors. But despite the good pay, attractive digs, and other amenities, GP was still getting a sub-zero "cold shoulder" from New York's media professionals.

The first person to hold the title of editor of the *Enquirer*, other than Pope himself, was an ex-gumshoe publicist for Madison Square Garden named Carl Grothmann. He assumed the title around 1955, although his journalism background was sketchy to nonexistent. Then, in the late 1950s, a young man named Nat Chrzan started "moonlighting" for the *Enquirer* to supplement his income from a menial newsroom job at the *New York World-Telegram*. Chrzan later became the first employee of a major U.S. daily to defect to Pope on a full-time basis.

A decade later, after Chrzan had ascended to the editorship of the *Enquirer*, and the *World-Telegram* Building was a vacant shell overlooking the Hudson River, he spoke gleefully to an interviewer about the job change.

"People at the *World-Telegram* laughed at me," he told *Editor & Publisher* in August 1969. "They wanted to know what I was wasting my time for.

They thought the *Enquirer* was an inky little sheet of about 40,000 circulation and couldn't pay lunch money. Well, I'm so glad the time finally came when they offered me a regular job at the *Enquirer*. I'm glad every day that I quit the *World-Telegram* and took it."

For the most part, though, to bring in the kind of professionals he needed to improve the paper in the early 1960s, Pope was forced to look overseas. Britain's hard-nosed journalists were far less squeamish than their Yank counterparts about writing and reporting for a paper of the *Enquirer*'s ilk—especially when Pope offered to pay them twice what they could make in the U.K., pick up all their relocation expenses, and arrange for them to get their immigrant "green cards" without a hassle.

Consequently, by mid-decade the vast majority of GP's twenty-member editorial staff were Britishers. Some of them didn't stay long, but a few stuck around to play important, long-running roles in the *Enquirer*'s emergence as the most imitated, most talked-about periodical of the century. Among these were Ted Mutch, who served as executive editor for several years and helped open a conduit that brought a long string of talented, gutsy Fleet Street veterans into the fold.

There were also a pair of Scotsmen, Iain Calder and William Dick, who were first hired to run a short-lived London bureau for Pope, then brought to the New York headquarters as articles editors. "He made us an offer we couldn't refuse," Calder would chuckle many years later.

Calder, in particular, a former assistant news editor at the *Glasgow Daily Record*, would leave a lasting mark as he rose through the editorial ranks to become Pope's right-hand man and closest confidant with the titles of editor in chief of the *Enquirer* and president of its parent company.

Meanwhile, rancorous labor disputes and the shrinking economic base of the daily press were working in Pope's favor on this side of the Atlantic. After the disastrous New York newspaper strike of 1963–64 shut down every daily in the city—and ultimately killed more than half of them— local journalists could never again afford to be as smug, spoiled, and snooty about where their paychecks came from as they'd been before.

The deaths of the *World-Telegram*, *Herald Tribune*, *Journal-American*, and *Mirror*, all within a three-year span, threw hundreds of newspeople permanently out of work. Meanwhile, newspaper mergers and closings in other cities from coast to coast left the jobless with few options elsewhere. Suddenly, that "inky little sheet" called the *Enquirer* became a desperately sought-after port in a storm, and Pope could take his pick from among some of the most respected writers and editors in America.

To Pope's credit, he didn't try to shortchange those he hired. In most cases, he paid them as much or more than they'd been making before. Notable additions to the *Enquirer* staff included Selig Adler, the last managing editor of the *Mirror*, and his brother, Mike, the *Mirror*'s last city editor.

Jim Donahue, another *Mirror* ex, was soon earning a reputed one hundred thousand dollars a year as a contract writer cranking out up to a dozen *Enquirer* feature articles per issue.

To GP, his newfound ability to attract "star-quality" professionals was proof that the *Enquirer* had "arrived" among the country's top echelon of papers. This gave him tremendous psychological satisfaction, but there were far more urgent reasons as well for beefing up his staff.

The most difficult test ever faced by the *Enquirer* lay just ahead. Unless it passed the test, it probably wouldn't survive over the long term, much less grow to fulfill the expansive vision that its owner had for it.

$$* \quad * \quad *$$

Pope had foreseen the trouble coming for years—long before any of his upstart competitors sensed its approach—and by late 1966, it was looming larger with every passing month. Far-reaching changes were taking place in the nation's retail structure, and some of those changes had particularly ominous overtones for publications like the *Enquirer*. They could jeopardize the whole future of GP's newsprint brainchild unless he found some way to circumvent them.

The traditional newsstands that had been fixtures in every city and good-sized town in America for as long as anyone could remember were rapidly disappearing. So were thousands of neighborhood mom-and-pop stores. Like a huge vaccuum, the chain stores and supermarkets were sucking away the little guys' business and forcing them out. Between them, the newsstands and the mom-and-pop stores were the mainstays of tabloid marketing, and their steadily dwindling numbers were a primary reason that *Enquirer* circulation had hit a stone wall. Unless a replacement could be found for them, all the weekly tabs were going to die on the vine, and Pope knew it.

"In one year [during this period] 25 percent of the newsstands in Manhattan and the Bronx shut down," Pope would recall a few years later. "What were we going to do? Sit and die or get up and do something? We discovered supermarkets—that's where papers and magazines are sold. But we had to have a product that a housewife could put in her food cart and take home to her family."

At the moment, that product was definitely *not* the *National Enquirer*, with its chopped-off heads and stomped-on hearts. As the undisputed cesspool of American journalism, it would've been about as welcome in the nation's supermarkets as a leprosy epidemic or a closeout sale on hand grenades.

Pope realized all this, but he had a plan to get around it. The "Sultan of Slime" would simply clean up his act.

"There are only so many people out there who get off on gore," he told his minions at a staff meeting early in 1967, "and they're all reading our paper already. We've got to find something with broader appeal, something any American will be interested in and won't hesitate to pick up and take home."

Later that same year, the redemption and reincarnation of the *Enquirer* began in earnest as GP issued the most sweeping "papal decree" of his career: No more gore!

From now on, he declared, the *Enquirer* would be known instead for inspiring stories about heroes. Uplifting stories about people who overcame handicaps or worked their way from rags to riches. Heartwarming stories about animals and children. Touching stories about love and patriotism. Informative stories about medicine, science, and technology. Revealing stories about social issues. Enlightening stories about the great, the famous, and the forgotten. And lots and lots of stories simply designed to make people exclaim, "Gee whiz!"

"I'm envisioning a *Reader's Digest* in tabloid form," Pope said.

The proposed transformation was so extreme that it defied the imagination of everyone but the man who conceived it. No publisher in history had ever tackled such a drastic makeover. A totally new readership would have to be found and cultivated, while present readers would be alienated in droves. Circulation was bound to nose-dive. Yet Pope Gene was unwaveringly confident of success.

To his "troops," he seemed to be saying matter-of-factly: "All we have to do is sanitize this stinking cesspool we've spent years filling with poisonous filth. First we deodorize it till it smells like a rose, then we turn it into a sparkling fountain of purity and wholesomeness. After that, the rest is as easy as making a silk purse out of a sow's ear."

It sounded impossible, preposterous—downright crazy. But if they could pull it off, it would be the biggest "gee-whiz" story of all time. Nothing in "Ripley's Believe It or Not!" would be more amazing or incredible.

And that's precisely what they set out to do.

FOUR
MIDNIGHT MADNESS BREAKS OUT IN MONTREAL

Opposites attract, they say, and within this short, simple adage lurks the peculiar chemistry that led to the birth of one of history's most phenomenally successful publishing ventures.

This age-old truism was undoubtedly in effect almost a half century ago when a bespectacled would-be playwright named John Vader entered into a business partnership with Joe Azaria, a Baghdad-born dandy with a lust for women and whiskey. On the surface, they were about as different as two guys could be, but in tandem, they generated a restless, reckless kind of energy.

The year was 1954, and neither Vader, who was a couple of years out of Canada's Concordia College, nor Azaria, who was waiting tables at a Montreal restaurant and trying to peddle stories to detective magazines, had two spare coins to rub together (Azaria later told friends he had exactly sixteen dollars to his name at the time). But they were full of youthful vigor, enthusiasm, and testosterone, and so, against all odds and logic, this unlikely duo decided to start publishing a very small but very racy local tabloid in Montreal.

For someone with the voracious fleshly appetites attributed to Azaria—rumors persist that he once had sex with a secretary on a conference table in the midst of a staff meeting—relatively little is actually known about the man. His father was a fairly well-to-do owner of an import-export business who immigrated with his son from Iraq to Canada when the boy was ten years old. Joe was smooth-talking, swarthily handsome, and a reasonably good writer—although not good enough to land a cub reporter's job at the daily *Montreal Gazette* when he applied there in the early 1950s.

According to some reports, Azaria had at least casual contact with gangsters connected to Montreal's Cottroni Mafia family, and there's little reason to doubt it since most of the city's nightclubs were controlled by the Mob. As Vader has phrased it: "If you did a lot of nightclub reporting, you got to know those people, and naturally, you wanted to stay on their good side because, if for no other reason, they were good for free drinks and news tips."

At any rate, the two unlikely partners called their paper *Midnight*, a name as dark as its apparent future. Unsupported by money, experience, or expertise, it ranked among the most tenuous of shoestring operations, and with every issue, it took a near-miracle to get its sixteen pages off the press and onto the street. But somehow it managed to keep struggling along, at first on an every-other-week publishing schedule, and a few thousand curious people began to buy it.

At the time, Vader and Azaria had never heard of the *Enquirer* or Gene Pope, but they'd observed several sensational weekly tabs that were being published out of Toronto at the time, and they used them as models. These included *Confidential Flash*, which thrived on exploiting fear and hatred of "pinkos and commies" ("Rape the women and burn the men," *CF*'s editor once exhorted his readers, "that's the way to bring these scum into line!"); *Justice Weekly*, which appealed to a hard-core deviate market of sado-masochists, necrophiliacs, and boot fetishists; and *Hush*, a semipornographic sex sheet.

Neither partner knew that the name they'd chosen for their paper had first been used thirty-two years earlier on a smutty and short-lived magazine owned by Bernarr MacFadden, and even if they had, they probably wouldn't have cared.

"Azaria came up with the original idea for the name," Vader reminisced on a recent spring afternoon in south Florida, where he now lives in retirement. "He was always talking about starting some kind of paper. I was twenty-four years old, with dreams of having a career in the theatre. I had a couple of close friends who were trying to break into show business with a nightclub act, so I was interested in publishing something that focused on night life and the more risqué types of after-dark action in Montreal. Later, the name *Midnight* caused us a lot of problems, but at that time, it seemed perfectly suited for what we had in mind."

Their idea was to loosely copy the format of the existing Canadian tabloids; outdo them whenever possible by pulling out all the stops on sex, sleaze, gossip and scandal; steal whatever they could find from other publications; and try to sell enough papers to pay their next printing bill.

As haphazard as it sounds, it turned out to be a highly effective approach, one that would place *Midnight* among the major publishing success stories of the twentieth century. By the time its name was changed to *Globe* in the late 1970s, it would rank among the largest-selling periodicals in the world.

It was extremely rough sledding at first, however. In fact, it's hard to imagine how it could've been any rougher.

"There were five of us originally—four guys and Azaria's girlfriend," Vader recalled, "and nobody got paid or even thought about getting paid. Azaria got his father to back us with a few hundred dollars worth of credit, but there was no money for salaries, or much of anything else, really. Our printing bill was $400 an issue, which is one reason we could only afford to publish every two weeks for a while. Joe struck a deal with a small print shop with a secondhand press and got the printer to give us credit for a couple of issues. After that, we had to rush around and collect from the newsstands before we could go back to press."

The print shop grew, too, by the way, largely as a by-product of *Midnight*'s own growth. Its owner now heads Quebecor, the second largest printing conglomerate in North America.

*   *   *

Just a few weeks into the operation, a young out-of-work nightclub comic named Jack Tabatch joined the staff and became, literally, a Jack-of-all-trades.

"I wrote articles, did layouts, and then delivered bundles of papers to the newsstands by truck," Tabatch recalled in an April 2000 interview. "There was always something that needed to be done."

For Jack, it was the beginning of a sixteen-year association with *Midnight*, during which he would become a sort of "unofficial third partner" in the enterprise, as well as the workhorse-architect of the company's early circulation strategy. A decade later, Tabatch was circulation director of the continent's second largest weekly tabloid with average sales of more than 300,000 copies.

Now retired and living in Pompano Beach, Florida, Tabatch has the distinction of owning the only known surviving set of the earliest issues of *Midnight*.

"Even though I wasn't there at the very beginning, I held onto the very first issue and got everybody who worked on it to sign the copy," he said, "and I've kept all the rest of the original issues, too."

That first *Midnight* cover, dated November 27, 1954, was dominated by a headline that read: "MONTREAL'S 2,000 LADIES OF THE EVENING." Issue number two, dated December 11, 1954, followed up with a graphic story and cover headline on "MONTREAL'S UNSOLVED MURDERS." The third issue, dated December 25, 1954, offered a rare Christmas treat for readers headlined "McGILL STUDENTS HOLD SEX ORGIES."

The initial print runs were 20,000 copies, but paid circulation usually didn't reach a third of that figure. Most of the sales were in mom-and-pop stores and traditional newsstands in central-city Montreal and around McGill University, and by the time the retailers took their cut, the fledgling publishers had enough to pay the printer, with maybe $200 left over to cover the next week's other expenses.

"That's the way it ran for quite a while," Vader said, "but we had a lot of fun in those days, too. None of us was married, and work was like one big party. Nobody cared what time it was, and if we wanted to go out for drinks or chase chorus girls until the sun came up, we just did it. Then we came back to the office and started working again."

Azaria's father soon got tired of financing this circus act and told Joe he was on his own. After that, things really got tough.

"Our main problem was that we never seemed to have any money," Vader remembered, "and when we did get a few dollars in, Joe always wanted to spend it on liquor and ladies. He'd say, 'Let's get some girls and have a party.' I was much less flamboyant and more conservative. I'd say, 'Let's pay some bills and then have a party.' "

This precarious situation continued for months, with weekly sales averaging no better than about 7,000. The company seldom occupied the same office space for more than two months in a row—except for once, when Azaria worked out a deal that involved sleeping with the rather rotund landlady in exchange for rent. When this arrangement fizzled, the company operated out of Azaria's apartment for a time.

Then, in the spring of 1955, the partners stumbled, quite accidentally, on an approach that almost tripled *Midnight*'s circulation overnight and helped Vader come up with an editorial formula that eventually produced dramatic financial success. A key ingredient was something the paper had never had much use for in the past—an element called truth.

"We'd been trying a wide assortment of sexy stuff on the cover, but most of it was just fluff without any real substance," Vader said. "We'd run a big photo of a busty model in a bikini with a headline something like 'I WANT TO BE HANDLED BY A REAL MAN!' and have some kind of made-up story on her inside. It just didn't have much substance."

As Vader recollects it, someone brought an attractive woman to the office and announced that she was willing to have sex right there on the spot with anybody who was interested. Some people *were* interested—it was that kind of place—but when Vader talked to the woman, he discovered an utterly bizarre, but totally true, story.

The woman and her husband had been a more-or-less typical middle-class couple working at ordinary jobs when they'd found themselves hopelessly deep in debt and beseiged by angry creditors. In desperation, the couple resorted to the only way they could think of to regain their solvency—both became prostitutes.

"We ran their true story, with photos, along with a cover headline that

said 'HUSBAND, WIFE PROSTITUTE SELVES TO GET OUT OF DEBT,' "
Vader said, "and the issue sold almost every copy we printed. That was
when we finally realized, hey, this is what we have to do. We had to keep
the subject matter hot, but it also had to be more personal and less general.
We had to tell authentic-sounding stories about real-seeming people in
believable situations—even if we had to steal or fabricate every word."

The next issue's cover headline was "SEX MACHINES REPLACE MEN," a
pseudodocumentary, liberally spiced with made-up "case studies," about the
allegedly growing popularity among women of battery-powered vibrators.
Others that followed included: "FIENDISH FATHER RAPES DAUGHTER"
and "SEVEN MEN ALL MARRIED SAME WOMAN AT SAME TIME."

"Again, sales were very high," said Vader. "After that, the worst was over.
Before long, Joe and I were each able to take $100-a-week salaries out of the
company, which wasn't bad money for the time."

But because of Azaria's ongoing preoccupation with wine, women, and
song, plus a general lack of concern with paying overdue bills, *Midnight*
wasn't out of the financial woods yet.

"We had to go through two bankruptcies before we finally got on solid
ground," Tabachnik recalled. "Each time we reorganized, we started over
with volume one, number one of *Midnight*, so my collection contains a
total of three 'first editions.' "

According to Vader, the "bankruptcies" were actually a calculated
means of cancelling piled-up bills by creating a new company, transferring
the old company's assets to the new one, then dissolving the old debt-
ridden one. This happened twice within *Midnight's* first year of operation.

"It was all highly illegal, but quite a few people were doing it and getting away with it, so we decided to try it, too," Vader said. "Joe had set up
the first company and called it Glendale Publishing, and when it reached
the point where we simply couldn't pay our bills, he had his girlfriend
charter another company, the name of which escapes me now. Pretty soon,
we found ourselves right back in the same situation all over again, so this
time, I went down and set up a third company called Midnight Publishing."

As it turned out, the third time was the charm. The company formed
by Vader would remain the publisher of record of *Midnight* for more than
twenty years and become a multimillion-dollar property. And since Vader
was originally listed as its sole owner, he would've stood to reap vast profit
from the situation—except for one thing.

"I signed it all away," he said wryly some four and a half decades later.
"Since the company was in my name, people kept telling me I should take
care of myself, protect my own interests. They said I should insist on
keeping 10 percent or 20 percent, maybe even 50 percent, but in the end, I
took nothing. After three years, I signed the company back over to Azaria,
and that was that."

According to those close to the situation, Vader didn't come away completely empty-handed, however. In the years since, he's mentioned having an "understanding" with Azaria, although he never spelled out exactly what it was. After Azaria sold the company to Michael Rosenbloom, it was widely rumored that Vader had some sort of ongoing contract under which he could never be fired—an allegation that he flatly denies. "I never had any kind of arrangement like that with Rosenbloom," he said recently. "I think he liked me, but there was no deal."

As a matter of record, when Azaria sold the company a dozen years later, the reported price was $4 million. By 1999, when it was sold again to American Media, the announced price was $105 million, and the seller, Rosenbloom, had previously amassed profits from the company estimated at $500 million. When reminded of this, Vader merely shrugged. "It sounds corny, I know, but I was never that interested in money for its own sake," he said. "For me, the challenge was always the big thing."

$*$ $*$ $*$

For five years, from 1955 until 1960, *Midnight*'s circulation remained basically static, hovering around an average of 20,000 sales, enough to keep the doors open but not enough to show any real profit. As the new decade began, it seemed painfully obvious that any chance for long-term growth depended on expanding the paper's circulation territory, since the local market seemed pretty well saturated.

At about this same time, Vader, Azaria, and Tabatch started getting occasional glimpses of Gene Pope's newly renamed *National Enquirer*. They were immediately impressed by the caliber of its crime coverage. They were also struck by the expansive implications of the word "national" in its title.

The sensible way to grow *Midnight*, Tabatch decided, was to reach out into new, untapped areas in search of more readers. So, early in the summer of 1961, he took on the formidable job of trying to find circulation outlets for the paper in cities and towns far beyond Montreal. He loaded his wife and two small children into an old Nash Rambler and set out on an epic transcontinental journey. As a result of that trip, *Midnight*'s sales would soon begin a steady rise, and the company would never be faced with insolvency again.

As Tabatch recalls it: "We put the kids in a playpen in the back seat, and just started driving. Every day, we'd hit another city, track down the local wholesale news dealer, and try to talk him into handling our paper. At the time, we didn't know anything about national distribution networks, but whenever we got someone to agree to distribute *Midnight* in another locale, it meant added exposure and higher sales. We built our own network of wholesalers that way, one dealer at a time."

The trek lasted for several weeks, and took Tabatch and his family all the way to the Pacific coast. When it was over, Tabatch had established a national presence for *Midnight* all across Canada, and the positive results began to be borne out each week as sales figures drifted in. Those figures, which remain in Tabatch's personal files today, show rapidly escalating print orders and mushrooming net sales beginning in mid-1961.

Before the end of that year, weekly sales passed the 50,000 mark for the first time, and at this point, Tabatch turned his attention southward and began making distribution forays into the United States.

"I thought if the paper sells in Quebec, Ontario, and Alberta, there's no reason it can't sell in Vermont, New Hampshire, and upstate New York, which were just across the border and a logical place to start," he said. "We picked up distributors in Buffalo, Rochester, Syracuse, and Utica. Later, we gradually moved on down to Boston, Providence, Hartford, Pittsburgh, Philadelphia, and so forth."

Some weeks, they replated the cover for the U.S. edition because the Canadian edition was considered too "tough" for the south-of-the-border market, but basically, Tabatch's assessment proved accurate.

Six months later, in June 1962, sales hit 72,000. Within another six months, the issue dated December 14, 1962, became the first to soar above 100,000. The takeoff was almost unbelievable, and the numbers just kept climbing. By early March 1964, *Midnight* was selling more than 220,000 copies a week, a tenfold increase in just over three years.

Not only had the wolf had been permanently banished from the door, but Azaria and company suddenly had more cash flow than they knew what to do with. Now there was plenty to cover all the wild parties Azaria wanted to throw, and they still had bundles of money left over.

Part of the growth could be explained in purely geographic terms: More outlets in more cities added up to more sales. That was more or less automatic. But the percentage of sale—the number of copies sold out of the total number of copies printed—was the real key to profitability, since unsold papers cost just as much to produce and ship as those that did sell. And no matter how efficient they may be, neither circulation departments nor wholesale distributors have much influence on percentage of sale.

High scores in this area depend almost entirely on how adeptly writers, editors, layout artists, and photographers do their work and how the target audience perceives it and reacts to it. To sell, any given issue of a paper first has to catch the eye of the casual passerby and turn him, almost instantly, into a potential buyer. It has to make him stop for a closer look, then persuade him to reach out and pick the paper up. Most importantly, it has to convince him to lay his money on the counter and take the paper with him.

It's an intricate, almost mystical process involving a maze of interwoven visual, graphic, linguistic, informational, psychological, and emotional components—and *Midnight* was scoring consistently high marks in this area. Unlike its early, struggling days when sales had seldom topped 35 percent, they were now averaging 65 to 70 percent.

One key reason was John Vader. In the long, checkered history of American tabloids, many observers agree, no editor ever mastered the process of turning lookers into buyers more thoroughlly than Vader.

For much of his career, and especially during *Midnight's* salad days, Vader had less to work with in terms of money, staff talent, physical resources, and direction from the top than the editors of most rival tabs. But he made up for it with boundless imagination, complete disregard for convention and conformity, unerring insight into the heart and soul of tabloid readers—and a relentless drive to give them exactly what he knew they wanted.

These rare traits produced some of the most intriguingly outrageous editorial concoctions ever seen on this planet. They also, in the words of one longtime eyewitness, made Vader and *Midnight* as "inseparable as a pair of siamese twins joined at the brain stem."

$$* \qquad * \qquad *$$

Among those who worked closely with him over the decades, Vader has often been called the "mad genius" of tabloidism. His rare skill at inventing, embellishing, tweaking, and doctoring stories has made him a legend among his peers, and it could, indeed, be considered a form of genius.

Meanwhile, though, his thick-lensed spectacles, which gave him a perpetually wide-eyed look; his long, seldom-combed hair; and his abrupt flurries of motion when an idea hit home undoubtedly contributed to his reputation for being somewhat "weird." But like the rumors of Mark Twain's death, Vader's "madness" was grossly exaggerated. It was inevitably based on perfectly sane deductions, sound reasoning, and keen instincts.

"Editorially, Johnny could do more with less than anybody I ever knew," says one veteran American journalist who spent four years working for Vader as a *Midnight* staff writer in the 1970s. "And mentally he was always about ten miles ahead of everybody else. That's why some people thought he was a little nutty."

In the late 1950s, Vader made a trip to New York for the express purpose of studying the *Enquirer* and trying to figure out ways to duplicate Pope's gory, grotesque type of crime coverage without having to pay freelance writers or buy photographs.

At the time, the New York Public Library was keeping back copies of the *Enquirer* in file binders, along with all other locally published papers (a practice that was discontinued at some point where the *Enquirer* was concerned), and Vader spent hours mining these volumes for ideas.

"Up until then, almost all the crime stories we did were sex-related," he said, "but our constant emphasis on sex was wearing thin and getting repetitious, and I knew we needed to broaden the mix. We didn't have any money to spend on freelancers, and none of the photo agencies would even deal with us, so our approach was to lift stuff from any source we could find, and I found lots of material in the *Enquirer* that we could recycle in one form or another. It was a very worthwhile trip."

Vader became notorious for his blatantly perceptive thievery. "We lifted material in wholesale lots from every conceivable source—*Cosmopolitan*, *National Geographic*, *Time*, you name it—then added our own little touches," said Tabatch. "For us, it was a way of life."

The practice continued unchecked throughout the 1960s. Bill Bates, whose job as an *Enquirer* photo editor involved paying large fees for supposedly exclusive picture packages, was often frustrated by Vader's larceny. "Those guys at *Midnight* would steal anything that wasn't nailed down," he said ruefully. "They'd rip off our material, change it a little, fake a few pictures, and away they'd go."

Not long after he returned from his New York "research expedition," Vader hired a talented Canadian writer named Dick Sair especially to turn out crime stories loosely based on cases previously reported in the *Enquirer*. Changing the names of the persons involved was easy enough, and so was making slight alterations in the details of the crime. A bigger problem was finding a believable locale. Vader felt it was risky to pick cities at random as the scenes of such lurid crimes.

He solved the problem in typical Vader fashion—by inventing a nonexistent town named Greenview, Quebec, and having most of the crimes occur there.

"Over the next year or so, there was a terrible wave of murders and mutilations in Greenview," Jack Tabatch recalled. "At least half of the crime stories we ran took place right there, but if any of our readers ever realized it was a phony town, they didn't bother to tell us."

Recently, a mellow Vader talked with total openness about some of the other classic "tricks of the trade" that fueled his fame, both as a sensationalist and as an improviser.

"Whenever I went to a motel, I'd sign some famous person's name to the register and keep the room keys," he said, recalling one favorite ploy. "Then we'd manufacture an off-the-wall story about this big star being caught messing around at such-and-such motel.

"Elvis Presley was taking America by storm at that point, and he was the most controversial figure in show business—the women all loved him, and the men all hated him—so I signed his name several times. In the next issue, we'd have a headline that said something like 'ELVIS FOUND IN MOTEL ROOM WITH SIX GIRLS AT ONCE.' For a while, we were getting most of our celebrity coverage that way."

Vader's mission, first at *Midnight* and later as editor of the *National Examiner* and the *Sun* (another creation that he took from scratch to a peak circulation of 500,000, again with a skeleton staff and virtually no freelance budget) can be summed up in one word: Entertainment.

He never promised his readers the truth, but he saw entertaining them as his sacred duty. To him, a successful tabloid story had a lot in common with a good play.

As Vader himself once put it: "You know the play's not an actual event, but while you're there, you want to believe it. It's a willing suspension of disbelief. So we make a deal with our readers. We won't tell you what's true or not true—and you won't ask."

In a sense, even through more than forty years as a tabloid editor, Vader never stopped being a playwright at heart.

*   *   *

By late 1968, *Midnight* was regularly selling up to 500,000 copies per week and showing no signs of topping out. As circulation climbed and the money rolled in, Joe Azaria's flamboyant style became as much a trademark of the paper as its peculiar arabesque logo, studded with moons, stars, and other symbols.

Like his paper, Azaria had a flare for the dramatic and unorthodox and a knack for arousing curiosity and drawing attention. A prime example of the "Azaria touch" was the small plane he bought and christened "Miss Midnight" and the British bush pilot he hired to fly it.

"It was partly for business and partly for pleasure," said Tabatch. "Now that we had some money, Joe liked to do his partying in places that were more exotic than Montreal. He dreamed up the idea of flying down to Guadeloupe and French Martinique to do 'research' on a French-language version of *Midnight*. Of course, the whole thing was just a ruse. Although we did start a French edition not long after that, there were plenty of French-speaking people to test it on right there in Quebec. Joe just wanted to kick up his heels in the Caribbean."

But the plane, a twin-engine Beech 18, also served some legitimate and useful business purposes, Tabatch was quick to add.

"Joe McDermott, the pilot, flew me all over the country to meet with wholesalers, and the plane created a great impression, especially when we landed in smaller cities and towns," he said. "Not many businesses had their own airplanes at that time—and certainly not businesses as small as we were—so it really got us noticed when 'Miss Midnight' came flying into someplace like Brownsville, Texas.

"We'd take the local wholesalers up for a spin and show them their houses from the air. They ate it up. But the plane also enabled me to get to points in the United States that I might've never reached otherwise. It was an extravagance, sure, but as a circulation builder, it was a worthwhile investment, and it served its purpose well."

*   *   *

At about this same point in time, Azaria was feeling flush and confident enough to start expanding his publishing operations. In the early 1960s, he bought three tabloid titles—*Spotlight, Close-Up,* and *Examiner*—from a defunct publishing company in the Boston area. The latter two papers were published sporadically and never amounted to much, but the third would evolve into the *National Examiner* and become a lucrative second-tier tabloid, posting significant sales in its own right. Later, after Azaria sold the company, the *Examiner* would reach a peak circulation of nearly 1 million.

Everything was coming up roses as the 1960s wound down, but Azaria was getting restless. His company was fifteen years old now, and its early struggles were only a distant memory. The ragtag offices and middle-of-the-night relocations had long since given way to a luxurious high-rise office suite at 1440 St. Catherine Street, West, in the heart of downtown Montreal. In contrast to the hand-to-mouth existence of a decade ago, the company now had $750,000 in cash in the bank, and the balance was swelling every week.

The secretaries were just as cute and sexy as ever, and Azaria could have his pick of them any time he wanted, but somehow it wasn't the same. The whiskey was still good, too, and now he could afford the very best, but it wasn't the same, either. He could spend the winters in Florida now, which beat the hell out of fighting the bitter winds that blew off the St. Lawrence and the bitter, sub-zero cold that turned the river's water to steam wherever it wasn't covered by ice. But Azaria kept hearing a small voice inside his head asking the same persistent questions over and over: "Is this all there is? Is this as good as it gets?"

Azaria was pushing forty, and he was bored. There was no way he'd ever want to go back to the old grind, but he did want something—a new challenge, a fresh start.

Recently, he'd entertained thoughts about selling the company, and he knew somebody who was interested. He'd tried to shrug off the idea at first, but now, with every passing day, he found the prospect more tempting.

Things had started to change in the tabloid world. The *Enquirer* was trying to get its foot in the door of the supermarkets, and Tabatch said that was the way *Midnight* would have to go, too. Otherwise, sales would eventually flatten out, maybe even start to fall.

Azaria didn't like to think about that. Maybe it was time to get out and try his hand at something else.

FIVE
PAPA JOE AND THE PULASKI ROAD "GOOFBALLS"

On the surface, Joseph Sorrentino's qualifications for founding a chain of national periodicals seemed to add up to absolute zero. He was neither a perceptive intellectual like Gene Pope nor a nervy young risk taker like Joe Azaria. He was a simple, middle-aged, family-oriented man with a slight Italian accent and a limited education.

Sorrentino had grown up in Chicago. He'd been a successful businessman there for the better part of twenty years, but as of early 1962, when he decided to try his hand at tabloid publishing, he remained a virtual nonentity. Where Chicago's business community was concerned, he was unknown and practically invisible—and he had no apparent Mob connections, either.

But in the mid-1950s, Sorrentino had established Allied News Company, a small, independent distributor of magazines and paperback books. It was a modest operation at first, but it grew steadily, partly because of a willingness to handle publications that were too off-color for other distributors. Over a period of nearly two decades, Allied became one of the more profitable periodical distributorships in the Midwest. It made Sorrentino comfortably wealthy, if not filthy rich.

Appearances meant little or nothing to "Papa Joe" as long as the cash kept flowing, and long after he could have afforded to move his company to more impressive quarters, Allied continued to operate in the same dingy gray, unmarked, two-story building on North Pulaski Road where it had started.

"I own dis building," he would say proudly. "Why should I pay rent somewhere else?"

Papa Joe first ventured into periodical publishing in the late 1950s when he started a so-called photography magazine with the thinly disguised motive of printing pictures of naked women. For the period, it was as racy as any magazine of its type, and it turned a healthy profit with minimum outlay. The "editorial office" and "staff" consisted of one subsistence-wage employee, one desk, one typewriter, and one filing cabinet stuck off in a corner of Allied's Al Capone–era warehouse. Except for printing costs, the only other expense was for the photos themselves, and there were hundreds of hungry photographers with bushels of nude pictures that they were willing to sell dirt-cheap.

The experience whetted Papa Joe's appetite for more, and after he brought his sons, Frank and Robert, into the business, they began kicking around ideas for other publications that might also be a natural adjunct to their distribution business. When the *National Enquirer* began showing up on newsstands in the Chicago area, it immediately caught the Sorrentinos' attention. And when Papa Joe heard about the millions that another Italian entrepreneur in New York was making off the *Enquirer*, he decided to jump into tabloid publishing.

It wasn't as easy as it looked. The main immediate problem was that the Sorrentinos had only the foggiest notion of how to design and produce a paper that would appeal to tabloid readers. Nude photos more or less spoke for themselves, but a tabloid needed stories, headlines, and layouts that not only sizzled but also made reasonable sense.

But an even bigger stumbling block was Papa Joe's determination to hold expenses to a bare-bones minimum. Pinching every penny had always been the cornerstone of his business philosophy, and it had served him well as a distributor. But this was a whole new ball game. His tightfistedness kept his papers trailing far behind the competition for years, and they might never have found a footing in the marketplace if the old man didn't finally retire in late 1971 and turned the company over to his sons. Even then, that footing was never as secure as it might have been.

At any rate, Papa Joe had a few more secondhand desks and typewriters hauled up to the second floor of the Allied warehouse, struck a deal with a floundering print shop in the southside suburb of Lansing, Illinois, and doled out enough money to hire a few drunks, weirdos, and wannabe writers as staff. The elder Sorrentino habitually referred to his editorial employees of this formative period as "dem goofballs," and with good reason. Rarely, if ever, has a more inane, rattlebrained collection of journalistic misfits been assembled under one roof.

They were assigned to rip and clip stories from the daily press or simply make them up as necessary—nobody really cared which. They were also given a small budget for photos (at the time, most newspapers were willing to sell previously published pictures to just about anyone for ten to twenty dollars per print). But beyond this, nothing was allotted for the agency pictures and freelance acquisitions on which the *Enquirer* thrived.

Allied's new *National Insider* made its inauspicious debut in the tabloid market in June 1962 with an inaugural issue that placed heavy emphasis on sex, freaks, gore, and celebrity scandal.

At best, it was a thin, tawdry little sheet that was plainly inferior to the *Enquirer*, even at the most cursory glance. At worst, it was a hellacious mess—a crazy quilt of semiliterate stories, disjointed headlines, freakish layouts, and pathetic photo reproduction with an overall effect approaching printed insanity. Sometimes, readers searched in vain for the articles to which blaring cover headlines referred. The reason they couldn't find the stories was simple—there were no stories there.

Meanwhile, shoddy platemaking and presswork caused some pictures to come out as indistinguishable black blots and cast a pervasive pall of "muddiness" over the whole paper. They made the subject matter seem even darker and more oppressive than it actually was—if that were possible.

But because of its similarity in name to the *Enquirer*, the *Insider* managed to attract some attention—and buyers—almost in spite of itself. A couple of years later, its modest success prompted Papa Joe to start a virtually identical paper called the *National Tattler*, which first showed up on newsstands in June 1964.

"Hell, with two papers we'll make twice as much money," he told Frank and Robert confidently. It didn't quite work out that way, but it was a concept that the elder Sorrentino continued to embrace for as long as he headed the company.

*   *   *

Certain small typographic touches in the early *Tattler* and *Insider* simply defied explanation. Liberal and repeated use was made, for example, of decorative borders made up of lines of small swastikas—either because of someone's quirky ideology or out of sheer stupidity. This led to assumptions that the papers were neo-Nazi propaganda sheets, but if the effect was intentional, it's unlikely that it originated with Allied's ownership. Papa Joe's personal political philosophy was often described as "slightly to the right of Attila the Hun," but he probably had nothing to do with picking the borders. In fact, some observers doubt that he even noticed such inconsequential details.

"There was nothing devious or indirect about Papa Joe," said one former *Tattler/Insider* writer. "He was about as subtle as a sledgehammer, and if he'd been a big Hitler fan, he would've come right out and said so."

On occasions when he took part in weekly cover conferences, Papa Joe's advice was invariably blunt, brutal, and straight to the point.

"Just say, 'He Rape, Kill Her,' " he advised one of his goofballs during a headline-writing session. "Dat's always good."

Another time, he stormed out of his office, slammed a fresh-off-the-press copy of *Tattler* onto an assistant editor's desk and bellowed out a blistering critique of the issue's racial balance.

"Too many niggers in dis fuckin' paper!" he yelled, stabbing a forefinger at several photos of blacks on the cover.

If there was, indeed, a calculated message behind the swastika borders, a likelier place to go searching for a culprit was in the long line of anonymous editors who came and went at Allied during the 1960s. A few were known for extreme sociopolitical beliefs, occasionally bordering on psychosis. One, in particular, had a penchant for wearing army surplus camouflage uniforms and cartridge belts to work, talking about the small arsenal of weapons he kept at home, and glancing nervously over his shoulder every few seconds. Coworkers recall him cursing the "pinko" Supreme Court, muttering under his breath about brainwashing by the CIA, and angrily blaming the Kremlin for the Kennedy assassination. He was known less than affectionately by his underlings as "Colonel Crackers."

Even in the midst of all this, though, Papa Joe did have one major advantage over other aspiring tabloid publishers: Allied News Company *was* an efficient nationwide distributor of periodicals, with tough, experienced field men who knew their business. As trashy, amateurish, and overinked as they were, the *Tattler* and *Insider* were soon being displayed right up there next to the *Enquirer* and *Midnight* in newsstands and candy stores all over mid-America.

And as amazing as it seems, quite a few people actually bought them. By the end of the sixties, although they still languished far behind the competition, combined sales of the two papers reached an estimated 65,000 to 70,000 copies in an average week. To Gene Pope, this would've been strictly small potatoes, but to Papa Joe, it meant a tidy profit after expenses of around $3,500 a week—not a bad return from a bunch of goofballs.

But before the Allied papers could have a deeper impact on the market, some significant—and costly—changes would have to be made.

*   *   *

As the *Insider/Tattler* odyssey was unfolding on Chicago's Northwest Side, another member of the Sorrentino family was also making his mark in tabloid publishing a few miles away. Papa Joe's nephew, Vince Sorrentino, was still in his early twenties and a recent business graduate of Marquette University when he set up shop in a dusty, hangarlike building on the South Side and started publishing the *National Informer*.

Because of its resemblance to the *Tattler* and *Insider*, many people assumed the *Informer* was owned by the same publisher. In reality, Vince was in bitter competition with his uncle and cousins, and there was no love lost between the two branches of the family. The *Informer* and its cleaned-up successor of the 1970s, *Modern People*, would remain thorns in the side of Allied News Company for a long time to come.

Like his uncle, Vince was eager to hop on the gravy train that Gene Pope had set in motion and siphon off some of the gravy for himself. But unlike Papa Joe, Vince came into the game with a fairly clear idea of what he wanted the *Informer* to be and how to give it—despite its copycat name—a separate identity from the growing crop of other tabs in the marketplace. There were two basic tenets to his publishing philosophy.

Tenet Number One: Sex sells best, and it never gets old.

Sex would be the *Informer*'s foundation—and its floor, walls, ceiling, and roof, too, for that matter. Vince didn't mind mixing in some gore and freaks here and there for variety, but sex was the overriding theme. Blatant, unabashed sex. Weird, kinky sex. Light, comical sex. Heavy, sordid sex. Twisted, depraved sex. Every kind of sex readers could imagine, and some they probably couldn't.

As Vince told a writer for *Playboy* in 1969: "We go after all the sex we can get, although sometimes we do have to draw the line." To illustrate his editorial restraint, he cited a recently rejected article involving carnal relations between a horse and a nymphomaniac. "There's only so many of your perverted people who'd be interested in that kind of thing," he explained.

Sexual no-nos were few and far between at the *Informer*, however. Articles about necrophilia, incest, torture, and perversion highlighted every issue, along with such banner headlines as:

"I WAS RAPED EIGHT DAYS BY THREE MEN AND A LESBIAN"

Even most of the ads were sex oriented, and some of them were pure come-ons. When readers sent in their money for mail-order products called "Instant Peter" and "Instant Pussy," what they actually received were tiny sponges in the shape of either a rabbit or a cat, which expanded in volume several times when placed in water. A disclaimer in the ad stated: "This [product], of course, is synthetic and is not designed to replace the original. However, in a pinch, we hope it will prove to be a satisfactory substitute."

As sadistic and perverse as some of the sexual content was, the *Informer* often read like one massive dirty joke. Its tone, as the *Playboy* writer described it, was one of "jovial depravity."

Tenet Number Two: Truth is troublesome and unnecessary. It should be avoided whenever possible.

Vince saw immediately that it was much quicker, easier, and less expensive to fabricate stories than to seek out factual ones. He was also smart enough to know that made-up people never filed lawsuits, no matter what you said about them.

"I don't think most people care that most of our stories are phony," *Informer* editor Joe Reece told *Playboy*. "In fact, a lot of them write and say that while they didn't believe a specific story, they enjoyed reading it. Others send in ideas of their own, many of which are a bit strong even for us."

Of course, fictitious characters are seldom as interesting as real flesh-and-blood celebrities, and the *Informer* had some ingenious ways of trumping up stories about them, too. One favorite ploy was imaginative innuendo, as in this front-page headline:

Ann-Margret XXXXed
By Nine Guys in Wild Scene

The story inside made it clear that the Xs stood for "kissed" and that the "wild scene" was on a movie set. Chances are, it still wasn't true, but what film star would go to court over such silliness?

Vince realized, just as other tabloid publishers did, that there were two overwhelming reasons why no celebrity of any stature would stoop to suing a gutter-level publication like the *Informer* even in clear-cut cases of libel. For one thing, the publicity surrounding this type of suit could prove a thousand times more damaging than the original fabrication. For another, the publisher probably didn't have any money to pay damages, anyway.

Only after the tabloids attained great wealth and influence—and became much more aggressive in their quest for celebrity scandal—would suing them become an option exercised by an increasing number of famous people. (We'll discuss some of the landmark lawsuits in a later chapter.) And by then, the *Informer* would have sunk back into the dark void from whence it came.

While it lasted, though, it definitely found an audience. In early 1969, Vince told *Playboy* with a straight face that his paper had a circulation of 500,000. According to the best available estimates, it's doubtful that weekly sales were ever more than 75,000 or 80,000. Even so, for a time, the paper published by the "other Sorrentino" may have been as profitable as any tabloid in the country, based on net return per dollar invested.

Maybe the *Informer*'s brashest misrepresentation of all—and its biggest joke on readers who believed it—was the slogan that appeared on its front cover each week just below the logo.

"Truthful News of All Facts of Life," it said guilelessly.

*   *   *

And then there was *Candid Press*, the publication that nobody at Allied News Company wanted to talk about, much less claim credit for. It was a strident, smirking strumpet of a paper—the only tabloid ever to be printed on hot-pink paper with a content to match. The Sorrentinos tried for years to keep their association with it under wraps, but *CP* had a way of popping forth at the most inopportune moments, like a perverted bastard child who enjoys taking his clothes off in public.

During the first half of the 1970s, as Allied fought to legitimize itself and win acceptance for the *Tattler* in the nation's supermarkets, *CP* became a horrendous example of how mistaken excesses of the past can cast a permanent cloud over the future. And even after it ceased to exist, its ghost kept resurfacing to play a key role in Allied's disintegration and eventual downfall.

When *CP* initially appeared in the spring of 1966, it looked to be just another example of Papa Joe's habit of starting a new paper every couple of years. But it soon became obvious that this one would be far different from the rest. Its editorial direction was unquestionably inspired by the success of *Screw*, the New York porno sheet that blazed hitherto unexplored trails in salaciousness, and possibly by that of the *National Informer* as well.

Just who was responsible for guiding *CP* along this route isn't clear, but the underlying concept—obscene as it was—seems almost too sophisticated to have originated with Joseph Sorrentino. More likely, the architect was someone else in the Allied organization, but if there was money to be made from it, Papa Joe would've been the last person on earth to veto the idea on moral grounds.

To give the devil its due, *Candid Press* had a talented and creative editor, who went under the pseudonym "John Horgan," and one or two clever writers who took a perverse delight in the paper's—and their own—notoriety.

From time to time, *CP*'s covers resembled those of other run-of-the-mill sex tabs—except for their vivid coloration, of course. One of the tamer ones was published on June 16, 1972, when Allied was making a concerted, and increasingly desperate, effort to tone down its "hot-pink one," as its staff called it. It featured the alleged "confessions of a Washington housewife/secretary" under a banner headline that read:

"I Had Illicit Sex With a U.S. Senator"

But such stuff was much too "ordinary" for regular *CP* readers, and Horgan and his cohorts were at their best when they concentrated on raunchy satire and obscene-but-outlandish spoofs of oft-repeated sexual themes. Most *CP* articles read like restroom graffiti, but there were threads of vulgar humor woven into them that could make even a hardened (pardon the pun) sex addict chuckle.

"Part of it's pretty disgusting, but, damn it, part of it's funny, too," observed the late John Moulder, an award-winning Texas newsman who joined Allied as a *Tattler* articles editor/investigative reporter in early 1973. "I'm embarrassed to tell anybody it's published by the same outfit I work for, but I can't resist sneaking a look at it, either."

The satire was at its sharpest in such every-issue *CP* features as "The Enema Column by Ben Dover" and "Toilet Talk by Herb Cann" (a crude parody on nationally famed writer Herb Caen's syndicated column in the *San Francisco Chronicle*). Crack-up cover headlines like the following were also a specialty:

Jackie's Gynecologist Tells All!

Exclusive Photos:
LESBIAN HOTDOG LICK-IN

SEVEN-HOUR ENEMA
TURNS BLACK GIRL WHITE!

"If we can make even the horniest reader laugh his ass off at the cover before he flips inside to read the story, we feel like we've done our job," Horgan once explained with a sly grin.

Unlike most other tabloids, *CP* had a fairly large mail-out subscription list—obviously because many devoted readers wouldn't have been caught dead picking up a copy of it in a public place. In retrospect, it seems surprising that its second-class mailing privileges were never revoked by the U.S. Postal Service. The paper's humorous tone may have been one chief reason why they weren't. By the early seventies, society was much more sexually permissive than a decade earlier, and satire—even the most pornographic sort—could be passed off as art and protected as free expression.

After the *Tattler* established itself as one of the "big three" national tabs, the competition used its relationship to *CP* as an effective weapon against Allied with the chain stores. Unfortunately, though, *CP* was also a substantial moneymaker for the company throughout its seven-year life span, and as long as Papa Joe remained in active charge, he adamantly refused to get rid of it. When the company reluctantly killed off the hot-pink one after Papa Joe's departure, Allied's weekly cash flow took a major hit.

Ironically, an effort to salvage *CP*'s second-class postal permit by transferring it to a respectable new paper with a similar name also turned into a financial disaster for Allied.

In a perversely fitting way, the demise of *Candid Press* foreshadowed the death of the entire organization.

*   *   *

Right up until the time of his retirement, Papa Joe clung stubbornly to the notion that "more was better" when it came to the number of tabloid nameplates his company could throw into the marketplace. Up to a point, he was right.

Tabloid buyers seldom bought any other types of periodicals, but they had a clearly demonstrated tendency to purchase several different tabs at once. So, with *Tattler* and *Insider* circulation pretty much stalled as the 1960s wound down, the quickest way to bump up total sales, according to Papa Joe's logic, was to keep starting new papers. *Candid Press* seemed to prove his point.

At the height of its popularity, *CP* sometimes outsold its older, more widely distributed counterparts, and the elder Sorrentino hoped for similar results when he ordered the creation of yet another entry into the tabloid field. Instead of specializing in sexual extremes, this one would offer the ultimate in sadistic crime, sinister cults, hideous monsters, repulsive freaks, and general vileness of the darkest, ugliest variety.

Businesswise, the idea was basically sound. In the mass-circulation tabloids' frenetic rush to clean up their acts, a large void had been left behind. To fill it, Papa Joe aimed to create a paper in the mold of the old *Enquirer*, only more so. Rougher. Tougher. Harsher. Nastier. More mean-spirited.

Of course, he didn't want to spend any money on it. With Papa Joe, that was a given.

But some people still wonder why he saddled his new paper with such a god-awful, derogatory, almost derisive name. For reasons known only to Papa Joe himself, when the first issue hit the stands in mid-1969, the name on the cover was the *National Exploiter*.

Around the end of 1971, the patriarch handed over the reins of Allied News to his two sons, and a few months later, he retired to Florida to oversee his real estate investments there. At that point, it was left to Frank and Robert to figure out what to do with the old man's latest addition to their growing stable of publications.

One of the first decisions they made was to try to soften the *Exploiter*'s name and make it a little less exploitive. It took them a bit longer to drop the axe on *Candid Press*, but they finally made that painful decision, too.

*   *   *

Frank and Robert Sorrentino were a study in contrasts. Rumor had it that Frank, a dour, introspective man who was several years older than his brother, had once studied for the priesthood. He spent his days going through endless reams of sales reports and other paperwork—and, some said, keeping a running log on employees who were late getting to work or took more than the allotted hour for lunch.

"What's that big, thick book that Frank's always writing stuff in?" a recently hired writer once asked an assistant managing editor.

"We call it the 'Guinea's book of records,'" the editor replied with a soft laugh, "and you'd just better hope you never end up in it. All it takes is three entries, then a guy with a baseball bat comes in and breaks your kneecaps."

The editor was kidding, of course, but the truth was, Frank did keep a constant, hawkish eye on the comings and goings of the editorial staff—and all other Allied employees, for that matter. He was also the guy who controlled the company purse strings and generally carried on the fiscal policies established by Papa Joe. No major monetary outlays could be made for equipment, personnel, freelance purchases, or other editorial expenses without the number one son's okay.

Although Frank was usually pleasant enough—in a detached, distant way—there was nothing warm or outgoing about his personality. He rarely spoke to members of the editorial staff, seldom came out of his small office, almost never smiled, and had no direct dealings with any of the publications. His name, for example, never appeared on *Tattler*'s masthead, where Robert was identified as "Editor and Publisher" and even Papa Joe was listed as "Founder." If Frank had an official company title, none of the employees knew what it was, but he clearly had plenty of input and influence in just about everything that happened.

Robert Sorrentino, meanwhile, seemed almost the exact opposite of Frank in appearance, personality, and mannerisms. Where Frank was staid and conservative, Bob—as he liked to be known among his employees—projected youthful vigor and enthusiasm. Where Frank was plain-looking and crew-cut, Bob was handsome and wavy-haired. Where Frank was silent and uncommunicative, Bob was polished and articulate. Where Frank came to work in his shirtsleeves, Bob was always sharply dressed in stylish suits and designer ties.

Bob liked to think himself as progressive, pragmatic, fair-minded, receptive to new ideas, even idealistic, and to a degree, he possessed all these qualities—certainly more so than his father or brother. Beneath the surface, however, he also shared some of the other Sorrentino's less desirable traits. Behind Bob's easy smile, as members of his editorial management team quickly learned, lurked more than a trace of his father's dictatorial nature and hardheadedness. According to some who worked closely with him, he also had a tendency to be overly impressed by high-profile individuals with flashy credentials that weren't always backed up by ability.

But one of Bob Sorrentino's most important strengths, observers say, lay in knowing what he didn't know. He understood that, despite studying business in college, he had neither the journalistic ability nor the editorial expertise to make Allied's papers a long-term success in the marketplace. To achieve that, he needed a crew of highly skilled professional editors and writers. This would mean paying whatever it took to hire and keep them—a "tough sell" to the old man and Frank—but he plunged ahead anyway.

In early 1972, Bob did something that no one else in the tabloid field had ever done before: He hired a professional head-hunting firm to locate the nucleus for what would become a whole new editorial staff.

For most of its first decade as a tabloid publisher, Allied had had almost no success attracting competent, experienced newspaper or magazine journalists, much less any with exceptional ability or qualifications. Occasionally, a journeyman who'd worn out his welcome with the dailies through repeated episodes of drug abuse, alcoholism, or other personal problems showed up on the company's doorstep in search of employment. Usually, such applicants got hired if they were reasonably sober and willing to work cheap. Most tended to drift on after collecting a few paychecks, but once in a while, one would stick around indefinitely.

From 1962 through 1971, roughly 80 percent of all Allied editorial staffers had next to no actual media experience. A few had worked part-time for some suburban weekly; others were would-be novelists or poets willing to hack for peanuts while they pursued their art; some were fresh out of college with degrees in English lit, political science, or other areas where job opportunities ranged from scarce to nonexistent; others had brief experience on service papers while in the military; still others had cranked out releases for public relations agencies; and so on.

There were some notable exceptions, though. After the demise of the *Indianapolis Times* in 1965, several former staffers came Allied's way looking for work, and a couple of them—writer Evan Crawley and copy editor Richard O. (Rob) Bacon—became valuable additions to the staff. A little later, Tom Valentine, a veteran reporter with a knack for digging out "gee-whiz" stories, grew tired of doing routine assignments for *Chicago Today* and hired on as an Allied staff writer at what was then reputedly the highest editorial salary the company had yet paid.

Then, in the spring of 1972, came a major breakthrough. Bob Sorrentino persuaded Patricia de Jager, a former editor of *Photoplay*, the most widely read movie magazine of the 1960s, to accept the newly created position of chief articles editor of the *Tattler*. Admittedly, Sorrentino was helped out by circumstances, since de Jager had just married a Chicago man and moved there from New York, giving up a post as editorial director of Ideal Publishing Company in the bargain. Still, it was far and away the biggest editorial employment coup ever scored by Allied up to that time. It brought invaluable recognition to the *Tattler*, and de Jager's contacts in the entertainment industry opened doors for the paper that might otherwise have remained locked and barred for years.

It was far from the last coup, however. Over the next twenty months, award-winning members of some of the most highly respected news-gathering organizations in North America flocked to join Allied. During that period, the size of the company's editorial staff increased by almost 50 percent, and its editorial salary budget more than doubled.

In the process, the "goofballs" of Papa Joe's era disappeared forever—and so did the ragtag papers that had been their trademark.

SIX

HELLO SUPERMARKETS, GOODBYE SEX AND GORE

T he suddenness of the *Enquirer*'s transformation of 1967–68 caught Gene Pope's imitators completely by surprise. The magnitude and totality of the change left other tabloid publishers blinking their eyes, scratching their collective heads, and wondering if Pope had taken leave of his senses. By the time some of them figured out what was happening, *Enquirer* display racks were already being installed at scores of supermarket checkouts, and its outflanked competitors were left to play a desperate game of catch-up.

At a casual glance, the "new" *Enquirer* still looked pretty much like the old *Enquirer*. It still had the same splashy photo layouts, blaring headlines, circus makeup ,and breezy, rat-tat-tat writing. But the difference in tone and subject matter was like the difference between night and day. Now, instead of "MOM BOILED HER BABY AND ATE IT," it was "YOU CAN'T GET A DOCTOR WHEN YOU NEED ONE" and "Outraged Public and Authorities Demand . . . GET TOUGH WITH COLLEGE RIOTERS."

In Chicago, Joseph Sorrentino's initial reaction to Pope's big makeover was typically blunt and outspoken.

"What's dis guy think he's doin'?" Papa Joe reportedly growled. "Has he gone nuts or somethin'? Where's all da chopped-up bodies?"

In Montreal, *Midnight* cofounder John Vader was equally puzzled.

"When I saw the cleaned-up *Enquirer*, I couldn't understand what was going on," Vader recalled many years later. "My first reaction was shock, but then I got excited. The stuff they were using was so blah I couldn't see how they could keep from losing sales, and I figured that could only help us. Obviously, I was wrong. Only Jack Tabatch saw the writing on the wall right away, and he told us we were going to have to soften up, too. Otherwise, we wouldn't be out there on the racks; we'd be shoved under the counter out of sight."

Across the board, the other tabs were slow to react, and even slower to grasp the method in Pope's apparent madness. It took several months before the real significance of the transformation began to sink in. During this interim period, as Vader observed, the *Enquirer*'s abrupt departure from gore and grotesqueness had all the earmarks of a major windfall for rival publications.

Midnight tallied by far the biggest short-term circulation gains when disillusioned sleaze addicts turned to new sources for their fixes. If anything, Vader and his staff actually turned up the heat a few notches as they rushed to capitalize with such cover headlines as:

Boy, 14, Kidnaps Tot to Rape Its Mother

At first, the *Enquirer*'s circulation plummeted sharply, just as the naysayers had predicted, and it continued to decline for several months. From average weekly sales of slightly more than 1 million in mid-1967, the figure fell to around 775,000 a few months later. *Midnight*'s circulation, meanwhile, jumped from about 350,000 to nearly 450,000, and *Tattler* and *Insider* posted smaller but significant gains, boosting their combined sales above 150,000 for the first time.

But the celebration was short-lived. As Pope had figured out, the traditional newsstands were rapidly fading away. Each time one closed, *Midnight*, *Examiner*, *Tattler*, and *Insider* lost another outlet. Meanwhile, Pope had anticipated this temporary setback, and he was well prepared for it. Years of reaping vast profits had given the *Enquirer* a huge "war chest" for riding out the tough times, and even when circulation bottomed out, it was still selling almost twice as many papers as its nearest competitor.

In 1968, as the *Enquirer* began showing up in a number of high-traffic chain stores in the Northeast, the negative trend reversed itself and sales again started to climb. By year's end, sales were once more hovering around the 1-million mark.

At this point, Pope also made sure that no one dared challenge the accuracy of his circulation claims. The *Enquirer* became the first national tabloid to hold membership in the highly respected Audit Bureau of Circulations, whose figures are accepted as "law" throughout the print media industry. From now on, while other tabloid publishers continued to resort to glowing generalities in talking about their circulations—but scrupulously avoided specifics—the *Enquirer* could present irrefutable proof of its sales, down to the very last copy.

The executive bean counters who held the power to decide what would and wouldn't be sold in the nation's supermarkets were deeply impressed with the *Enquirer*'s ABC-audited figures—just as Pope had known they'd be. Allowing an outside agency to tabulate and publicly report these numbers was obviously a display of confidence that only a trendsetter and front-runner could afford. Unless the also-rans were willing to follow suit—and at this point they clearly weren't—many supermarket officials would turn a deaf ear to their unsubstantiated sales claims.

All of a sudden, the *Enquirer* was back in the driver's seat and heading full speed for the checkouts at Kroger, Safeway, Shop-Rite, and Winn-Dixie.

Meanwhile, the other guys were lying back there somewhere in the dust, brushing themselves off and wondering what to do next.

* * *

In mid-1969, Pope made yet another strategic move that widened the gap still further between the *Enquirer* and its pursuers. He lured William Hall, one of the country's foremost supermarket executives, away from his position as nonfood merchandise manager for the entire Kroger chain and made him executive vice president of the *Enquirer*'s parent company, Best Medium Publishing.

In his new post, Hall ranked second only to GP himself in the corporate chain of command, and although he had no experience in publishing in general or tabloids in particular, his contacts throughout the supermarket industry were considered invaluable. Rumors placed Hall's starting salary in the $400,000-a-year range, plus stock options and other perks.

At the time Hall was hired, the *Enquirer* was already being sold in about twenty supermarket chains—some with more than a hundred stores, others with only a dozen or so. But Pope foresaw the day, in the not-too-distant future, when his paper would be displayed at every checkout counter in every supermarket in America. As the man in charge of "mass-market distribution," Hall was expected to achieve that goal.

Within a decade, GP would come very close to realizing his objective (by 1979, close to 100 percent of all chain supermarkets carried the *Enquirer*), and Hall played a major role in this saturation marketing. But Iain Calder, the Scotsman who rose through the editorial ranks to become editor of the *Enquirer* and president of the parent company—passing Hall in the corporate pecking order in the process—credits Pope himself with planning and engineering the supermarket blitz that started in 1969.

"Bill Hall was important because of his contacts in the industry," Calder said in a March 2000 interview. "He gave us a foot in the door, so to speak, but Gene Pope was the real architect of the supermarket campaign. He was the one who designed it and carried it out. He spent years studying the logistics, and I don't think anyone else in the country could have done it as well."

But the tens of millions of dollars that Pope had available to pour into the campaign were probably the biggest single factor in its success. As the other tabs were about to learn, the supermarket game was brutally expensive. It was also one in which the chains held all the aces, and while other tabloid publishers may have been capable of executing a supermarket strategy as well as Pope did, none of them had anywhere near as much money.

For some of them, it was destined to be a fatal shortcoming.

*   *   *

Virtually everything was now changing at the *Enquirer*. In the mid-1960s, Pope had already built his own printing plant in Pompano Beach, Florida, and by 1968, there were growing indications that the whole operation would end up in the Sunshine State within a few years.

In the meantime, in the fall of 1968, Pope moved the business, production, and editorial departments out of midtown Manhattan into a pastoral suburban setting on aptly named Sylvan Avenue in Englewood Cliffs, New Jersey. More in keeping with its freshly scrubbed image, the *Enquirer*'s new home was in a modernistic low-rise building, nestled on a tree-shaded knoll a stone's throw from the Palisades Parkway and the Hudson River. Across the street was Prentice-Hall, one of the giants of the book-publishing industry.

At the time, much of GP's editorial staff was comprised of longtime Manhattan residents, most of whom took a dim view of the move. To dyed-in-the-wool New Yorkers, New Jersey was a primitive, uncultured wasteland, and they hated the idea of having to commute there, especially those who lived within walking distance or a short subway ride of the old Madison Avenue headquarters.

It was, of course, much more convenient for GP himself, since he spent most of his time at his palatial home in neighboring Englewood, just a couple of minutes from the new offices. But the logic behind the move involved more than the boss's personal convenience.

One of Pope's top current priorities was to assemble an editorial staff that was second to none in the United States, and he was prepared to pay whatever it took to do this. But to get the "all-American" flavor he was looking for, he'd decided to look beyond New York City's jaded journalistic community and even beyond the trans-Atlantic conduit that had brought so many good British newsmen to the *Enquirer*.

The local situation had changed markedly since the days of the *New York Enquirer*. A sizeable percentage of the city's journalists were still without regular, full-time jobs in the wake of the newspaper catastrophe of a few years earlier, but Pope had no intention of building his staff of the future out of the scraps in the unemployment lines. He'd already picked up several of the best out-of-work newsmen in New York and managed to hire away one of the *Daily News*'s more popular columnists, Joe Cassidy. But other high-profile staffers of the remaining New York dailies had resisted his job overtures.

For two or three years, for example, he incessantly wooed Theo Wilson, the premier criminal courts reporter for the *Daily News* and one of the nation's most highly regarded female journalists, but all to no avail. Theo often spent her accumulated "comp days" from prolonged trials moon-lighting for the *Enquirer*—sometimes for weeks on end—at about twice the pay she earned from the *News*. But she never once allowed her byline to appear in Pope's paper, much less considered taking a full-time job there.

Now, with the supermarket campaign moving ahead at full speed, Pope turned his attention elsewhere. The best way to staff a paper that would one day fulfill his dream of selling 25 million copies a week, he decided, was to tap the vast journalistic talent pool in the cities and towns of mid-America.

But top-notch writers and editors in places like Fort Worth, Indi-anapolis, Atlanta, Milwaukee, Kansas City, Des Moines, and Columbus—even Buffalo and Ithaca—were often apprehensive about taking any job in the heart of the nation's largest, dirtiest, meanest, most expensive, most unforgiving city. And if that job happened to be with a paper with a lin-gering reputation as the epitome of sleaze, forget it.

By escaping the perception of congested, crime-ridden concrete canyons in the city and substituting the "sylvan green" west of the Hudson, Pope hoped to make the move from the hinterlands less psychologically and culturally threatening to the media professionals he was targeting. In many cases, the ploy worked.

"But I don't think I could stand to live in New York," a prospective recruit from Tulsa or Tacoma would invariably say when a job overture came. "It's just too big and crowded—too different from what I'm used to."

"But it's *not* New York," the recruiter would explain. "It's suburban New Jersey, and there's no similarity, believe me."

From 1968 until the long-anticipated relocation to Florida in 1971, the *Enquirer* frequently ran help-wanted ads for writers and editors in *Editor & Publisher*, the *New York Times*, and other publications. It was standard pro-cedure to pay all expenses to bring promising job candidates (and their spouses, too, if they wished) to Englewood Cliffs for a weeklong tryout at a salary that was usually at least twice what the prospective employee earned back home.

During this period of roughly three years, a constant stream of news-paper and wire service personnel from the boondocks took advantage of Generoso's generosity. Many had no intention of actually taking a permanent job at the *Enquirer*, but the offer of a free week in the Big Apple, plus a fat paycheck, was frequently too good to pass up. Once they got there, however, more than a few of them changed their minds. It turned out to be an offer they couldn't refuse.

"I'd heard all the horror stories about New York City, and I came up here prepared to hate the place and the paper, too," said one Texan who took the bait. "But then I was amazed at how much I liked it. The atmosphere wasn't all that different from the suburbs around Dallas, except it was classier. Besides, it was a chance to make triple the pay for half as much work. How could I say no?"

By 1970, the *Enquirer* was paying the highest across-the-board editorial salaries in America. They ranged from $18,500 to $60,000 a year for writers, reporters and articles editors and up to $150,000 for top editorial management positions. These figures may not sound overly impressive today, but to put them in perspective, the average annual wage of daily newspaper reporters and copy editors with five to ten years' experience was approximately $10,000 at that time, and only about 2 percent of all U.S. wage earners made $20,000 a year or more.

Pope also instituted an attractive profit-sharing/retirement plan that basically cost individual employees nothing, since all contributions were made by the company. Editorial staffers who quit or got fired at any point after three years of continuous employment received 10 percent of their accumulated profit-sharing funds for each year of service completed, and they became fully vested in the plan in just ten years.

As word about the handsome salaries and perks spread, hiring competent editorial help ceased to be a problem for the *Enquirer*. But there were other stumbling blocks that no amount of money could eliminate, and there were other tabloid publishers who didn't have Pope's millions to use as leverage.

*   *   *

In Montreal, *Midnight* publisher Joe Azaria was facing a different kind of dilemma. By purposely keeping the paper's content as "hot" as possible, Azaria had seen *Midnight*'s circulation climb to unprecedented heights. By 1969, the paper was regularly selling 450,000 copies a week or more, and Azaria was raking in more money than he'd ever thought possible. That was the good news.

The bad news was that, in its present format, *Midnight* didn't have a prayer of gaining admission to the supermarkets. Its staff, from editor John Vader on down, showed no interest whatsoever in altering that format, and Azaria wasn't sure himself if it was such a good idea. If they toned down the product too much, sales were sure to plummet and it could mean financial disaster—like killing off the goose that laid those golden eggs.

Still, something had to be done soon to get the paper into more outlets. Circulation already seemed to be stalling because there simply weren't as many places to buy it as there once had been. As the number of outlets kept dwindling, sales would dwindle, too—regardless of how much sex and gore they packed into *Midnight*.

Azaria's position was further weakened by the fact that his company was based in Canada. This made *Midnight* a foreign commodity and an even harder sell where U.S. supermarkets were concerned. With the *Enquirer* already neatly racked in hundreds of supermarkets coast to coast, Azaria still had no clear-cut marketing plan. Worse yet, he didn't even have a product that was fit to show to a supermarket buyer.

Azaria solved his dilemma in 1970—and simultaneously became a rich man—by selling *Midnight*, the *National Examiner*, and their parent publishing company to his former accountant, Michael Rosenbloom, for a reported $4 million.

At the time, Azaria seemed to have pulled off the deal of the century. Rosenbloom had some money, but not a lot, and under the terms of their agreement, he had to come up with a $300,000 payment every six months until the note was retired. If he defaulted, as many observers expected, the whole kit and kaboodle would revert to Azaria. If not, Azaria walked away a multimillionaire who no longer had to worry about the supermarkets.

Either way, it looked as if Azaria couldn't lose—but looks can be deceiving. He couldn't foresee that Rosenbloom would reap tremendous wealth from the company, even before selling it in 1999 for a reported $105 million. If he had, Azaria might've changed his mind.

He used part of the money he received from Rosenbloom to establish a local weekly called the *Sunday Express* and buy several old-line U.S. magazines that had fallen on hard times, including *Police Gazette* and *Pageant*. But after *Midnight* and *Examiner*, none of Azaria's publishing ventures was very successful. In the mid-1970s, he sold out and moved to Central America.

✳　　✳　　✳

Mike Rosenbloom may have lacked Azaria's adventurous spirit and flamboyant personality, but he had other attributes that would prove even more valuable. "Rosie," as his minions referred to him when he was out of earshot, had an exceptional head for figures, keen business instincts, and total dedication to the bottom line. He was an outwardly shy, soft-spoken, nervous man, but beneath his Caspar Milquetoast exterior lurked a fierce, cold-blooded competitor who could be thoroughly ruthless when necessary.

He'd earned his business success the hard way, working his way through college by driving a taxi, then establishing an accounting firm that developed into one of the most profitable in Montreal. Azaria had become one of the firm's clients when his publishing operation was still in its infancy, and Rosenbloom had been in a unique position to observe its growth at close range over the years. So he wasn't buying a pig in a poke. He knew full well what he was getting into, and he was at least as aware as Azaria—and probably more so—that *Midnight*'s future depended on getting into the supermarkets.

Even before the sale was finalized, Rosenbloom had formulated a strategic plan aimed at that objective, and once the deal was done, he made a rapid-fire series of moves to implement it.

One of his first steps was to create a new corporate entity known as Globe Communications, Inc., to serve as an umbrella organization for other publications Rosenbloom planned to bring into the fold. This brought together a hodgepodge of real and dummy subsidiary corporations—among them Midnight Publishing, Beta Publications, Ltd., and Summit Publishing. It also provided a fresh, onus-free cover name that could be used for everything from contacting chain store executives to interviewing news sources. (At the same time, other major tabloid publishers were taking similar measures. More on this a little later.)

He ordered Vader and his staff to eliminate all sex, gore, and freaks from *Midnight* and concentrate on celebrity and government scandal, consumerism, unexplained phenomena, medical and scientific breakthroughs, courage and heroism, and the like—a mix similar to what the new *Enquirer* was using.

But Rosenbloom always believed in hedging his bets, so to offset *Midnight*'s anticipated loss of sales, he beefed up the *Examiner* by shifting most of the "better" gore, freak, and horror stories into it. He also launched a third tabloid, the *National Bulletin*, which would be comprised almost totally of made-up sex stories bordering on hard-core porn. Meanwhile, the highly profitable French-language edition of *Midnight*, which was circulated only in Quebec, would remain as hot and spicy as ever.

And, most important of all, Rosenbloom began picking up key people from the *Enquirer* staff for the kind of specialized expertise he knew he had to have in marketing, design, and editorial content. He had nowhere near the financial resources to compete with Pope's overall pay scale on a head-to-head basis, but what he *could* afford to do was offer exceptionally attractive salaries to a few key *Enquirer* people in hopes of luring them north to serve as the foundation blocks of his organization.

Only weeks after taking over the company from Azaria, Rosenbloom scored his first—and probably most far-reaching—victory in this campaign. Rumors had reached Montreal that Aubrey Burke, the *Enquirer*'s vice president for circulation, was being forced out and might be interested in making a change if the money and circumstances were right.

The source of Burke's troubles was believed to be William Hall, the supermarket guru that Pope had brought in with the title of vice president for corporate development. Theoretically, Burke and Hall were to be equals in the company's power structure, but Hall's supermarket contacts had given him a decisive edge. Burke had been instrumental in signing up two dozen supermarket chains, but now he was being squeezed out of the chain of command.

"Bill Moriarity, who was also one of the *Enquirer*'s circulation people, put me in touch with Aubrey," said former *Midnight* circulation director Jack Tabatch. "I went down to Jersey and interviewed him, and I hired him on the spot."

It's impossible to overstate the importance of Burke's departure from the *Enquirer* in the spring of 1970 and his acceptance of the newly created position of circulation director for Globe Communications. In one fell swoop, Rosenbloom had shifted the whole playing field by adding one of the most knowledgeable figures in tabloid marketing to his team—and one who knew all the *Enquirer*'s trade secrets, to boot.

Gauging just how severely Burke may have been missed at the *Enquirer* isn't easy, given Hall's impeccable credentials and Pope's carefully calculated plan (Hall was immediately elevated to executive vice president). But Burke's impact on *Midnight*'s fortunes could hardly have been more dramatic. He instituted a marketing strategy that started paying dividends with the big chains almost immediately, and signed a distribution contract with Fawcett, one of the largest companies in the field. Because of these developments, Rosenbloom now felt secure enough to follow Pope's lead and make *Midnight* a member of the Audit Bureau of Circulations.

(In another of the bitter ironies that are such an inseparable part of the supermarket tabloids' story, Burke's presence at Globe Communications and his clout with the supermarkets led directly to the end of Jack Tabatch's career there. Soon after hiring Burke, Tabatch said, "I became yesterday's news, and he became the wave of the future." Tabatch found himself in almost exactly the same situation that Burke had been in at the *Enquirer*. In the spring of 1971, after building *Midnight*'s average weekly sales from less than 7,000 to more than 550,000, Tabatch left the company. He moved to Toronto, where he bought the Canadian tabloid *Confidential Flash* and published it until 1980, when he got out of the tabloid business for good.)

Rosenbloom's next urgent priority was upgrading the editorial staff and giving it a new sense of direction and leadership. Burke's contacts also proved valuable in this effort as they paved the way for other successful raids on the *Enquirer* staff.

Up to this point, most of Globe's writers were young, inexperienced hippie types with limited skills. The Vietnam War was raging at the time, and Montreal was overrun with draft dodgers and college dropouts from the United States who were willing to work for almost any wage in order to stay in Canada. An overabundance of them had found jobs typing amateurish trash at Globe. The staff also included a few immigrants from India, Australia, and the Middle East and one or two old burnouts from Canadian dailies.

Overseeing this conglomeration was John Vader, whose wild imagination, creativity, and hard work had been instrumental in making *Midnight* the second-largest-selling weekly tabloid on the continent. Rosenbloom respected Vader's abilities as an editor, and he wanted to continue drawing on them. At the same time, he considered Vader too laid-back and unconventional to oversee the kind of editorial department Globe required.

In the summer of 1970, with Burke serving as a go-between, several experienced journalists simultaneously jumped ship at the *Enquirer* and joined Globe in a group. Among them were: (1) a new editor in chief, who would be in charge of all company publications but whose main job would be to reform and reshape every aspect of *Midnight*; (2) a chief articles editor to coordinate story processing and compete for the prime agency photo packages that had always been beyond reach in the past; and (3) two seasoned senior writers, who could handle most major cover stories and also help show less experienced writers how to improve their work.

Within weeks, *Midnight* had a whole new look. It also had a whole new lease on life.

$$* \quad * \quad *$$

Creating innocent-sounding "cover" organizations to disguise their true identities and keep their scabrous pasts from coming back to haunt them was a ruse used by all the major tabloid publishers. As mentioned above, Mike Rosenbloom lost no time adopting the name Globe Communications, Inc., mostly for this very purpose.

A similar cover name conceived some years earlier by Vader and used even more frequently by the Montreal operation was Globe Newspaper Group. Many sources and freelancers in the United States, where most of the company's dealings were taking place, assumed that this name referred to a group of Montreal dailies. Most Americans didn't realize that *Midnight* was published in Canada, anyway, since its mailing address was listed as Rouses Point, New York.

Rosenbloom was, of course, far from alone in this subterfuge. He had plenty of company "down south" in New Jersey and Chicago.

The Sorrentinos of Allied News Company used a whole string of dummy corporations to distance themselves from the unsavory aspects of their business and avoid embarrassment when dealing with outsiders. The publisher of the *Tattler* was listed as Publishers Promotion Agency, Inc., while *Candid Press* and *News Exploiter/News Extra* were published by Novel Books, Inc. The *Insider*, published by National Insider, Inc., was the only forthright one of the bunch.

But the cover name utilized most often by Allied editorial staffers was National Features Syndicate, Inc. It sounded sedate and businesslike, and it was easily confused with such highly respected entities as United Features Syndicate, Universal Press Syndicate, and King Features Syndicate. Most importantly, it enabled reporters and articles editors for Allied's tabloids to contact news sources all over the world by phone without ever mentioning the *National Tattler,* much less the company's other tabs.

If pressed to explain exactly what National Features Syndicate was, the staffer's standard response was: "We provide editorial material for a number of national publications."

If the source insisted on knowing which of these publications would be running the story in question, then—and only then—would the staffer mention the *Tattler.*

Surprisingly enough, the *Enquirer* had more trouble with its cover organization than the rest of the tabs put together. Despite Pope's wealth and resources, *Enquirer* staffers were forced during its transition and for quite a while afterward to rely heavily on the cover name Worldwide Features, Inc. But then, without warning in the fall of 1969, they lost the legal right to use the name and had to start telling people the truth.

It happened in this sudden, yet roundabout way: Jim Donahue, a former reporter and editor for the *New York Mirror* had formed Worldwide Features in the mid-1960s, at a time when he was under contract with Pope to produce the bulk of the feature material that ran in the *Enquirer.* By mid-1968, this service was reportedly paying Donahue $150,000 a year, less minor fees that he passed along to other freelancers who supplied him with information or helped with the writing.

As the move from Manhattan to New Jersey was being finalized, Pope hired Donahue as the *Enquirer's* full-time executive editor—at the same salary, but now without having to share any of the money—and when Donahue came aboard, he brought Worldwide Features with him. After that, every articles editor on the staff started using the name numerous times each week in making assignments to freelancers all over the country.

The routine often began with a phone call to a daily newspaper city desk somewhere in America. "Hi, this is Mike Adler with Worldwide Features in New York," the greeting went. "We're looking for somebody to do an interview for us out there in _____. The assignment pays a $150, and it shouldn't take more than a couple of hours to do. You interested?"

Since the stated fee was close to a week's pay for many smaller-city reporters, they usually jumped at it without asking questions. Worldwide Features was an especially effective cover name because it was so similar to Wide World, the photo agency operated by the Associated Press. Besides, it just had a solid, authoritative ring to it. People who encountered the name for the first time had a tendency to think, "Oh, sure, I've heard of them."

Even the checks issued to freelancers bore the Worldwide Features logo, and usually neither the freelancer nor the person(s) he interviewed were ever the wiser. On at least one occasion, the freelance work of a daily reporter out in the hinterlands was so impressive that *Enquirer* editors offered him the customary expense-paid, weeklong tryout. The reporter's first inkling that there was more to Worldwide Features than met the eye came when he received an advance expense check through the mail in an *Enquirer* envelope.

Puzzled, he put in a call to Joe Cassidy, the articles editor who had given him his last assignment. "What's going on, Joe?" he asked. "What's the connection between Worldwide Features and the *National Enquirer*?"

"Aw, don't worry about it," Cassidy said evasively. "Just come on up, and we'll explain the whole thing to you when you get here."

The reporter took Cassidy's advice—and when he was offered an *Enquirer* staff writing job at the end of his tryout, he took that, too.

Normally, when someone got curious enough to ask questions about Worldwide, the stock reply was: "We supply stories and photos on American subjects to some of the largest magazines in Europe—*Oggi, Der Stern, Paris Match* [and others that most yokels had never heard of]."

Donahue, Worldwide's originator, was a gifted writer, but he was also a man plagued by severe personal problems and erratic behavior patterns. After he went for weeks without spending more than an hour or so a day at the office, and let story folders pile up on his desk by the hundreds in the interim, GP finally laid down the law. Under the circumstances, he would've fired anyone else without batting an eye, but he really liked Donahue—"Jim's like a son to me," Pope told one writer sadly—so he gave him forty-eight hours to shape up and start doing his job.

Instead, Donahue went on a two-day drunk.

"Pope can't fire me," he slurred confidently to a small group of coworkers at a nearby saloon that evening. "He wouldn't dare. I own Worldwide Features, and the *Enquirer* would dry up and blow away without it."

But Donahue was wrong. Pope could, and the *Enquirer* didn't.

The following Monday morning, Donahue was officially declared dead meat, and a "papal decree" came down from GP. From then on, all staff members would identify themselves straight out as representatives of the *National Enquirer* and let the chips fall where they might. Anyone caught hiding behind the Worldwide Features name, Pope warned, would immediately join Donahue among the ranks of the unemployed.

It was a scary moment, but after a few days, most staffers agreed that "coming out of the closet" wasn't nearly as traumatic as they'd expected.

"I can tell you this much, it sure gets their bloody attention," said reporter Harry Edgington, referring to the faceless voices at the other end of the phone line. "I had a couple of hang-ups this week, but I didn't have to tell anybody twice where I was calling from."

For the record, Globe Communications turned out to be a far more legitimate and longer lasting name than any of the others that were originally designed as covers. It survived for almost three decades, until Rosenbloom sold the company to American Media in 1999. Along the way, it also lent its name to *Midnight*, which became *Midnight Globe* in the late 1970s, then simply *Globe*.

✳   ✳   ✳

For Allied News Company, meanwhile, the problems loomed even larger than those of its competitors, and they were sometimes complicated by indecision. The Sorrentinos debated at length, for example, over whether the *Tattler* or the *Insider* should become Allied's primary entry in the race for the supermarkets. Continuing to push both papers equally, as had generally been the company's policy in the past, had now become too expensive, and would probably be counterproductive, anyway. One paper had to become the "flagship" while the other was relegated to "tramp steamer" status—but which?

The *Insider* was the older of two, had what might be considered the stronger name, and frequently outsold the *Tattler*. But the *Insider* was also known as the sexually "hotter" paper, while the *Tattler* had leaned more heavily toward the bloody and bizarre. And since sex was absolutely taboo with the supermarkets, the decision eventually went in favor of the *Tattler*.

Because of the resulting delay, only a handful of small supermarket chains in the Chicago area were handling the *Tattler* as of late 1972, and it was running a distant third in the scramble for the checkouts. But by now the company had launched a couple of major incentives to increase the paper's visibility and distribution, and both were slowly beginning to pay dividends.

For one thing, the caliber of the *Tattler*'s editorial staff and the overall quality of its editorial product were steadily improving. The paper's appearance, story content, and readability were now at least on a par with *Midnight*, and the gap between it and the *Enquirer* was gradually closing. Not only was the writing and editing better, but changes in graphics and typography, plus improved presswork, had given the *Tattler* a lighter, fresher look.

For another thing, Allied's staff of "road men" had been doubled in size, and all the new personnel were devoting their full attention to the campaign to sign up the chain stores. The company still had no specialist with direct contacts to the upper echelons of supermarket management, but it had added some skilled marketing people to present the *Tattler*'s case.

By fall 1973, impressive progress had been made on both fronts, and the *Tattler*'s circulation was taking off accordingly. Weekly sales were averaging around 500,000 copies and occasional issues were nudging the 550,000 mark. The editorial department had grown to about thirty full-time employees with staff-manned news bureaus in New York, Los Angeles, Washington, and London. And along with the standard tabloid fare of celebrities, psychics, UFOs, unsung heroes, and wacky inventions, *Tattler* was introducing an element of serious, thoughtful journalism that was largely missing from the other tabs.

A special issue on the tenth anniversary of the John F. Kennedy assassination in November 1973 looked and read more like a newsmagazine than a tabloid. Its cover featured a montage of famous (and expensive) agency photos formed into a large profile of JFK's face and a subdued but effective headline:

THE KENNEDY TRAGEDY:
A DECADE OF DOUBT

The issue sold almost 600,000 copies during its week on the newsstands and supermarket racks, plus thousands of additional copies by mail order later (at double the newsstand price). The attendant boost in cash flow so impressed Bob Sorrentino that, from that point on, offering back copies of big-selling issues and putting out one-shot *Tattler* special editions became part of Allied's standard operating procedure.

If anything, the *Tattler*'s transformation in 1972–73 was even more amazing than the *Enquirer*'s about-face of 1967–68. Even the mainstream media couldn't help but take notice. The conservative *National Observer* offered the following observations in June 1973:

> The *Tattler*'s operation appears less prosperous, less formal, and less ostentatious than the *Enquirer*'s, but these qualities seem to give its 28 editorial staff members a noticeably keener esprit de corps. With a circulation that's just above 500,000, the *Tattler* is the underdog in the three-way check-out scramble, although its editors predict a close race with the *Enquirer* within a few years.

The *Observer* article also included a quote from *Tattler* assistant editor Tom Lutz: "I think the best way to overcome the bad image of the tabloid is to put out a good one. Mr. Pope did one thing by cleaning up the *Enquirer*. We're going one better."

The *Tattler* even drew praise from *Editor & Publisher*, considered the ultimate compliment in the newspaper trade. "Weekly tabloid newspapers have been abandoning the 'mother eats babies' school of journalism to become 'family weekly newspapers,' " noted *E&P* writer Margaret Fisk. "One of the leaders in this trend is the *National Tattler* . . . published out of Chicago.

"In the past year or so, the *Tattler* has revamped its makeup and its story content. Many journalists from top dailies are now on the *Tattler* staff. . . ."

Late in 1973, the *Tattler's* average paid circulation was inching toward 600,000, but despite its steady growth and the spate of favorable media attention, it remained far behind the *Enquirer*, with average sales now running above 3 million and well behind *Midnight* with about 1.1 million. The situation prompted Bob Sorrentino to make a brutally frank assessment of the situation during a management meeting: "We're still only a pimple on the *Enquirer's* ass, and we'll never be anything more until we crack the biggest national supermarket chains."

In the meantime, there was a heavy price tag attached to all the *Tattler's* progress. By the end of 1973, freelance acquisitions alone were costing upwards of $8,000 a week—more than the entire editorial salary budget of just over eighteen months earlier.

These enticing fees had been the key to making regular contributors of such respected journalists as Fred Sparks, winner of the 1951 Pulitzer Prize for international reporting, as well as such sought-after Hollywood gossip-mongers as Toni Holt, who was now a featured *Tattler* columnist.

The *Tattler* had become a better paper than anyone—its owners included—had had any right to expect less than two years earlier. But the mounting costs of doing business were steadily leading Allied News into deeper and more turbulent economic waters.

And if Allied did, indeed, intend to crack those major chains, the heaviest financial demands were yet to come.

SEVEN
THE JACKIE O MIRACLE AND THE DAWN OF CELEBRITYITIS

Ff you've spent much time standing in supermarket checkout lines over the past quarter century, you know one thing for sure: Celebrity scandal and supermarket tabloids go together like bread and butter, chips and salsa, chili and beans. Like cholesterol and heart attacks. Today's tabs and the celebs they feed on are so inseparable in the public mind that they're practically synonymous. It's easy to imagine that if you got rid of the first one, the other one would automatically disappear, too—and maybe it would.

But the surprising thing is, it wasn't always that way. For the first decade after the tabloids infiltrated the chain stores in significant numbers, celebrity coverage was an important, but still relatively small, part of their total editorial mix. They devoted far more space and attached much higher priority to stories that embodied the "gee-whiz" factor—unexplained phenomena (space aliens, UFOs, psychics, telekinesis, out-of-body experiences, life after death), unsung heroes, rags to riches, wacky inventions, weird pastimes, people overcoming handicaps, and the like. Even medical breakthroughs, government waste and skulduggery, burning social issues, and self-help articles were often played above celebrity pieces.

"There was a balance between the 'gee-whiz' stories and the celebrity stuff," says Iain Calder, who shaped the *Enquirer*'s editorial direction for two decades as its editor and president. "At the time we went into the supermarkets, it was the 'gee-whiz' stories that fueled our popularity, but now the balance is gone, and the tabloids are more like movie magazines."

Nothing illustrates this loss of balance more dramatically than a comparison of two *Enquirer* covers published almost exactly thirty years apart.

On the front page of the issue dated April 5, 1970, the main headline was "3 Top Psychiatrists Talk About . . . ADDICTION . . . Why Drug Use in U.S. Is Much Greater Than in Other Countries." Other headlines on the same cover included: "Deadly Weed Killer Is Still Being Sold Despite Govt. Order"; "U.S. Lost $16 Million Last Year in Loans to Small Businesses"; "Why Universities Are To Blame for Violent Rebellion by Students"; "Archaeologist Says We May All Be Descendants of Men From Mars"; and "How to Improve Your Memory." The lone celebrity-related item on the entire cover was a large photo of actor Lee Marvin's famous profile with a low-key caption that read: "Birdwatcher, Purple Heart and Oscar winner, top Hollywood idol Lee Marvin reveals his real self in interview on page 5."

Now, to show how things have changed, let's fast-forward to the *Enquirer* cover of March 28, 2000, and a set of headlines that are far more familiar to today's supermarket shoppers: "HILLARY'S SECRET BREAK-DOWN—MOM RUSHES TO HER SIDE"; "KATHIE LEE & FRANK—HIS SISTER TELLS ALL; FAMILY BATTLE ERUPTS! 'They're both phonies who deserve each other' "; "EXCLUSIVE PHOTOS—INSIDE VINCE GILL & AMY GRANT'S WEDDING"; and "KEVIN SPACEY'S SECRET LIFE."

Unlike the abrupt departure from sex and gore, this transformation didn't happen overnight. It was a considerably more gradual change, one that fed on itself over a period of years, and yet it all has its roots in a single event that took place in the late 1960s. At the center of this event was the woman who became the single most captivating female personality of the twentieth century—Jacqueline Kennedy Onassis.

The moment he heard about Jackie's stunning marriage in October 1968 to Aristotle Onassis, a billionaire Greek playboy nearly twice her age, Pope smelled a circulation bonanza in the making. In an interview some thirty-two years later, longtime *Enquirer* photo editor Bill Bates vividly recalled GP's reaction to the news.

> It was about eight o'clock at night, and several of us from the *Enquirer* were having after-work drinks at a bar not far from the office when Pope phoned the place. He told me he'd just heard that Jackie and Ari were honeymooning at a resort in Peapak, New Jersey, and he said, "Get some photographers over there as fast as you can. Charter some helicopters and fly them in. I don't care what it costs. Just send in the helicopters and make sure they get some pictures." I'd never heard him sound so excited.
>
> I didn't say anything to Pope about it, but I nixed the helicopter idea right away. I knew if helicopters showed up making all kinds of racket, everybody in the place would duck for cover and we'd never get anything. I contacted one of our guys who lived in New Jersey and arranged to have him meet a couple of photographers there very quietly. They managed to

get some shots—nothing really great, but some stuff of the buildings and grounds and one or two of the Onassis party at a distance. The next day, I had to defend my decision about the helicopters. I thought I was gonna get fired for sure, but I didn't.

Many of Pope's employees—Calder and Bates included—insist to this day that their boss had a kind of sixth sense for measuring reader response to certain subjects. And GP's intuition about Jackie did prove uncannily accurate. Public emotion about her marriage ran the gamut from disbelief to revulsion, but it was only after the *Enquirer* began applying a negative spin to stories about her that the real dividends began to show up.

In its issue of January 19, 1969, most of the *Enquirer*'s front page was devoted to an arresting photo of the late President Kennedy with his son and daughter, John-John and Caroline, and Caroline's pet pony, Macaroni. Above the picture was a bold banner headline:

JACKIE BLASTED BY NURSE WHO BROUGHT UP JFK'S CHILDREN

Inside was a three-page spread of text and photos in which former Kennedy nanny Maud Shaw bemoaned Jackie's marriage to Onassis, portrayed the former First Lady as an arrogant, self-centered vixen, and predicted a life of neglect and disastrous consequences for Caroline and John-John. Pope had paid one of the highest fees in the paper's history for exclusive rights to the package, outbidding a half dozen other publications in the process. To many media people, including some on Pope's own staff, it seemed like a waste of good money. Did American readers really care about the spiteful grumblings of a grouchy old Englishwoman?

Apparently, they did care—a lot. A few weeks later, when final circulation figures for the issue were delivered, even Pope was amazed at how accurate his intuition had been. At the time, the *Enquirer* was selling an average of just over 1 million copies per week. But the issue with the "Jackie Blasted" cover had logged in at close to 1.3 million—a jump of almost 30 percent and a new all-time sales record.

Pope was elated, but there was only one way to prove it wasn't some kind of fluke. "Put out the word to freelancers around the world," he decreed. "We've got to have more tough, hard-hitting Jackie stories and pictures."

It was a simple formula, but it worked. And it kept on working, month after month. "Whenever we run a major story on Jackie, our circulation goes up by two or three hundred thousand," Pope told his editorial staff. "If there's any way to do it, I want her on the cover at least every couple of weeks. I want us to go after every Jackie story we can find."

Inspired by the *Enquirer*'s big fees and seemingly inexhaustible demand, freelance journalists and photographers rose to the bait in droves. They swarmed around Jackie and Ari like flies wherever they went. A new term—"paparazzi"—entered the world's vocabulary as other sensational publishers followed Pope's lead and the international chase intensified.

Sets of six or eight pictures of the jet-setting couple snapped in New York, London, Paris, Athens, and Rome routinely brought $5,000, $10,000, even $15,000 apiece. Then there was often a mad scramble to find some sort of text to accompany the photos. Some of the stories contained a few grains of truth. Many took a single molehill-sized fact and embellished it into a mountain of mostly fictional controversy. Others were undocumented, unadulterated BS from start to finish.

An itinerant British journalist named Dennis Eisenberg was one of the most prolific—and handsomely paid—of the Jackie followers.

"All I have to do is call Dennis and tell him what pix we've got," articles editor Bill Dick confided to a writer. "He always manages to dig up something to back them up."

Eisenberg's "diggings" frequently arrived in the form of cablegrams long enough to stretch from one side of a writer's office to the other. They were studded with lengthy quotes from anonymous sources ("a close confidant of Ari told me," "a good friend of Jackie said," "a bell captain at the couple's hotel revealed," and so on). *Enquirer* staffers marveled at Eisenberg's ability to produce such voluminous reams of copy—all without a shred of documentation.

"It was a game we played, and everybody knew what the rules were," said one longtime *Enquirer* writer. "If somebody claimed we were fabricating stories about Jackie and Ari, Pope could always say, 'We bought them in good faith from reliable freelancers,' and the freelancers didn't give a damn as long as the money rolled in. Most of them were three or four thousand miles away, anyhow."

Except for the Jackie stories, everything else that went into the *Enquirer* was scrupulously—almost obsessively—checked and rechecked for accuracy, and writers and articles editors knew better than to try to fudge on the facts. If a medical, scientific, or sociopolitical article lacked sufficient documentation, it didn't stand a chance of seeing print after the editors and fact checkers got through with it, yet they knew to look the other way when a Jackie story came across their desks.

Even John J. Miller, whose celebrity gossip column had run continuously in the *Enquirer* for more than a dozen years, was subjected to rigorous scrutiny. And when Pope's "truth police" found a number of unsubstantiated items in Miller's copy just as the "Jackie miracle" was coming into full bloom, the column was dumped, despite his long friendship with GP dating back to the "Uncle Frank" Costello era.

"By being so picky about all the other copy, Pope thinks we strengthen the credibility of these off-the-wall Jackie stories," veteran articles editor Mike Adler quietly explained to new writers. "So don't think you can get away with pumping a lot of spiced-up quotes into the other stuff you write. There's a very obvious double standard at work here."

True, false, or somewhere in between, all the Jackie stories had one thing in common. They sold papers, and that was all that mattered.

Over the next two or three years, the *Enquirer* gave its readers a steady diet of Jackie O in stories, pictures, and headlines that ranged from nitpicky to slightly silly to downright nasty: "JACKIE'S ANTICS TURN ARI'S HAIR WHITE"; "Jackie and Ari Are Separated From Her Kids Most of the Time"; "Onassis Loses His Cool" (a full-page cover picture showed him slugging a photographer); "ROSE KENNEDY FLEW TO GREECE IN ATTEMPT TO SAVE JACKIE'S MARRIAGE"; "Exclusive Photos of Jackie-Ari Showdown Over Maria Callas"; "Amid European Press Reports of Trouble . . . ONASSIS DID NOT SPEND CHRISTMAS WITH JACKIE."

The other tabs weren't able to match Pope's freehanded spending, but they eagerly jumped into the fray with their own hoked-up stories backed by inexpensive stock photos. "JACKIE SECRETLY CHANGED RELIGION— She Did It to Please Ari," shrilled one *Midnight* cover. " 'Pot Garden' Blooms at Jackie's House—Cultivated by Kennedy Kids," leered another.

And through it all, the readers just kept howling for more.

In staff meetings, Pope offered this explanation for the hugely profitable Jackie phenomenon: "She's gone from being the country's number one heroine—a murdered president's tragic widow—to the world's number one fallen angel. It's like she spit in the whole country's eye by marrying Ari, and people who used to love her can't stand her anymore. They read our stories and shake their heads and say, 'Just look what that low-life broad's up to now!' "

*   *   *

Journalistic celebrity chasing—and celebrity bashing—didn't originate with Jackie, of course. Sensationalists have always been fascinated and infatuated with celebrities. Mostly, it's a simple matter of supply and demand.

As Hearst and Pulitzer repeatedly proved more than a century ago, a certain segment of the public is endlessly curious about the assorted bad habits, social excesses, secret vices, violent outbursts, budding affairs, and broken romances of the rich and famous. Generation after generation, in good times and bad, "Enquiring minds" have been willing to pay to view the skeletons hidden in celebrity closets, and sensationalists have profited accordingly.

Such old adages as "Misery loves company," "Too good to be true," and "The bigger they are, the harder they fall" also come into play in this equation. Millions of nonentities who spend obscure lives working at drudging jobs and struggling to survive are perversely gratified to learn that the great, the powerful, and the superwealthy have their troubles, frailties, and heartbreaks, too. A wide mercenary streak runs through the public psyche, and when the "great unwashed" exclaim, "Oh, how the mighty have fallen!" the words usually ring more with jubilation than sympathy.

All of which helps explain why negative stories about famous people are so much more sought after than positive ones.

While the public's desire to peek into the most intimate nooks and crannies in the lives of the great and near-great is nothing new, it's more prevalent today than ever before, and so is the media's willingness—make that eagerness—to accommodate it. And more than any other factor, it was the "Jackie miracle" of the late 1960s and early 1970s that set these trends in motion.

Today, it often seems that someone of note accommodatingly gets caught with his or her pants down just about every week. But thirty-odd years ago, the big problem with shock-value stories involving major celebrities was their scarcity.

For the better part of two generations prior to Watergate, the mainstream U.S. media had followed an unwritten policy of nonaggression and nonintrusion in their coverage of public figures. Beginning in the FDR years, when a protective press had concealed the true extent of a popular president's invalidism, there was almost a conspiracy among highly placed newspeople to "hear no evil, see no evil, speak no evil" where society's movers and shakers were concerned.

This hands-off posture was still very much in effect at the time of the Kennedy assassination, which is why the indiscretions, infidelities, and shady associations later linked to JFK and RFK were largely unknown to the public during their lifetimes. Political muckraking, adversarial journalism, and even honest investigative reporting had all but vanished from the American scene. Consequently, the tabloids—always kept at arm's length by the establishment and its power brokers—got no help at all from their mainstream brethren in sniffing out celebrity dirt.

As Iain Calder puts it: "By and large, American newspapers in the 1960s were as dull as anything ever printed. It was hard for those of us who came from England and Scotland to believe how dull they were. The U.S. press didn't know or care anything about celebrity coverage. The *Enquirer* helped change all that."

In this atmosphere, "hot" celebrity stories with substance and legitimacy were like solid-gold coins—rare, expensive to obtain, and never within the reach of everybody who chased after them. Shiny, thinly plated imitations, however, could easily be mistaken for the real thing by a public that was more naive, more easily shocked—and much more easily conned.

Faced with a shortage of pure gold, the tabs of that era often resorted to plain old brass to keep the celebrity scandals flashing from their front pages. *Midnight*'s John Vader signing Elvis Presley's name to the register in a cheap motel, then inventing a story about Elvis's escapades there, is a classic—but by no means isolated—example. In literally hundreds of instances over the past three decades, the stuff the tabs sold their readers was mere "fool's gold" mined by journalistic opportunists specializing in counterfeiting and alchemy.

As the tabloids grew stronger and richer, they and their readers demanded an ever-increasing supply of more authentic celebrity coverage, supported by photos and confirmed by eyewitness accounts. And after Watergate, the mainstream media became as cynical and sensation seeking in their approach to celebrities as the tabs had ever been.

In combination, their mean-spirited pursuit of celebrity scandal and their relentless invasion of famous people's private lives finally snowballed into the same all-consuming mania that would one day kill Princess Diana.

When and where this aggravated case of celebrityitis ends is anybody's guess, but it unquestionably started with Jackie O.

$$* \quad * \quad *$$

For the uninitiated, it might be easy to assume that every personality who reaches center stage in America has equal potential for harassment and defamation by the tabs, but nothing could be further from the truth.

At times, a financier like Donald Trump may make hotter copy than any Hollywood superstar. At other times, an ex-jock whose most recent claim to fame is a series of rent-a-car ads becomes an ongoing cause célèbre, especially if he's accused of killing his estranged wife. Even a murdered six-year-old girl, unknown to the national media during her lifetime, can posthumously reign for months as a "cover queen."

In recent years, Frank and Kathie Lee Gifford have probably been on more tabloid covers than any other living couple. Yet neither has the background or credentials of a true superstar. Frank's fame is based on his tenure as an often-overshadowed commentator on *Monday Night Football*, and Kathie Lee is a run-of-the-mill talk show personality, but their ongoing marital crisis has been aired endlessly at America's checkouts.

On the other hand, there are massively popular personalities who stay in the limelight for years, even decades, without attracting much attention from the tabs. This is because they either command such public reverence that any negative coverage is likely to backfire, or they actually don't have any personal warts worth exposing. The pope, Billy Graham, Mother Theresa, Eleanor Roosevelt, and Dwight D. Eisenhower immediately come to mind as prime examples of this celebrity type. But many others also fit the category—Bob Hope, Bing Crosby, James Stewart, Henry Fonda, John

Wayne, Katharine Hepburn, Gregory Peck, Ronald Reagan, and Jimmy Carter, to name a few.

Then there are those who, for reasons often difficult to pin down, just don't "click" with tabloid editors or their readers. When Johnny Cash suddenly burst onto the national scene in 1969 with his top-rated *Johnny Cash Show* on ABC-TV, he seemed like a natural for tabloid treatment. He was an admitted former drug addict who'd been kicked off the *Grand Ole Opry* for his violent, self-destructive outbursts. En route to stardom, he'd ditched his first wife and kids. He'd been busted for drugs, spent time in jail, and come close to killing himself before God and second wife, June Carter, got him straightened out.

At the time, Gene Pope was going through one of his "tell me what people are talking about" phases, in which he called the *Enquirer* editorial staff together at regular intervals to pick their brains for ideas. When someone mentioned Johnny Cash during one of these meetings, Pope didn't even know who he was. But as GP learned more about the singer and his show's high ratings, he called for a major cover story on Cash.

When the story ran a couple of weeks later, it was a resounding flop—probably because Cash had been so open and forthright about his past problems that they were old hat to most people who watched him on TV and bought his records. The lackluster sales figures for the issue sealed Johnny's fate as far as Pope was concerned, and Cash was notably absent from the *Enquirer* from then on, except for a few of those patented "brave fight for life" pieces after the singer got old and sick.

Cary Grant reigned as a Hollywood icon for close to half a century, yet he was pretty much a dud as a tabloid "cover boy." The tabs dutifully followed his May-December marriage to actress Dyan Cannon, their subsequent divorce, and the custody fight over their six-year-old daughter, but the coverage did nothing to spur sales. The rest of the time, they tended to steer clear of Grant.

As big a star as he was, Marlon Brando was never a favorite of tabloid audiences, either. Part of the reason may have been that his sexiest films (*On the Waterfront*, *The Wild One*, *A Streetcar Named Desire*) were behind him by the time the tabs became a national presence, and he'd withdrawn into a shell of privacy that the media seldom bothered trying to penetrate. But when the *Tattler* tried to get some mileage out of a cover piece on Brando's 1973 starring role in *Last Tango in Paris*—billed as "the dirtiest movie of the year"—the issue bombed big time. After that, the tabs generally honored Brando's desire to be left alone.

A few celebrities have had even greater tabloid reader appeal in death than they did in life. Elvis Presley and Marilyn Monroe represent the all-time pinnacles of such postmortem notoriety. The fall 1978 issue of the *Enquirer* that carried a cover photo of Elvis in his coffin sold close to 7 million copies and still ranks as the largest-selling issue of any tabloid ever published in

America. And later reports of mysterious Presley sightings around the country would periodically boost tabloid sales for years to come.

Marilyn Monroe's after-death popularity has been even more enduring, however. As the most celebrated Hollywood sex goddess of the post–World War II era, Marilyn's death in 1961—officially from an overdose of sleeping pills—came just as the tabloids were starting to draw national attention, and it wasn't gory enough to get them very excited. (The decapitation of Monroe look-alike Jayne Mansfield in a horrendous auto crash was much more in tune with tabloid editorial tastes during that period.)

But in the years since, by virtue of her alleged relationships with John and Robert Kennedy and the lingering mystery surrounding her death, Marilyn has appeared on tabloid covers as often as any living star. And she still has the capability to sell papers.

Among living Hollywood legends, Elizabeth Taylor indisputably stands alone as the all-time darling of the tabloids. Her many marriages and flings, several brushes with death, breathtaking beauty, outspoken views, and endless guile kept the tabs nipping at her heels for a third of a century and placed her in a class by herself.

Other entertainers with strong perennial appeal who ranked just a half step below Liz in cover chemistry include: Richard Burton, mostly because of his on-again, off-again romance with Liz; Frank Sinatra, whose brawling, womanizing, alleged underworld ties, and leadership of the famed "Rat Pack" were tailor-made for the tabs; Sophia Loren, whose striking face and sexy figure were splashed on the *Enquirer* cover at the slightest pretext (Pope's editors swore the man was utterly obsessed with her); and Johnny Carson, whose rapier wit and long run on *The Tonight Show* made him one of the world's most familiar figures for two decades.

Fame is fleeting, of course, and in show biz, the celebrity scene is constantly changing. This year's brightest star is often next year's has-been. Over the span of more than thirty years, hundreds of names and faces have been paraded across tabloid covers, some scores of times and some only once.

But the celebrities with the greatest staying power and reader appeal—the ones the tabs simply can't leave alone—have nothing to do with Hollywood or network TV. Their "star quality" springs instead from a base of power, wealth, sophistication, style, good looks—and politics.

England's royal family has been the centerpiece—and favorite whipping boy—of the British national tabloids throughout their existence. No small group of people on earth is as ruthlessly and relentlessly hounded by the sensationalist press, and the reason is obvious. Nothing apparently excites working-class Britons more than reports of princes and princesses caught in torrid love affairs, tawdry drug-and-sex escapades, and other assorted tomfoolery, especially if it involves commoners.

The British journalists who came to work for the U.S. supermarket tabs during their formative years naturally assumed their American cousins would be equally excited, so they continued to report on palace scandals back home and did their best to popularize royalty watching in the United States. But the whole idea of crowns, thrones, and divine right to rule was strange and foreign to people in this country, whose forebears had fought a long, bitter war two centuries earlier to divorce themselves from that same British monarchy. Yanks were intrigued at times by misbehavior in the House of Windsor, but in general, public interest was noticeably diluted on this side of the Atlantic.

Neither Princess Margaret's fling with a captain in the RAF nor her marriage to and divorce from a society photographer caused more than a slight ripple in America on the Richter scale of celebrity scandal. And when the paparazzi caught chubby Sarah Ferguson skinny-dipping at some posh resort, it was mildly amusing, but so what? After all, it was just those nutty British going at it again.

It remained that way until the "battle royal" erupted in the mid-1990s between Prince Charles and Princess Diana. After that, it was a different story.

✳   ✳   ✳

What many Americans of a romantic nature did seem to want in the 1960s, however, was a "royal family" they could claim for their very own—one that embodied all the glamour of the English version, but one that was also 100 percent American. They came very close to finding it, too. Appropriately enough, they called it Camelot.

JFK, their urbane, charismatic "King Arthur," held the most powerful job on Earth. Jackie, his beautiful "Guinivere," and their two picture-book children were with him in the White House, where they set the styles and social patterns for the whole civilized world. Prince Bobby was riding high as attorney general. Prince Teddy was the youngest member of the U.S. Senate. Patriarch Joe and "Queen Mother" Rose held court at Hyannisport. And the various other lords and ladies of the regal, rowdy, incredibly rich Kennedy clan seemed to be everywhere at once.

Then, on a November noon in 1963, in the space of six seconds, Camelot came crashing down. Five years later, Jackie also crashed. Instead of remaining the courageous widow, devoted mother, graceful tender of the eternal flame at JFK's gravesite, and gentle symbol of a nation's lost innocence, she was suddenly wearing tight slacks and bikinis, sailing off on a yacht with a swarthy (and most likely horny) old Greek, and hanging out in Paris nightclubs until the wee small hours.

If the Statue of Liberty had suddenly shed her robe to reveal a pair of pink neon nipples, the country's over-forty female population—the same women who did 90 percent of its supermarket shopping—couldn't have been more outraged.

Not only was Jackie a "fallen angel," as Pope observed. She'd also committed the unpardonable sin of trying to get on with her life and have a little fun. For shame!

Other tabloids were quick to jump onto the hate-Jackie bandwagon. A 1969 broadside from the *National Tattler* accused her of taking pep pills and "speed treatments" while she was First Lady. "The true picture of Jacqueline Kennedy Onassis is beginning to emerge from the Camelot legend—like a slap in the face," the *Tattler* editorialized. The same article described her as a "selfish, demanding, materialistic and relatively unfeeling woman."

Even *Tattler* readers got in on the act. "She never did like our country," fumed one letter writer in the July 26, 1970, issue. "She left our country for a rich Greek."

Not to be outdone, *Midnight* published an alleged quote from JFK's personal diary saying "Jackie can be a real bitch" and confiding that he'd considered divorcing her. *Midnight* also labeled her "the world's merriest widow" and described the world as being "shocked at her behavior."

In June 1969, hard on the heels of Jackie's tumble from grace came Teddy's nightmarish episode at Chappaquiddick—and with it, a massive change in public attitude toward the Kennedy clan in general.

Up to that time, except for a hard core of unreconstructed segregationists and embittered right-wing radicals, most Americans had regarded the Kennedys with sympathy, awe, and admiration. Joe Jr. had died defending his country. John and Robert had been cut down in their prime by assassins' bullets. Joe Sr. was paralyzed from a stroke. Rose was a saintly mother figure to much of the nation. Even if you didn't agree with their politics, they were worthy of respect.

But Jackie's remarriage, coupled with Mary Jo Kopechne's death and Teddy's shadowy role in it, were to change that perception quickly and permanently. Respect was replaced by suspicion, sympathy by cynicism. With breathtaking suddenness, the Kennedys in general—including the slain JFK and Bobby—became the tabloids' favorite targets for abuse and exploitation.

Today, the Kennedys remain the closest thing the media sensationalists and the U.S. public have ever found to an American royal family. Pecking away at their wounds and weaknesses has been royal sport for the tabs ever since Jackie married Ari and Teddy drove off that bridge.

Beyond those two monumental missteps, the Kennedys have contributed to their own transcending notoriety in two distinct ways:

(1) Both their self-inflicted traumas and the catastrophes that regularly befall them "out of the blue" have convinced the public of a real curse hanging over the whole clan. Thus, the rape charge against William Kennedy Smith, the death of Robert Kennedy Jr. in a freak skiing accident, and the fatal plane crash that killed JFK Jr., his wife, and sister-in-law are all seen as part of the same terrible preor-

dained plot—and the public is always waiting to find out what happens to them next.

(2) Early on, the word got out among tabloid journalists and publishers that the Kennedys were a totally "safe" subject. In other words, anything the human mind could possibly conceive about them—no matter how bizarre, demeaning, or injurious—could be published as fact with total impunity, because the Kennedys would never sue. Like the British royal family, the Kennedys saw themselves as an institution, and filing a lawsuit was beneath their institutional dignity. Unlike the royal family, though, certain members of the Kennedy clan have sometimes had ample reason to fear that testifying in open court would only add to their troubles.

For these reasons, no family has ever been the victim of more vicious, tasteless, outrageously phony stories than the Kennedys. And although Jackie was far and away the most maligned of the lot, and Ted holds second place by a wide margin, no member of the family has been totally spared.

The tabs have never allowed JFK to rest in peace. Even today, nearly forty years after his death in Dallas, they still occasionally dredge up "startling new information" about his life and death.

"We still do Hitler now and then, and he's been dead just about forever," said one writer for *Weekly World News* who asked not to be identified. "But I think President Kennedy'll be around as cover material even longer."

Former *Midnight* editor John Vader talked very candidly in a March 2000 interview about what was probably the most outlandish JFK fabrication of all time.

"We'd been toying for months with the idea of doing a cover story to the effect that Kennedy hadn't really been killed in Dallas, after all," Vader recalled. "He'd been severely wounded, obviously, but with Ari's help, Jackie and the family had managed to spirit him away to a secret hiding place where he'd been living as a semivegetable all those years.

"We had this staff writer whose profile was very similar to JFK's, and we got a wheelchair and some other props, and took them and the writer up to a deserted spot on top of Mount Royal [the peak that rises above downtown Montreal]. As the sun was going down and the light was starting to fade, we bundled the guy up in a robe, posed him slumped down in the wheelchair so that just his shadowy profile showed, and started shooting pictures. It was amazing how authentic it looked."

When the "scoop" appeared in mid-1972, the entire front page of *Midnight* was covered by one of those pictures and a huge, black headline that read:

**JFK IS ALIVE
ON SKORPIOS!**

The issue and its flagrantly creative lie sold more copies than any *Midnight* ever published up to that time, and it made other tabloids eager to share in the spoils. Previously, the tabs had contented themselves with periodic pieces on alleged "new evidence" of a conspiracy in Kennedy's murder, but *Midnight*'s audacity led to a full-fledged posthumous assault on JFK.

Within a few weeks, no less than three tabloids came out simultaneously with slightly different versions of the same bogus story, a fantasy loosely based on innuendo published by the sensational French weekly, *France Dimanche*, and the German magazine *Stern*.

In their issues dated November 12, 1972—timed to hit the stands on the eve of the ninth anniversary of Kennedy's assassination—all three tabs carried cover spreads with nearly identical headlines:

JFK AND MARILYN MONROE HAD BABY IN 1962
(Midnight)

MARILYN MONROE HAD JFK'S BABY GIRL
(National Insider)

MARILYN MONROE WAS MURDERED
BECAUSE SHE HAD JFK'S BABY (Candid Press)

The floodgates were open, and the race was on to see who could come up with the most far-fetched storylines. At this stage of the game, the bottom-of-the-barrel tabs, in particular, threw caution to the winds, declared open season on anyone connected with the Kennedys and allowed their warped imaginations to run free. Among the let's-see-you-top-this headlines dreamed up in *News Extra*'s booze-fueled Wednesday night cover conferences were such gems as:

JET-SET CAFE WHERE JACKIE DINED
SERVED HUMAN FLESH!

TED & ETHEL: THE TRUTH BEHIND
THOSE AWFUL RUMORS

ARI KICKS OUT MAN HE HIRED
TO GET JACKIE PREGNANT

ROSE KENNEDY, 71, TO WED WAITER, 23;
TEDDY IS FURIOUS

DRUNKEN JOAN GOES ON RAMPAGE WITH POWER
MOWER—Cuts Down Neighbor's Hedge & Scalps Pet Dog!

JOAN WANTS TO RUN FOR PRESIDENT!

Poor Joan. By this time, the only thing she and most of the other Kennedys wanted to run for was someplace to hide.

*   *   *

By and by, the worst of the lunacy ran its course. After Onassis's death, the tabs' obsession with Jackie tailed off, and they allowed her to spend the last years of her life in relative peace and quiet. With his presidential aspirations doomed by Chappaquiddick and his campaign for the White House abandoned, Teddy also lost his glitter and was left to bury himself quietly in the Senate.

Then, in the 1990s, the sensationalists rediscovered JFK Jr., and the cycle seemed destined to repeat itself until his sudden and untimely death. Still, as they did with his father, the tabs have kept digging up the son for one last exposé. (Indeed, as this was written, the main headline on *Globe*'s April 4, 2000, cover was "I BLAME JFK FOR FATAL CRASH," based on a statement by a relative of John Jr.'s wife.)

Had John-John lived to fulfill a now-haunting 1970 cover prophesy in *Midnight*—"JFK JR. WILL BE PRESIDENT IN YEAR 2000 . . . Prominent Astrologer Predicts"—the saga might never have ended. But now, even the most persistent tabloid editors have to look somewhere else for their next sure-fire celebrity bombshell.

In all likelihood, there'll never be another Jackie, but as long as the tabs exist, they'll never stop searching for one. This is why they zeroed in on Princess Diana with such fierce tenacity in the first place. They thought that, just maybe, Diana possessed that elusive aura—part heroine, part victim, part "fallen angel"—to rekindle the Jackie magic. But she died too soon for the theory to be fully tested, and besides, the tabs were forced to share her with too many other celebrity chasers. It just wasn't the same—and it never will be again.

Now, ironically, the residue of public anger over the sensational media's perceived role in causing Diana's death may be as much a key to the supermarket tabs' undoing as the "Jackie miracle" was in their rise to prominence.

In a sense, if it works out that way, there couldn't be a more fitting end to the tabloid odyssey. It's just the kind of final, epic twist of fate that the tabs themselves have always thrived on.

EIGHT
THE POPE
AND THE MAFIA
A COZY, CONTINUING CONNECTION

Firings were a constantly recurring fact of life at the *Enquirer* during the 1960s and 1970s. The threat of them hung like an invisible sword over the head of every editorial staffer as a reminder that the fat salary (up to two or three times what major dailies were paying) and the good life it provided could end at any moment.

The list of things that could get you canned seemed almost endless. Several guys who had the temerity to adjust the thermostat in the editorial offices were booted with thunderclap suddenness, and at least one writer got the axe for merely opening a window. After those incidents, newcomers were warned early on not to mess with indoor climatic conditions. Nobody but GP himself was allowed to do that. He never passed through the editorial department without checking the thermostat setting and temperature. If either was off as much as half a degree, you could almost see the smoke start coming out the boss's ears. He was totally obsessive about it.

As a frequently whispered one-liner put it: "It makes you wonder if that's the only thing he learned at MIT—how to read a thermostat."

There was no question, however, about his ability to strike like a cobra over the most trivial transgressions. Maybe it was part of the training he'd gotten during his time with the CIA, or maybe it was something he'd learned at the knee of his wealthy Mob-connected father. Those who observed Generoso Jr. over the years weren't sure if he ever really *liked* anyone who worked for him. He respected only three qualities in an employee—skill, productivity, and loyalty. If he sensed a lack of any one of these, it was usually fatal for the lackee.

Even key long-term employees could fall from favor with alarming suddenness. Editor Nat Chrzan himself, who had been with the *Enquirer* since 1960, often broke into a visible sweat when summoned for a private confab in Pope's inner sanctum (an office roughly the size of the press box at the Meadowlands and furnished, in the words of a *Newsweek* writer, in "early Motel Gothic").

Selig Adler, a former managing editor of the *New York Mirror* who joined the *Enquirer* as chief articles editor after the *Mirror*'s demise during the calamitous New York newspaper strike of the mid-1960s, described Pope's dealing with his staff this way: "He likes to toy with people, like some sadistic asshole pulling the wings off live flies. He knows half the newsmen in the city can't find full-time work, so he dangles these high-paying jobs under their noses, then, once he hires them, he thinks he owns them body and soul."

One sufferer named Jim Allan traveled up and down the *Enquirer*'s slippery ladder of success at least three times, once rising as high as executive editor before being ousted and rehired as a lowly staff writer. "If he wants to see me squirm, then I'll squirm," Allan remarked calmly to a coworker. "He pays me double what I could make anywhere else."

"We're all just a bunch of whores," was a favorite observation of Mike Adler, Selig's brother and also a former *Mirror* executive, "but at least we're high-paid whores."

Selig himself rarely made it through a morning without pounding his fist on his desk and snarling, "Damn this fucking place." But he never uttered a cross word to GP.

Because he never wore a necktie, much less a jacket, and his shirts were always open at the collar, Pope looked more like a service technician than the owner and publisher of the *Enquirer*. But when a rookie employee mistook GP for a custodian and asked him to take care of an overflowing commode in the men's room, the foul-up brought swift retribution. The offender was bounced before the end of his first week.

A popular secretary was summarily dismissed after being ordered to type up Pope's daughter's school homework assignment—in addition to doing all her regular company work—and failing to complete it on time. A young editorial assistant was sent packing for pouring Pope too much coffee.

"I said half a cup," he told her, lighting one of his omnipresent Kent cigarettes with a solid-silver lighter the size of a hand grenade. "Is that half a cup?"

"I—I don't know, sir."

Thirty seconds later, Pope picked up the phone and called Chrzan's secretary. "Anybody who can't tell half a cup from a full cup is too stupid to work here," Pope told her. "Tell that broad to get the hell out."

Departmental secretaries and editorial assistants were often saddled with endless rounds of menial chores for Pope. The boss's personal secretary, meanwhile, was a nattily dressed young man who seldom seemed busy, never smiled, and had even less to say to the staff than GP himself.

Having a male secretary gave rise to occasional staff speculation about Pope's sexual orientation, especially among recent arrivals.

"Is he queer?" one wondered. "If he's not, why does he have a guy working in there instead of a good-looking chick?"

In response, more experienced and well-informed staffers usually offered two possibilities: (1) Pope's stunningly attractive second wife, Lois, a former showgirl, had forbidden him to have a female secretary, or (2) the young man was actually an underworld "plant," placed there to keep an eye on Pope and provide inside information to the Mob.

Most staffers tended to support the latter theory. And the longer they stayed around Pope, the more plausible the idea seemed. Pope's Mafia connections hadn't ended with the fall from power of "Uncle Frank" Costello. If anything, they had intensified. The difference now was that Pope could deal with Mob leaders not as someone begging for help but as a powerful equal.

✳   ✳   ✳

A single dissenting comment during one of the high-tension staff meetings held periodically in Pope's private office could send GP into a firing frenzy. "If he doesn't believe in what we're doing, then he's got no business here," he would growl. "Get ridda that guy." Likewise, an articles editor who once dozed off in a meeting woke up to find himself among the unemployed. "Now he can find a nice, comfortable bench in Central Park and sleep all day," Pope snapped.

One afternoon when GP was giving a pep talk to his assembled journalistic troops, he raised his voice from its usual soft semiwhisper to declare: "I want you people to disagree with me when we have a difference of opinion. If you think I'm wrong, I want you to tell me so."

Amid the rather uncomfortable pause that followed, a small voice piped up in the back of the room: "How much does the job pay?"

The questioner was a rotund copy editor and well-known office clown named Joe Dean. It had been Dean who first coined what eventually became a sort of informal philosophy of life for *Enquirer* staffers—"Shut up and take the money"—and now, heaven help him, Joe had violated his own bywords. The rest of the staff cringed and held its collective breath. For a few seconds, you could have heard a pin drop in the office. When Pope spoke, there was a frozen little smile on his lips, but his blue eyes were as cold as ice under his bushy brows.

"You can stay after the meeting, Joe," GP said softly, "and we'll discuss it."

Dean's face turned the color of a sheet of newsprint, and no one would have bet a nickel on his survival, although he had worked for Pope for close to ten years. However, when he emerged later from Pope's office, still white and shaking, other staffers were relieved to learn that GP had let him off with a warning.

"He said, 'I wouldn't want to think you were being insubordinate, Joe,'" Dean mumbled. "And I said, 'No sir, I wouldn't want you to think that, either.'"

Many other unfortunates weren't nearly so lucky. Science Editor Merwin Dembling was ousted because "his stuff's too scientific." Cartoon Editor Larry Barth was shown the door because, out of the hundreds of syndicated cartoons he submitted for approval each week, Pope couldn't find any he thought were funny.

"Show him a sackful of dead babies, though, and the warped bastard'd probably laugh his ass off," one of Barth's friends remarked sourly over an after-work drink in a bar that evening.

Actually, Pope hardly ever fired anyone face to face. Instead, his modus operandi was to summon one of his editorial overseers and hand the dirty job to him. Whenever you saw a grim-faced Nat Chrzan, Carl Grothmann, or Executive Editor Mel Snider heading for GP's office around 3 o'clock on a Friday afternoon, you knew another "get ridda that guy" decree was about to be carried out. In some Friday massacres, three or four people were given the gate at once.

In a 1969 interview with *Editor & Publisher*, Pope classified his revolving-door employee policy as an unavoidable part of upgrading the *Enquirer*'s content and refining its image. As *E&P* put it: "Reporters who had written flamboyantly about crime and sex, he said, couldn't write with clarity about finance, automobiles, and household needs. He had found it necessary to discharge some people and hire new ones.

"'I still haven't solved that problem,' Pope said. 'I'm still looking for good men.'"

Of all the irrational beheadings and executions, though, perhaps the most unforgettable—and certainly the most unforgivable in the minds of many observers—came on an early-summer Friday in 1970. Even today, more than three decades later, those who witnessed it still debate its true meaning. Only one thing about it is 100 percent certain: It illustrates, as clearly as any single incident in Pope's remarkable career, how strongly his relationship with the Mafia continued to influence his personal and professional life.

＊　　＊　　＊

When Mel Snider summoned him into his office that afternoon, Dominick Merle's first thought was that he was going to get a raise. "Man, was I in for a surprise," he recalled later.

At thirty-four, Merle had been a highly respected veteran reporter at the *Buffalo Evening News* up until the previous February, when he had come to the *Enquirer* for a week's tryout—a standard part of the hiring procedure— then accepted a writing job. Although he had been on the staff only about four months, Merle's work had drawn numerous compliments, and he had every reason to think of himself as being on the way up. So what Snider had to say hit him like a kick in the gut.

"I hate to be the one to have to tell you this, Dom," Snider said, chewing his lip, "but I've got no choice. I've been ordered to let you go, effective immediately. Mr. Pope wants you to collect your personal stuff and get out of the office as fast as you can."

For a few seconds, Merle was stunned speechless. Then, as the impact of Snider's words sank in, he could feel cold panic welling up inside him. He had a wife and four kids at home—all of them totally dependent on his salary—and now, suddenly, there *was* no salary. What was he going to do?

He shook his head. "I don't get it, Mel. What's this all about?"

Snider pushed his reading glasses up on his forehead and wiped his face with a handkerchief. "It's about that story you wrote—the one on the Mafia. I can't describe all the trouble it's caused over the past twenty-four hours. When GP found out it was in the issue that was already on the press, he called the printing plant in Florida and made 'em yank it. I've never seen him any madder—and I hope I never do."

"But, Christ, Mel," Merle protested hoarsely. "Pope approved the story himself. He okayed it weeks ago. It's been so long I'd forgotten all about it. Why should he be so upset now?"

Snider shrugged. "He claims he never saw it. That's all I know."

"Well, God, let me go in and talk to him. This has got to be some kind of misunderstanding. Maybe I can straighten things out."

"No, you don't want to go in there, Dom. That'd be the worst thing you could possibly do." He leaned forward and lowered his voice. "You didn't hear this from me, but the kind of rage this guy's in, he just might put a contract out on you, and that's no shit. I hear he's very well acquainted with guys who do that kind of work. The best thing for you to do is make yourself scarce."

"I just don't understand this," Merle muttered. "This is the craziest thing that ever happened to me."

Snider slid an envelope across the desk. "I'm sorry, Dom," he said, "but my hands are tied. Here's a check for two weeks' severance pay—it was the best Nat and I could do. If you need a reference when you start looking for another job, I'll be glad to give you one. Good luck."

Over the next few days, with the help of sympathetic former coworkers,

Merle was able to piece together the chain of events leading up to his dismissal. But even then, the reasons for it remained incomprehensible.

The story that caused the trouble was one Merle had written previously for the Buffalo paper. It was based on an interview with a prominent criminologist and university professor who claimed that, instead of being a vast, shadowy empire of interwoven underworld enterprises, the Mafia was basically nothing but a fabrication created by the FBI to enhance its own importance.

"The gist of what this expert was claiming was that every time the feds busted some petty crook with an Italian surname, they tried to make it look like part of some big organized crime operation," Merle explained years later. "He didn't deny that something called the Mafia exists, but he said its power was grossly exaggerated because of all the hype by the FBI and other law enforcement agencies."

Following the usual *Enquirer* routine for submitting a story idea, Merle had filled out a "lead sheet" describing the proposed article, attached a clipping of the piece he had done for the *Evening News* and routed it through the usual channels.

"At the time, the New York press was running stories about the Joseph Colombo family protesting that they were being illegally and unfairly harrassed by the FBI over alleged mob activities that the feds couldn't prove," Merle said. "I thought this would help create interest in my story."

As anyone associated with Pope's *Enquirer* was well aware, nothing *ever* went into the paper without being personally approved by GP. Every lead sheet had to receive his okay and initials. He read every word of every article, often several times. He reviewed every page proof and, in an era when fax machines were unknown, bragged loud and long about the speed and efficiency with which these proofs could be transmitted via telecopier from the Florida plant to the editorial offices in New Jersey.

As Chrzan had told *Editor & Publisher* in an interview several months before Merle's firing: "Pope is the kind of publisher newspapers ought to have more of. He's here 365 days a year, just about. He's supposed to take a two-week vacation in Florida, but when he does he spends all his time in the printing shop down there. He looks over the copy every day. It was the same when he took his vacations at the Hamptons on Long Island. We sent all the stuff out to him. He wants to see everything before it gets into the paper."

According to what Pope told his editors, however, he had never laid eyes on the Merle article until he was sitting at home in Englewood, New Jersey, on a Thursday evening. Pope claimed that his wife was leafing through a hot-off-the-press copy of the *Enquirer* which had just been delivered by air express from Florida.

"What's this?" she allegedly demanded, pointing to a headline on an inside page toward the back of the paper. "How did this get in here?"

It was only then, according to Pope, that he got his first glimpse of the Merle story and the riveting headline above it:

THE MAFIA IS A MYTH!
—Famed Criminologist Says

Pope later told several *Enquirer* editors that he threw down the paper and rushed to the phone to call the printing plant in Florida, shouting, "Those bastards have been trying to get me to print this story for almost twenty years, and whoever's responsible for this is going to pay!"

But at least one editor recalled hearing a radically different account of this episode. In this version, GP was first made aware of the Merle story and headline not by his wife, but by a gleeful telephone call from someone in the New York Mafia who had managed to get hold of an early copy.

By Pope's own account at the time (despite conflicting accounts that surfaced later), more than 700,000 copies of the *Enquirer*—roughly a third of its press run—were already printed before he could order the presses shut down and the story killed. All copies remaining in the printing plant were destroyed, but an undetermined number were already en route to wholesalers across the country and couldn't be recalled. No one knows to this day how many "tainted" copies actually found their way onto newsstands and supermarket racks. Only the "abridged" version is to be found in the paper's surviving files.

Among insiders, Pope's motives for doing what he did have been examined and debated for more than thirty years. To other staffers, GP angrily accused Merle of being either a paid agent of one of the powerful New York–New Jersey Mafia families specifically assigned to penetrate the *Enquirer* staff and plant an editorial "bomb" in its midst, or "the stupidest sonofabitch that ever lived."

But it was common knowledge among virtually all *Enquirer* journalists that Merle had been set up as a convenient scapegoat in a deliberate, cynical plan that spanned at least several weeks. Among the strongest evidence was the fact that no articles editor had ever been assigned to the Merle story. At the time, the division of responsibility between articles editors and writers was total and clearly defined. AEs gathered information. Writers wrote. And never the twain should meet.

Every story lead was automatically assigned to an AE for development and research, and only when this phase was completed was it passed along to a writer. The single exception that anyone could remember was the "Mafia Is a Myth" story. Nobody had the slightest doubt that Merle, the only Italian-American on the editorial staff at the time, had been sacrificed as a pawn in a much larger game. The question was "Why?" What purpose could it possibly serve?

After lengthy and surreptitious discussion, some staffers claimed to know the answer. One explained it this way:

> Pope was playing both ends against the middle. He's got important anti-Mafia friends in the Italian community, but he's also on intimate terms with a bunch of Mafiosi whose muscle helps keep competing tabloids locked out of the New York–New Jersey–Connecticut market. He needed some way to demonstrate his loyalty to both groups, and this was how he did it.
>
> Now he can say to his Mafia friends: "See what I did for you? I ran that story you'd been trying to get me to run for so long. I did it as a special favor for the family." But he can also tell his anti-Mafia friends: "Hey, look, when I found out about that damned story, I made them stop the presses in the middle of the run, and I fired the guy responsible."

In other words, it was apparently another chapter in the same tightrope-walking act that had caused Pope to fall from grace with the mayor of New York some twenty years earlier.

In all probability, no one will ever know how close this theory comes to the truth, but it's as plausible an explanation as any. And everyone associated with the incident agreed on one thing: However twisted his reasoning may have been, Pope knew exactly what he was doing—and why.

The week after the firing, Merle consulted several lawyers to see if he might have grounds for a civil suit. A couple of them discouraged him for the usual practical reasons—the case could drag on indefinitely and cost a fortune in legal fees and court expenses. But one Manhattan attorney advised Merle to forget the whole thing for his own future well-being.

"Pope's got a lot of powerful friends," the attorney said, "and some of them would as soon break your legs as look at you. They could make things very unpleasant if you persist. If I were you, I'd just drop it and get on with my life."

The events that unfolded over the next week or so convinced Merle to take the lawyer's advice. He was offered, and quickly accepted, a job as a staff writer at *Midnight* at a slightly higher salary than he had been getting at the *Enquirer*, and within a few days he was in Montreal cranking out stories again. This not only proved his journalistic competence and restored some of his confidence, but also allowed him to adopt a more philosophical attitude about what had happened.

"Since I was able to land on my feet so quickly, I just more or less stopped thinking about it," he said. "I never had any reason to feel very bitter because I ended up in a better job in a place I really like."

For almost three decades after the episode, Merle continued to work in the Montreal corporate headquarters of Globe Communications, publisher of *Globe, Examiner,* and the *Sun,* as editor of North America's last surviving string of detective magazines. He retired shortly after the company was sold to American Media in late 1999.

Meanwhile, those who personally remember the "black Friday" when Merle was fired at the *Enquirer* still wonder about it and shake their heads.

✳   ✳   ✳

While Merle's firing was a unique event, it was only one of many incidents that revealed Pope's intricate involvement with high-ranking Mafiosi.

Many employees at the tree-shaded suburban office building on Sylvan Avenue in Englewood Cliffs, New Jersey, where the *Enquirer* was headquartered from 1967 to late 1971, noticed the chauffeur-driven limousines that pulled into the rear parking lot at regular intervals to discharge Mafia capos and their well-heeled bodyguards. Joe Colombo dropped by periodically. So did Vito Genovese, Carlo Gambino, Joseph "Joe Bananas" Bonanno, and others.

The late William Dick, who spent more than fifteen years in Pope's employ in New York, New Jersey, and Florida, described a typical visit.

> You'd see a pair of these big black cars drive up, and as soon as they were stopped, these huge bodyguards would jump out and open the door for some little man in a fedora and a dark suit. Two bodyguards would come with him up the back stairs to Pope's private office, and the little guy would go in while the others hung around outside in the hall with their hands stuck in their coats. At least two more guys always stayed downstairs with the cars.

These same shadowy underworld bosses were also frequent visitors in earlier years when the *Enquirer* offices were at 655 Madison Avenue in Manhattan. Although they were able to slip in and out of that busy midtown location without being nearly as noticeable as they were in the quiet setting of Englewood Cliffs, the enforcers who accompanied them often made their presence painfully obvious.

Reginald Potterton, a former *Enquirer* articles editor, described some of these comings and goings in an April 1969 article in *Playboy*:

> He [Pope] rarely left his office and was accessible only to key executives, to his barber, who called once a week, and to an intermittent procession of pinkie-ringed male visitors who arrived in twos and threes wearing white–on–white and expensive shot-silk suits and who would sit in the reception area, backs straight and with manicured fists resting on their knees, while waiting to be ushered into Pope's office.
>
> "Who are those guys," a writer once asked another staffer.
>
> "I think they're connected with charity," he was told.
>
> I once passed one of them, who had evidently lost his money in the

cigarette dispenser that stood outside the washroom. He was kicking the machine, intently, methodically and with great force, all the while holding it with both hands and rolling a toothpick slowly from one side of his mouth to the other.

The legend surrounding Pope's close personal relationship with Costello was handed down from veterans to newcomers among several generations of *Enquirer* staff members. Rookies were always intrigued to learn that Pope had been among the last persons to see Costello before the fateful attempt on the mobster's life in 1957.

"Was Costello really his godfather like they say?" the newcomers would invariably ask.

"That's what everybody says," the old-timers would answer. "Maybe you ought to go down the hall and ask him about it."

Stories were also repeated about Pope's father, Generoso Sr., being one of Costello's oldest and closest friends and also having had his fingers in a number of Mafia-flavored pies.

A longtime Hearst reporter named Joe Faulkner, who was hired as an *Enquirer* staff writer when he was late in his career and rather deep in his cups, once stunned everyone—GP included—during his first editorial staff meeting by brashly introducing himself to the boss with these words: "Hello, Mr. Pope, I'm Joe Faulkner. I was covering the federal courthouse in New York the day your father was convicted of racketeering."

Eyewitnesses to this bizarre encounter were amazed that Faulkner wasn't axed on the spot. "Jesus, we knew Joe was crazy," said writer Ralph Mahoney, another former Hearst newsman who had helped Faulkner get his job at the *Enquirer*, "but not *that* crazy, for Chrissake."

When Faulkner *was* fired several weeks later, it was ostensibly for drinking on the job, and few staffers could argue with the verdict, since Joe spent most of his afternoons using his typewriter for a pillow and snoring like a beached whale.

As far as any of his employees can remember, Pope never once mentioned Frank Costello's name. He didn't talk much about his father, either, but when he did, he described the elder Pope as an astute businessman and generous philanthropist who had bequeathed some $3 million to a small Catholic college in Elizabeth, New Jersey.

A dozen years after the assassination attempt on Costello, Thomas "Tommy Ryan" Eboli, a racketeer with a long history of Mafia associations, was found on a Brooklyn sidewalk with seven bullet holes in him. There was no overt evidence that Eboli had any connection with Pope. But old hands at the *Enquirer* pointed out that Eboli lived in nearby Fort Lee, only a mile or so as the crow flies from both the office and Pope's Englewood mansion. Some thought they had seen Eboli among Pope's periodic visitors.

It's doubtful that anyone who worked for Pope ever had the nerve to ask him straight out about how close his relationship to Costello really was. But occasionally someone did broach the question to Chrzan.

"I don't know and I care less," Chrzan told one curious articles editor in 1968. "If you're smart, you'll care less, too."

While it proves absolutely nothing, it's also interesting to note that, of the key early officers in the *Enquirer*'s parent company—it was called Best Medium Publishing in those days—almost all were Italian Americans. They included Dino Gallo, the goateed little man who followed Pope from *Il Progresso* to serve as secretary; Vince Manzo as office manager; and Guy Gagliardo, who served until the mid-1990s as the company's treasurer. In no way does this mean that any of these men were directly connected to anyone in the Mafia. But it could indicate that Pope felt he could trust them not to see or hear too much of what went on in his inner sanctum.

The most obvious reason for Pope to have maintained a friendly relationship with the New York and New Jersey Mafia families during the 1950s and 1960s was to protect the *Enquirer*'s circulation base in the populous Northeast. It's a widely acknowledged fact that one of the Mob's earliest and most lucrative ventures into "legitimate" business after World War II was in the field of periodical wholesaling and distribution.

With Mafia-controlled distributors, under-the-table payoffs or other types of favors could assure that certain publications received the highest possible visibility in stores and newsstands. They also meant that competing publications frequently got "lost" by distributors and never saw the light of day at all.

Whether it was done for cold cash or simply to accommodate a friend, there is virtually no doubt that Pope's paper benefited tremendously from this arrangement. Circulation executives at Globe Communications often decried the "invisible wall" that kept sales of *Midnight* and *Examiner* far below par in the Northeast. And in Chicago, Allied News Company's Robert Sorrentino was bitterly outspoken about the circulation drought that afflicted his *Tattler* and *Insider* in that same area.

"Sometimes I think we'd be just as well off not to send any papers at all to New York or New Jersey," Sorrentino complained. "I don't think a single copy ever gets out of the distributor's warehouse."

As the tabs began to penetrate the supermarkets in substantial numbers and hired large numbers of their own "road men" and "detail people" to see that their papers ended up where they were supposed to, it became harder to stifle the competition's distribution. Meanwhile, though, Pope's near monopoly in the Northeast undoubtedly gave the *Enquirer* a major boost at a critical time in its development.

*   *   *

That Pope was extremely proud of his Italian heritage is beyond question. So is the fact that he reveled in the high-profile status bestowed on him and other members of his immediate family by the Italian community. He was neither as popular nor as handsome as his older brother, Fortune Pope, who remained editor and publisher of *Il Progresso* until the paper's demise in the 1970s. But GP nevertheless drew his share of salutes and admiring smiles whenever he entered any gathering of Italian American movers and shakers.

One of the first signs that an employee had "arrived" at a certain level in the *Enquirer* power structure and pecking order came in the form of an engraved invitation to the annual Sons of Italy Ball, a black-tie affair that was always held at one of Manhattan's premier hotels like the Biltmore, Ritz-Carlton, or Waldorf Astoria. It wasn't an invitation to be taken lightly, either. For anyone who wanted to continue in Pope's good graces, declining with regrets simply wasn't an option.

"Look, it's an honor, a sign Mr. Pope appreciates what you're doing," Nat Chrzan told a recently promoted Texas expatriate who had just received his first invitation. "Just buy your wife a nice long dress—you can afford it. Rent yourself a tux and go. It'll be an interesting experience, I guarantee."

Chrzan was right. The atmosphere was stiffly formal, the orchestra was sixteen pieces, the dinner was two hours and seven courses long. The celebrants included everybody from the Italian consul-general and a couple of congressmen to a diva from the Metropolitan Opera and, yes, Joe Colombo himself, accompanied by a small army of muscle. Sophia Loren and Frank Sinatra sent their compliments.

The annointed hirelings from the *Enquirer* sat self-consciously at one large, round table and tried hard not to whisper, point, or stare. GP smiled blandly as he passed by on his way to join the rest of the big shots, but otherwise didn't acknowledge their presence.

In its own flamboyant way, the Sons of Italy Ball was a revelation and an eye-opener for Pope's employees. It made them realize just how much clout this man had—and with how many different kinds of people.

It also gave them a reason to be grateful that, in the parlance of the *Enquirer*, "get ridda that guy" usually meant nothing worse than being fired. With Pope's connections and background, it could just as easily have meant something considerably more permanent.

*   *   *

So how and why did "Pope Gene" become such an unrelenting tyrant? How could he draw such apparent pleasure from casting some people into oblivion and creating a living hell for others? Even today, more than a decade after his death, no one really knows. Even those who spent most of their working lives in daily contact with him can only wonder.

His soft-spokenness and reserved manner were often interpreted as shyness, even insecurity. Possibly he was torn by deep inner conflicts: Embarrassment at being the son of a known racketeer, but pride in his feared underworld connections; a thirst for public admiration, but fierce anger at society for denying him admission to its highest echelons despite his wealth. At times, he lived up to his name by being generous to a fault, but he had an insatiable need to control and manipulate others.

By all accounts, his father was a stern man who probably dealt harshly at times even with his favorite son and who instilled the fear of God in young Gene in the tradition of many other Italian Catholic fathers. Maybe the old man's behavior set the pattern for GP in his dealings with his employees.

In the classic movie *Citizen Kane*—a thinly veiled and highly unflattering portrait of William Randolph Hearst—the main character's tyrannical personality is traced to his lost childhood. Kane's last word on his deathbed is "rosebud," a reference that becomes clear only in the film's last scene as a toy sled bearing that name is consumed by flames.

But GP was, if anything, an even greater enigma than Kane or Hearst. He could be charming one minute, vicious the next, but in either mood he never lowered his guard or removed his mask. Beyond his passion for the *Enquirer*, he never discussed his personal beliefs or disclosed his private sentiments about anything. Was he Republican or Democrat, liberal or conservative, believer or nonbeliever, optimist or pessimist, pro or con? It's still anybody's guess.

If Citizen Pope had a "rosebud" buried in his past, it has yet to be discovered.

NINE
THE WAR AT THE CHECKOUT

The game that played out between the tabloids and the supermarkets between 1968 and 1974 was strictly one of "give and take"—but it was the tabloids that did all the giving and the supermarkets that did all the taking.

In the chain store industry, space is the most valuable commodity of all, and the management and allocation of space approaches the status of a fine science. Every inch of the precious stuff contained in every shelf, bin, refrigerator/freezer case, and display rack is expected to produce revenue, and the demand for space is always greater than the supply. For each of the thousands of items stocked by the typical supermarket, others are squeezed out because their sales potential fails, in the estimation of the merchandising hierarchy, to justify the amount of space they'd consume.

Because of this, the competition for space was—and continues to be—merciless. And as of the late 1960s, the tabloids had virtually nothing to recommend them to the spacemeisters of the supermarkets. In the first place, no class of publications had a more unsavory, less appetizing reputation. What earthly advantage could there be in food stores stocking a product whose whole purpose, until recently, appeared to be turning people's stomachs?

But there were other, more practical considerations as well. For one thing, tabloids were nonfood, low-priority "impulse" items and inexpensive ones at that. At this juncture, the per-copy price of all the major papers was just fifteen cents, a figure that chafed the smaller publishers no end, but one to which the *Enquirer* held fast. Pope, too, would have liked to raise his cover price, but he was still making significant profit at fifteen cents. He was also far enough ahead of the pack to dictate what the standard would be, and he intended to put as much pressure as possible on the competition.

Even at fifteen cents per copy, the tabs made enough money that they didn't have to depend on advertising to show a profit. Pope, in fact, imposed a strict limit of eight pages per issue for display advertising and frequently bragged about turning away ads that exceeded this space allotment. Other tabs were less discerning, and the bulk of tabloid advertisers—the *Enquirer*'s included—were companies whose products and services weren't welcomed by the slick magazines. Psychic readers and purveyors of religious symbols or good-luck charms were among the more frequent users of tabloid ad space. Almost from its inception, *Midnight* derived significant income from lonely hearts ads in its in-house Sheela Wood Have-a-Friend Club, which still appears in *Globe* today.

(Cover prices would begin to creep upward a few years later, as the tabs became an accepted part of the supermarket scene and added color photographs, slicker paper, and other costly refinements. Today, tabloid cover prices are approximately a dozen times higher than they were in 1970. At that time, though, only the bottom-of-the-barrel papers, which had no chance in the supermarkets, anyway, dared deviate from the *Enquirer*-dictated price structure.)

For another thing, the tabloids' size demanded an inordinate amount of display space, especially for a fifteen-cent item. It was decided early on that stocking the papers in flat stacks simply wasn't a viable option, even if there'd been someplace near the checkout where this could've been done. They had to be placed in vertical racks so that they faced outward with their garish covers as close to eye-level as possible, and the racks had to be at the fingertips of shoppers waiting to have their groceries checked.

There was no possibility of using existing racks, because there weren't any. At the time, only two periodicals—*Woman's Day* and *Family Circle*—were sold routinely at checkout counters. Although they were conservative "slick" magazines whose dimensions were only about half the size of the tabloids', Pope and other tabloid publishers had studied them intensely. Both had been fixtures in grocery stores since pre–World War II days, and they were predictably heavy on recipes, full-color food photos, and home-making tips that encouraged the sale of other supermarket items. Their example caused all the top-line tabloids to make at least a cursory effort to include similar fare in their editorial mix. It led the *Tattler* to become the first tab to designate a staff writer (Connie Donnellan) as "food editor" and establish a regular recipe column.

At any rate, while *Woman's Day* and *Family Circle* had established a precedent of sorts for periodicals at the checkout, their example offered no practical assistance to the Johnny-come-latelies. Once permission was obtained to bring their papers into a chain of stores, the tabloid publishers would bear the full responsibility of designing, manufacturing, installing, and servicing their own display racks. Yet the chain would dictate all the terms as to style, specifications, construction, and location.

It was a big order, and the supermarkets made it clear from the outset that the hefty expenses involved would be borne solely by the tabloids themselves. In some cases, there was a possibility of splitting racking costs with other publications—notably *Reader's Digest* and *TV Guide*, which were also seeking wider exposure at the checkouts at the time. But such collaborative efforts were rare, and for the most part, each tabloid ended up paying between ten and fifteen dollars for each rack it installed.

But there were also "hidden" costs in the supermarket campaign that were even more oppressive and harder to justify.

* * *

"What the hell is a 'market placement allowance'—and why is it costing us so damned much money?"

It was late 1973, and the question was being posed from fifteen hundred miles away by Joseph Sorrentino, whose Florida retirement was feeling less and less comfortable and secure these days. Under the direction of his sons, Allied News was sinking incredible sums into the battle for the supermarkets, and the drain on the company's cash reserves was giving Papa Joe himself a sinking feeling in the pit of his stomach.

The elder Sorrentino knew full well how under-the-table payoffs worked, and he recognized that they were sometimes necessary. But the chain stores' demands seemed endless, while Allied's resources definitely weren't. Where did it all end? What sense did it make to get the *Tattler* into more and more supermarkets if they had to bankrupt the company to do it?

The market placement allowances, or MPAs, to which Papa Joe referred were actually nothing more than bribes demanded by the supermarket chains over and above the legitimate expenses involved in gaining admission to their stores, such as racking and adding "detail people" to service the racks.

No one outside the Sorrentino family knows how much Allied spent on MPAs between 1972 and 1975, but an educated guess places the probable total in the neighborhood of $300,000. According to figures compiled by Allied in July 1974, the *Tattler* was being sold in 21,875 national chain-store outlets in major metropolitan areas alone. The number of chain outlets in smaller markets would almost certainly have swollen the nationwide total to 30,000 or so—and the majority of these outlets exacted an MPA, a one-time payment of up to ten dollars per checkout before allowing the first papers to be racked.

"We just signed another big contract with a three-hundred-store chain in the Midwest," Bob Sorrentino confided to his top editorial management people at about that same time, "but I'm not sure if we ought to be celebrating or not. At ten dollars per checkout and an average of eight checkouts per store, we're having to shell out $24,000 just for the MPA."

When racking expenses were figured in, the short-term cost of this "victory" was close to $50,000. At about seven and a half cents per copy—Allied's share of the cover price after the retailer's cut—it would take some 670,000 Tattler sales just to break even on a deal like this. At an average of ten sales per checkout per week, this translated to six or seven months of red ink before the company earned a cent.

Gene Pope and the *Enquirer* could take such blackmail in stride. After all, GP had been paying "gratuities" for special treatment for more than two decades, and the MPAs were basically the same thing under a different name. Even Mike Rosenbloom at Globe could accept the financial bite as one of the built-in liabilities of doing business with the giants of American retailing.

But for Allied News, it increasingly meant living on the edge of a steep and slippery slope.

"We're betting on the come," Bob Sorrentino told his management people, "but it's the only thing we can do if we want to stay in the race."

$*$ $*$ $*$

As the war at the checkouts heated up, it became more and more apparent that limited financial resources weren't the *Tattler*'s only problem in the marketplace. Rivals were also successfully using its own name against it, and the culmulative effect was starting to smart.

Far more than the *Enquirer* or even *Midnight*, the name *Tattler* implied sneakiness, skulduggery, eavesdropping, and tale-telling, and despite the paper's clean look, quality writing, and upbeat content, it was an implication that was hard to shake. Pope's army of "roadmen" constantly poked fun at the name in their dealings with supermarket buyers, and the Sorrentinos again had cause for serious second thoughts about their decision to push the *Tattler* rather than the *Insider*.

The Sorrentinos gave serious consideration to changing the paper's name, and Bob held a series of executive meetings to brainstorm the pros and cons of the idea. The company had already carried out two name changes—a sudden one with *Candid Press*, which had become *Candid Viewer* overnight, and a gradual one in which the *National Exploiter* first became the *National News Exploiter* and finally the *National News Extra*.

But after several months of debate, the idea of doing the same to the *Tattler* was rejected. It was simply about two years too late for such drastic action. Tons of money and countless manhours had been poured into the effort to familiarize the supermarket-shopping public with the existing name. Changing it now, it was decided, could damage the paper's identity severely enough to jeopardize its entire future.

It didn't help that, near the peak of this ongoing discussion, the "other Sorrentino"—cousin Vince, founder of the scurrilous *National Informer*—launched a new squeaky-clean tabloid of his own called *Modern People*. Vince guessed correctly that the *Informer* was beyond redemption where the big chains were concerned, so he decided to start over from scratch. He also seemed to have an uncanny knack for timeliness, since he managed to copyright the new name shortly before Time-Life's *People Weekly* made its initial appearance. Otherwise, Time-Life could have easily proved infringement.

Modern People was particularly galling to Bob Sorrentino, not only because it belonged to Vince, but because its name seemed so perfectly in tune with what the *Tattler* was trying to be.

"God, I wish we could've thought of that name first," Bob lamented during a meeting with his editors. "It captures everything we want to say in two words."

As he'd done earlier with the *Informer*, Vince was also able to turn *Modern People* into a short-term financial success. It found its way into a number of drug and convenience store chains, and even a few supermarkets, and while no hard-and-fast circulation figures are available, some issues may have sold 150,000 copies or more.

Modern People had excellent reproduction and was among the first tabloids to use a touch of color on its covers, but its overall quality was never on a par with its major rivals, and it was never able to establish a true national presence. After Rupert Murdoch's *National Star* entered the struggle for checkout space in 1974, *Modern People* became lost in the fray. Despite its seemingly near-perfect name, it found itself increasingly squeezed out of the marketplace. Within a few years it vanished.

In the meantime, the urge to tinker with the *Tattler*'s name continued to resurface periodically for as long as the paper lived, but it was never changed. To smooth away some of its unfavorable edge, however, Allied tried several less drastic steps, including a new slogan, "The Most Respected Name in People-To-People Journalism," which was added in small type below the cover logo. The following pledge also began appearing at the bottom of page two in every issue:

> The *National Tattler* conforms to the highest standards of modern reporting, while also carrying on a tradition of incisive personal journalism dating back to the original "Tatler," established in London, England, in 1709. Today's *Tattler* and its staff are dedicated to total, truthful coverage of today's people and the world in which they live.

These measures didn't get rid of all the negative connotations, and they didn't quiet the caustic comments from the competition, but to some extent, they did at least manage to dignify and legitimatize the *Tattler* name.

Midnight had ongoing problems with its name, too, and there was talk about making a change as early as 1970. Joe Azaria and John Vader had liked the "after-hours" aura of the name, and it had been highly appropriate in the beginning, but for many it had dark, sinister connotations, and Mike Rosenbloom would've perferred something a bit tamer. Most of the national tabs were referring to themselves as "family weekly newspapers" by now, and the name *Midnight* definitely didn't fit that image.

Once the paper won acceptance by several national supermarket chains, however, pressure to find a new name eased off. Finally, in 1978, Rosenbloom began a months-long transition from *Midnight* to the most logical possible substitute and the name under which the parent company had operated for nearly a decade—*Globe*. During this process, the paper bore the rather awkward interim name *Midnight Globe* for a number of issues, but there was little or no ill effect on sales. By the time the paper became simply *Globe*, hardly anyone seemed to notice.

＊　　＊　　＊

The headlong rush by the tabloids to reflect wholesomeness, morality and "family values" was now as intense as the quest for gut-wrenching gore had once been. Articles with positive religious themes were eagerly pursued, especially if they could be attributed to some noted spirtual leader. Both the *Enquirer* and the *Tattler* featured lengthy bylined pieces by Billy Graham and never missed an opportunity to splash the famed evangelist's name across their covers.

If the power of the Almighty and a big-name celebrity could be linked together in the same story, so much the better. The *Tattler* scored major points in this category, for example, with such cover headlines as "MICKEY ROONEY SAYS: 'LIFE WAS MEANINGLESS UNTIL I FOUND GOD' " and "GEORGE FOREMAN SAYS: 'GOD AND ASTROLOGY GUIDE ME.' "

Divinely inspired healing was another supermarket-suitable subject that was always in demand. The *Enquirer* paid a hefty fee in early 1970 to serialize the book *God Can Do It Again* by Kathryn Kuhlman, the best-known faith healer of the era. The other tabs knew they couldn't outbid Pope for this type of high-profile material, but they carried stories on faith healing and psychic healing in almost every issue.

Stories about Christian relics and artifacts were also much in demand. Between 1970 and 1975, virtually all the major tabs published stories and photos about the Shroud of Turin, an ancient cloth that was supposedly used to wrap the body of Jesus following the crucifixion

LOCAL HUSBANDS SWAPPING WIVES

Councillor Frames Cops

MARRIED A FAIRY

Gigolo Exposed

VOL. 1 — No. 1   MONTREAL, APRIL 2, 1955   10 CENTS

Midnight cofounder John Vader in the late 1950s.

dnight

VOL. 1 — No. 2   MONTREAL, APRIL 9, 1955   10 CENTS

FIENDISH FATHER RAPES DAUGHTER

Call Girl Racket Smashed By Cops

WAITRESS FACING HOMICIDE CHARGE

Early *Midnight* covers paired pinup photos with sensational headlines. Its beginnings may have been humble, but by the time *Midnight* changed its name to *Globe* in the late 1970s, it was one of the largest-selling periodicals in the world.

Future *Globe* publisher Michael Rosenbloom (left) with *Midnight* circulation manager Dave Silverman in the early 1960s.

The December 8, 1974, *News Extra* cover inspired the title of this book.

BREAST TRANSPLANTS

Poor Peasant Girls Being Disfigured for Life so Wealthy Jet-Setters Like Jackie Can Have Their Aging, Diseased Bodies Reconstructed

THE NATIONAL

NEWS EXTRA

50¢

VOLUME 11, NUMBER 23 DECEMBER 8, 1974

Soviets Torture Spaceman For Secret of Building a UFO
—Lurid Details, Page 15

A Mother's Tale of Horror:

'I Watched A Wild Hog Eat My Baby!'

WORLD EXCLUSIVE--FIRST PHOTO INSIDE!!!

Girl Raped by Abominable Snowman Gives Birth to a Hideous Beast-Child

ELVIS IS IN LOVE WITH A DEAF-MUTE

WORLD'S TALLEST WOMAN IS 7-FT-5

The author (center), *Tattler* executive editor Tom Lutz (left), and publisher Bob Sorrentino pose a picture that ran in *Editor & Publisher* in 1973.

The author (seated) in the offices of Allied News in 1974 with assistant *Tattler* managing editors Ben Stevens (center) and Tom Ayres.

ENQUIRER

15¢ Vol. 44, No. 45, July 12, 1970

How to Conquer Your Frustrations

More Than a Year After Her Death...

JUDY GARLAND IS STILL NOT BURIED

JUDY GARLAND DEANS

s notable cover pictures future *Enquirer* editor n Calder covering a story as a young reporter.

ENQUIRER POLL REVEALS:

70 Percent Believe Parents Should Be Held Responsible For Illegal Actions of Children

NATIONAL

ENQUIRER

★★★★★ FEATURE 15¢

THE WORLD'S LIVELIEST PAPER

Vol. 40, No. 7, October 23, 1966

A VIOLENT CANNIBAL

KILLS PAL & EATS PIECES OF HIS FLESH

A classic cover from the *Enquirer's* "gore era."

Australian media mogul Rupert Murdoch got his start in the tabloids. The former *Star* owner's empire now includes print and electronic media.

Enquirer founder Gene Pope with his third wife, Lois, out on the town in New York City.

THE NATIONAL Insider

△ 25¢

Informative • Provocative • Fearless • Entertaining

VOLUME 21 NUMBER 20 — NOVEMBER 17, 1972

EXCLUSIVE:

How Astrology Will Replace 'The Pill'
See page 6

Nude Men Anger Gal Who Started Topless Craze
See page 12

Study Reveals Hitler's Secret Sex Perversions
See page 20

Homosexual Brothels New Rage In Europe
See pages 10 & 11

Marilyn Monroe Had JFK's Baby Girl

That's the real reason she committed suicide. According to two highly respected European publications, the West German Magazine Stern and The French newspaper France Dimanche, Miss Monroe and John Kennedy's baby is now living in Mexico. See the suppressed story on pages 4 and 5.

Nine years after JFK's death, the three major tabs came out with the same bogus story: Marilyn Monroe had given birth to JFK's baby.

THE NATIONAL TATTLER

20¢ △

Vol. 28, No. 26, *The World's Fastest Growing Family Weekly*, April 8, 1973

Donations Pouring In For Girl Who Can't Eat
—page 6

Under Joan's Very Nose...

Teddy Frolics With Jet-Set Beauty, 20

How You Can Haul IRS Into Court for Just $10

● Ben Johnson Says His Oscar Film Is 'Too Dirty for Mom'
—page 15

● Computers Join Hunt for Fabled 'Bigfoot' Monster
—page 16

● RFK's Son, 20, Takes Gov't Job To Support Himself
—page 24

THE NATIONAL TATTLER

25¢ △

VOL. 18, NO. 21, *The World's Fastest Growing Family Weekly*, NOV. 25, 1973

SPECIAL HISTORIC EDITION

THE KENNEDY TRAGEDY: A DECADE OF DOUBT

■ Jackie Onassis: Wife, Widow, Woman
By Pulitzer Prize winner Fred Sparks

■ JFK Wanted U.S. Out of Vietnam
By famed historian Theodore White

■ Where Fate Will Lead America Next
By acclaimed prophetess Jeane Dixon

■ My Son, the Accused Assassin
By Lee Harvey Oswald's mother

■ How I Would Have Saved Ruby's Life
By renowned attorney Melvin Belli

■ EXCLUSIVE
John Connally Says Let's End Official Secrecy

■ plus:
Congressmen Demand A New Investigation

Space Beings Warn U.S. and Russians: 'Stop Building A-Bombs or Be Destroyed'

THE NATIONAL NEWS EXTRA

50¢

VOLUME 11, NUMBER 29, DECEMBER 22, 1974

625-Pound Gospel Singer Marries 135-Pound Preacher
—Crushing Details, Page 4

ROSE KENNEDY, 71, TO WED WAITER, 23; TEDDY IS FURIOUS

3,000-Year-Old Man Brought Back to Life

Liz Has Vision of Heaven, Hears Angel's Stern Warning: 'Mend Your Ways or Else!'

The floodgates were open, and in the years since, the trials and tribulations of the Kennedy family have provided endless fodder for the tabs' mills.

From her marriage to Aristotle Onassis until her death in 1994, Jackie O was a big seller for the tabs.

Some popular personalities have very little tabloid-reader appeal. This *Tattler* issue, featuring a cover story about Cary Grant's messy divorce, was a bust.

Although they're known for their more sensational stories, on occasion the tabs find success with serious investigative journalism. This *Tattler* cover story about radioactive cargoes being transported on U.S. passenger jets earned praise from the floor of the U.S. Senate.

The three major tabs as they look today.

and bears a mysterious imprint that many interpret as the image of Christ's face.

Animals and kids—especially sick or endangered ones—were more sought after than ever. But in their zeal for appeal, the tabs sometimes painted themselves into uncomfortable corners from which there was no graceful escape. When *Enquirer* articles editor Joe Cassidy ran across the story of a lovable abandoned dog named Lucky in 1972, it led to one of the most ludicrous episodes in the paper's checkered history. It also stuck Cassidy with the unwanted job of playing nursemaid to a stray mutt for months on end.

Pope was so smitten with Lucky and the publicity potential he represented that the *Enquirer* ended up adopting the dog as its quasi-official mascot, much to Cassidy's chagrin. Special quarters for Lucky were constructed at Cassidy's home, and whenever the dog was scheduled for a promotional personal appearance, it was Cassidy's job to transport him to and from the assignment and generally guard Lucky with his life twenty-four hours a day.

"I haven't been able to work on a story in weeks," Cassidy groused to a friend. "I don't have time to do anything but baby-sit that damned mutt. If anything should happen to him, God forbid, Pope would have me boiled in oil."

Unfortunately for Joe, the saga of Lucky (which helped provide the inspiration for John Travolta's hit movie *Michael*, twenty-five years later) was destined to stretch on and on. First there was a series of articles detailing the animal's early plight, his rescue from certain death in the dog pound, and his subsequent ascent to a happy home and the soft life of a canine celebrity. Then Pope kept the saga alive with a series of contrived articles in which Lucky was "interviewed" on a seemingly endless range of subjects. Lucky also put in personal appearances at all major events staged by the *Enquirer* for promotional purposes—and wherever Lucky went, a weary Joe Cassidy was required to tag along.

Encouraged by stacks of fan mail from readers, GP even arranged to make the pooch the hero of a cartoon strip called "Life With Lucky" that appeared in every single issue of the *Enquirer* for nearly three years. According to Cassidy and other staffers, Pope had aspirations of making Lucky into a classic cartoon figure that would one day rank in national familiarity with Bugs Bunny or Donald Duck.

Pope personally approved all "Life With Lucky" episodes—as he did every cartoon that appeared in the *Enquirer*—and many of them reflected GP's odd sense of humor, or, perhaps more correctly, his lack of one. The brutal fact is that most of Lucky's cartoon adventures tended to be long on moral and short on laughs. When the strip was eventually allowed to lapse, there were a few complaints, but none of them came from Joe Cassidy.

The end to this bizarre story came when Cassidy grew tired of Lucky's sexually aggressive behavior and quietly had the dog neutered in an effort to cure the problem. When Pope discovered the truth—that Lucky could no longer produce an heir—he was so furious that he fired Cassidy. After that, Lucky slipped into an uneventful retirement and eventually died.

* * *

Benefit campaigns for children with rare, life-threatening illnesses became yet another tabloid staple during the scramble for supermarket acceptance. Such "humanitarian" crusades had been used for decades by sensational papers as attention-grabbing, circulation-building promotional devices. But they were an exceptionally effective tool during this period, when the tabs were eager to demonstrate that beneath their garish, celebrity-bashing covers lay compassionate souls and hearts of gold.

The *Tattler* was particularly active in this area, running major cover stories on several cute kids with unusual health problems, then conducting national fund-raisers to help pay their medical bills. The most dramatic of these—and the one that gave the paper by far the most PR mileage—involved an eleven-year-old New Jersey girl named Jennie Westerink.

When she was discovered by New York bureau chief Jeanne King in February 1973, the child was believed to be the only person in the country living with virtually no intestinal tract. As the result of an undetected congenital defect, Jennie had developed gangrene in her small intestine, and it and about half of her large intestine had been surgically removed to save her life. But the operation left Jennie unable to eat more than a few morsels of food each day, and her survival depended on a small transistorized pump that fed vital nutrients, drop by drop, directly into a main artery leading to her heart.

Incredibly, except for having to wear the pump and a plastic bag containing the life-giving intravenous fluid on a cord around her neck, Jennie was able to live a relatively normal life. She attended school, visited with friends, and played with her collection of stuffed animals like any normal girl her age. But the fluid, a mixture of sugars, salts, vitamins, amino acids, and an anticoagulant, cost nearly fifteen thousand dollars a year, and her father, a self-employed carpenter, was having a hard time paying for it—until the *Tattler* came to the rescue with a centerfold spread in its March 4, 1973, issue and a front page headline that read:

Join Tattler to Help
JENNIE
The Brave Little Girl Who Can Never Eat

The campaign stretched over a six-month period, with frequent updates and published lists of contributors, and it brought in close to

$10,000 in small donations from readers to a special "Let's Save Jennie" fund set up by the paper at a New Jersey bank. But the favorable recognition it generated for the *Tattler* was probably worth at least a hundred times that much.

$$* \quad * \quad *$$

Despite all the tabloids' various editorial gimmicks and publicity-hunting shenanigans, however, it took cold, no-nonsense economic logic to win the supermarkets over.

Having specialists on board who understood chain store psychology and who could talk in bottom-line terms to supermarket executives was vital, and Allied News Company had been at a decided disadvantage in this respect ever since the war at the checkouts had started. In early 1974, however, Allied finally managed to land its own supermarket whiz kid to pit against the *Enquirer's* William Hall and *Midnight's* Aubrey Burke.

His name was Drew Herbert, and his credentials and background seemed ideally suited to help Allied make up lost ground and put the *Tattler* in the thick of the fight for supermarket space and circulation. Herbert had twenty years of experience as a retailing executive with Kroger and King's Department Stores. He was handsome, youthful, and had a dynamic personality. He spoke the industry's language fluently, and he promised an aggressive, all-out merchandising campaign.

As of mid-1974, Allied claimed in trade publication ads that the *Tattler's* circulation had tripled during the past year, but this was a gross exaggeration. (The paper still wasn't subject to ABC audit, so its figures could be padded with relative impunity.) If the claim had been true, average sales at that time would've approached 1.2 million copies, but by best estimates, they were actually only about half that much—somewhere between 600,000 and 630,000. This still represented a healthy rate of growth, although it may have seemed rather puny next to the *Enquirer's* multiple millions.

Because of the *Enquirer's* wide lead and its obvious domination of the market, one of the biggest tasks now facing the *Tattler* sales force was convincing supermarket people that it was "good business" to stock more than one weekly paper. Getting this message across was a primary aim of an ambitious sixteen-page Allied advertising supplement in the July 1974 issue of *Chain Store Age* magazine.

As the supplement stated in part:

> Unfortunately, the message that weekly newspapers these days mean family reading has reached consumers more widely than retailers. . . . It's one of the chief reasons many supermarkets are still missing their share of lucrative national weekly newspaper profits. From a merchant's point of view,

the *National Tattler*'s major impact has been to transform what was essentially a static one-paper category into a thriving center of checkout activity.

The supplement also made a determined effort to shoot down "myths" that remained prevalent among chain store management:

> Supermarket executives, by and large, belong sociologically to the America which doesn't read these papers. So when they keep a publication like the *Tattler* out of their stores, blaming "sensationalism," they are generally making a judgment based on old impressions. . . . What's motivating their actions isn't current reality, but words from the past . . . a myth.

The supplement cited tests showing that (1) when two or more papers were displayed in an outlet, sales increased over those in which only one paper was displayed, and (2) almost two-thirds of shoppers surveyed said they'd buy a second paper in addition to their favorite if they liked the second paper's cover.

Information supplied for the supplement by a highly respected research organization showed that 67 percent of tabloid readers bought their papers in supermarkets, and that 93 percent of them liked to see the papers displayed at the checkout as opposed to other in-store locations. According to the research, tabloids outsold other "impulse" items normally displayed at the checkout (such as batteries, cellophane tape, and razor blades) by a wide margin. Also emphasized was the fact that tabloids were one of extremely few supermarket items with a 100 percent turnover once every week throughout the year.

Overall, the material presented in *Chain Store Age* was an effective testimonial, not just for the *Tattler*—although that was Allied's primary aim—but for all supermarket papers. It was among the earliest published documentation of the trend that would place the once-despised tabloids among the top profit makers in the nation's supermarkets.

Even so, there were now hints of growing panic in Allied's marketing pitch. Drew Herbert and his aggressive strategy were winning attention and gaining some converts, but they were also agonizingly expensive. Herbert's salary was a closely guarded secret, but educated guesses placed it in the $150,000-a-year range. His title of "executive vice president and chief operating officer" also led to speculation that part-ownership of the company was part of Herbert's deal with the Sorrentinos.

With the cash flow situation growing more tenuous with each passing week, Bob Sorrentino ordered the editorial staff to put together an ongoing series of *Tattler* special editions, to be issued at the rate of about one per quarter. The specials would be marketed in addition to the regular papers in hopes of generating significant extra income.

The specials would feature such hot topics as UFOs and new evidence in the JFK and RFK assassinations. But the first of them was going to be a real trendsetter—a blockbuster—Sorrentino assured his editors. It would be the first *Tattler* ever published with a full-color cover, the first designed to stay on sale for a full month, and the first with a legitimate shot at selling a million copies or more.

It would be designed to capitalize on rampant public curiosity about the new movie *The Exorcist*, and it would go on sale just as prerelease publicity of the most eagerly awaited film in years was at its peak.

In retrospect, observers say, there was something strangely, unnervingly prophetic about this whole project—because things were about to get really spooky at Allied News.

$$* \quad * \quad *$$

The war at the checkouts was still raging at fever pitch when Rupert Murdoch introduced his *National Star* to American readers in 1974 and permanently altered both the landscape of the marketplace and the complexion of the conflict. Murdoch routinely did things that other U.S. tabloid publishers had never considered doing—like running multimillion-dollar TV ad campaigns to coincide with the *Star*'s debut, for instance. Before making the decision to start a new publication from scratch, he also made a handsome offer to Pope to buy the *Enquirer*, which GP, of course, emphatically turned down. This failed attempt may have delayed the *Star*'s appearance by at least six months and possibly even longer.

In the past, Murdoch's modus operandi had been to take over an existing publication, even one considerably smaller in circulation than the established leader in the market, infuse it with money and talent, then use it to eat away at the larger rival and gradually overtake it. According to close associates, in fact, this was the first time in Murdoch's career that he'd taken on the job of creating a new media product out of whole cloth.

With this in mind, it's interesting to speculate why Murdoch, once he was spurned by Pope, didn't go after one of the smaller tabloids in the U.S. market in order to gain a toehold, but Murdoch apparently made no effort in that direction. Maybe it was because he thought the others were too insignificant to bother with, or maybe because he didn't like any of their names. In the case of *Midnight*, the drawback may have been its Canadian base and the fact that Murdoch wanted a presence identified as totally American (although the *Star* would be liberally staffed with Australians, especially at first).

Murdoch biographer Jerome Tuccille says that "no imitators (of the *Enquirer*) had yet been spawned," and "nothing remotely similar (was) available for purchase" at the time—which clearly wasn't the case. Had he bothered to look, Murdoch likely would've found much more receptive prospective sellers in Montreal or Chicago, where other tabloid publishers were caught in a vicious economic squeeze—one that was sure to become even tighter with a strong new player checking into the game.

The most unnerving part was that this new player had even deeper pockets than Pope, and he'd demonstrated again and again in Australia and Britain his willingness to spend whatever it took to achieve his goals. It was pretty obvious that he wasn't going to lose any sleep over those supermarket MPAs.

Murdoch's explosive entry into the battle for the chain stores rocked the whole tabloid field back on its heels for a while. Even Pope felt considerable heat, and he was forced to take measures to keep the *Enquirer* out in front that he might never have considered a few years earlier.

The *Star* would eventually become one of the most profitable properties in Murdoch's worldwide media empire, although it would never catch up with the *Enquirer* in circulation or readership. In the final analysis, by far the most disastrous impact of Murdoch's new paper would be felt at the lower end of the tabloid pecking order.

Because of it, the stakes of the game had increased astronomically overnight, and the days when a small player could enter the war at the checkouts with any hope of success were now gone forever.

TEN
SEEING STARS
THE CHALLENGE FROM DOWN UNDER

Ironically, Generoso Pope's greatest inspiration and the most serious challenge to his overwhelming dominance in the American tabloid market were destined to come from the same man—Australian publishing czar Rupert Murdoch.

It had been Murdoch's splashy British weekly, *News of the World*, with its 7 million circulation that first provided Pope with a pattern for what he wanted to do with the *Enquirer* and a vision for what heights it might reach in the future. Murdoch's example fueled Pope's belief that the *Enquirer* could also sell in the multimillions each week, and it prompted him to launch a grand strategy for achieving that end by penetrating the supermarkets.

By early 1974, although his paper was still nowhere near GP's announced ultimate goal of selling 20 to 25 million copies a week, its position had never been stronger. The *Enquirer*'s average weekly sales now stood at about 3.5 million, and although some of the rival tabs were also scoring substantial circulation gains, they'd slipped further behind than ever in terms of raw numbers.

Midnight was running a distant second, with sales approaching 900,000, and the *National Tattler* was considerably further back, with just over 600,000. None of the other also-rans was selling more than 150,000 copies on a regular basis. If you lumped together the circulations of all the other existing "national" tabloids in North America, the *Enquirer* was still outselling the whole pack combined by more than 1.5 million copies in an average week.

But none of the others had even a fraction of the resources and know-how at Murdoch's disposal. At the time, the Australian was virtually unknown in the United States, and he didn't own a single media property in North America, although he already controlled a powerful and far-flung international publishing empire. But the U.S. blitzkrieg that would establish Murdoch's News Corporation as the world's preeminent media juggernaut by the mid-1990s was about to begin.

For his first strike, Murdoch didn't aim at famous slick magazines, huge metropolitan dailies, nationwide TV networks, or Hollywood film studios, but all those would come later. Murdoch's holdings as of this writing include 20th Century Fox Film Corporation; the Fox Television Network and seven of its largest stations; *TV Guide*, the largest-selling weekly magazine on earth; and dozens of other periodicals, newspapers, book publishing companies, and commercial printing plants scattered across the English-speaking world.

But for his initial incursion into the United States, he chose the much-vilified weekly tabloid field, where the only potential adversary he deemed worthy of note was the *Enquirer*. Probably he did so because that was the area in which he felt the most comfortable and confident. According to friends and close associates, the "down-and-dirty" sensationalist press has always been "Rupe's" first love.

For the first and only time in his publishing career, Gene Pope was about to come head-to-head with a direct competitor who was at least as rich, canny, determined, and powerful as Pope himself—maybe more so. Like Pope, Murdoch had a reputation for sparing no expense, pulling no punches, and taking no prisoners. Also like Pope, he'd felt the antisensationalist hounds in his own industry nipping at his heels for many years and developed a thick enough skin to ignore them.

Unlike Pope, however, Murdoch had already owned many publications and would own many others in the future. GP, on the other hand, kept all his eggs in one basket. Except for *Weekly World News* (note the name's similarity to *News of the World*), which he started in 1980 to utilize his old black-and-white letterpress after the *Enquirer* switched over to color, Pope would never publish another paper or periodical. The *Enquirer* was like one of his children—no, even that's an understatement; it was more like his whole life.

Both men were used to winning, but of the two, Murdoch appeared to have the advantage of being more battle tested. He'd succeeded in buying *News of the World* in the late 1960s only by wresting it away from British media baron Robert Maxwell, who also had his sights set on it. Then, less than a year later, he'd also thwarted Maxwell's attempt to buy a money-losing London tabloid called the *Sun*. Murdoch acquired the struggling paper for a ridiculously low down payment of just $120,000 and turned it into one of the cornerstones of his empire—and Britain's largest-selling daily—beating out the *Daily Mirror*, the patriarch of all tabloids, in the process.

It's well known in the upper echelons of publishing that Maxwell and Murdoch didn't like each other very much. According to Murdoch biographer Jerome Tuccille, Rupert's enmity stemmed from some nasty cracks Maxwell made thirty-plus years earlier about Australians in general, plus a low esteem for Maxwell's journalistic abilities. As Murdoch once told a *New York Times* reporter about Maxwell: "He's brilliant, but he knows nothing about publishing newspapers."

Maxwell, however, clearly had more gnawingly personal reasons for bitterness toward his rival. Starting in the late 1960s, Murdoch was his biggest nemesis. In practically every confrontation between them, Maxwell had a disturbing record of second-place finishes, but no defeats were more painful than losing the *Sun* and *News of the World* and watching them take the U.K. by storm.

Without these triumphs and the enormous financial clout they supplied, Murdoch's decision to cross the Atlantic and challenge Pope on his own turf might have been postponed indefinitely. But with them, there was no further reason for delay.

It was going to be a helluva brawl between the titans of American tabloidism, one that would stretch out over the next fifteen years, cost the combatants tens of millions of dollars each, and end with no clear-cut victor. When it was over, Pope's *Enquirer* would still hold a million-copy circulation lead over Murdoch's *Star*, but the value of the two papers would be adjudged almost equal when they were purchased by the same bidder in 1989.

And Murdoch, although denied the decisive triumph he'd hoped for, would live to walk away to achieve far greater successes. Pope, on the other hand, would be dead.

Before the long fight was over, however, the *Enquirer* and *Star*, between them at their peak, would claim a total of close to 40 million weekly readers, and the term "supermarket tabloid" would hold a permanent niche both in our vocabulary and in our national consciousness.

*   *   *

Generoso Pope Jr. was a four-year-old toddler in Manhattan at the time of Keith Rupert Murdoch's birth on March 11, 1931, at a secluded family estate called Cruden Farm thirty miles south of Melbourne, Australia.

Where young Pope grew up in a Fifth Avenue world of doormen, elevators, limos, and high-rises, Murdoch spent his formative years in an imposing but isolated colonial-style house, surrounded by pastoral countryside. He reportedly learned to ride horses at the tender age of five, but he was also exposed to music, art, and a cultured, esthetic lifestyle. In a 1981 interview with the *New York Times*, his mother described his childhood as "very normal" and neither "elaborate" nor "overindulged."

Although they were born half a world apart and in sharply contrasting environments, Murdoch and Pope shared at least a few similarities in their early lives. Both were born into wealthy families with established media ties. Keith Murdoch, Rupert's father, was described by his son as "a great journalist who started as a reporter and finally became the chief executive of a company that he built, but was not a large shareholder of."

Both Pope and Murdoch also attended exclusive private schools as boys and prestigious universities as young men. Both lost their fathers to sudden heart attacks while they were in their early twenties, and both became owners of newspapers in their own right shortly thereafter.

They began their publishing careers within a year of each other. Rupert had just turned twenty-two when he came home from Oxford and a brief internship on the *Daily Express* in London to take charge of two smallish newspapers owned by his father in Adelaide, the *News* and *Sunday Mail*. Murdoch's mother had had to sell another paper, the *Courier-Mail* in Brisbane, to pay taxes on her husband's estate. It was 1953, less than twelve months after Pope had bought the *New York Enquirer*, and Rupert was ready and eager to jump into his late father's shoes.

"I was brought up in a publishing home, a newspaper man's home, and I was excited by that, I suppose," Murdoch told an interviewer in 1989. "I saw that life at close range, and after the age of ten or twelve never really considered any other."

Adelaide ranked as Australia's third-largest city, with a population at the time of almost 500,000, but the afternoon *News* inherited by Murdoch was barely showing a profit. The youthful publisher tackled the job of changing that with boundless enthusiasm and energy. He immersed himself in every aspect of the paper's operation, literally trying to do everything at once—writing stories and headlines, laying out pages, even setting type and working at the "stone," a concrete slab in the composing room on which page forms of hot-metal type were assembled.

As one associate put it, "The expression 'one-armed paperhanger' could've been invented to describe Murdoch" at this juncture. His editors and board members of his parent company, News Limited, frequently objected, but Murdoch made it clear he intended to do things his way or else, and he developed a hands-on management style that would still be evident when he invaded America two decades later.

Sensationalism was an integral part of Murdoch's editorial style from the start. As a student at Oxford, he'd become a great admirer of London's *Daily Mirror*. He'd even dreamed of owning it someday (and would make a concerted effort to fulfill that dream in years to come), and he tried hard to imitate its look and tone with the *News*. There were more than a few in Adelaide who were unsettled by his circus poster lay-outs and strident headlines, but there were many others who bought his papers and made them solidly profitable.

By 1956, after just three years as a publisher, Murdoch was ready to expand. He found a floundering red-ink paper, the *Sunday Times* , in Perth, a city of 350,000 on Australia's west coast, and paid for it with $400,000 in mostly bor-rowed money. He fired the bulk of the existing staff and tore the paper apart, determined to replace its tame appearance and tepid reporting with a bolder look and more colorful news coverage. Again, the sensational formula worked wonders. Circulation soared, and the paper was soon in the black.

But Perth and Adelaide were strictly "bush league stuff," even by Aus-tralian standards. The big time—the place where a shrewd, innovative, risk-taking young publisher could begin assembling a true media dynasty—was Sydney, the smallest continent's largest city. Predictably, that was where Murdoch turned his acquisitive attention next. It was also where he encoun-tered his first bare-knuckle battle with an entrenched media mogul—in this case, an ex-boxer and "tough old bastard" named Frank Packer.

In 1960, Murdoch bought one of four well-established Sydney dailies, an afternoon tabloid called the *Mirror*—how could he possibly resist a paper with that name?—paying the then-princely sum of $4 million for it, again largely in borrowed funds. He immediately began trying to reshape it in the image of its London namesake, but as his efforts began to pay off, they aroused the ire of Packer, whose *Daily Telegraph* was the dominant paper in the market.

Never one to mince words, the crusty Packer vowed to send his upstart twenty-nine-year-old rival "back to Adelaide with his fookin' tail between his fookin' legs."

But Murdoch was equal to the challenge. In the face of everything Packer could throw at him, he hung in. Within a few years, he built the *Mirror* into Sydney's number one afternoon paper and eventually ended up buying the *Telegraph* from Packer, too.

Next he established Australia's first national newspaper, the *Australian*, and the editorial tone he envisioned for it—sort of a cross between the *Wall Street Journal* and the *New York Times*—was an indication of Murdoch's maturing political ideology rather than any abandonment of the sensa-tional approach. Up to this point, he'd always been well to the left of center politically—at Oxford, where he reportedly kept a bust of Lenin on his win-dowsill, he was known by the nickname of "Rupert the Red." But now he began to shift perceptibly to the right, and by the time he started moving into the United States in the mid-1970s, he was an avowed supporter of Richard Nixon, Ronald Reagan, and other rock-ribbed conservatives.

About the time the *Australian* was born, Murdoch also began to take on some of the traditional trappings of wealth and prominence. He bought a yacht, some Rolls-Royces, a sheep and cattle farm out of Canberra, an interest in several Australian TV stations, and some more newspapers in New Zealand. His first marriage, to Patricia Booker, had been coming unraveled for some time, and now he started dating a young cub reporter for the *Australian* named Anna Torv, who would become the second Mrs. M. in 1967, two years after he and Patricia were divorced.

Rupert was now thirty-six years old, owned a business empire valued at $50 million, and stood alone as the major media force in the South Pacific region. He'd developed an impatient, autocratic manner to go along with his new status and, like Pope, he had no qualms about firing people he considered incompetent or uncooperative. But he still didn't mind rolling up his sleeves, getting his hands dirty, and doing the sort of work usually done by a lowly subeditor, and even while attending to nitty-gritty details, he never seemed to lose sight of the big picture. Observers credited him with an amazing capacity for keeping track of everything that was going on in his growing empire at any given moment.

Now, though, he was clearly chafing for bigger and better conquests beyond the confines of Down Under. The rest of the world was out there waiting for him to come and grab a piece of it. He could feel it waiting—and it wouldn't have to wait much longer.

$$* \quad * \quad *$$

For years before he published the first issue of the *National Star*, Murdoch had been intrigued with the idea of a true nationwide American newspaper. But as of the mid-1970s, the concept defied most conventional wisdom, and there was no successful precedent for it. The *Wall Street Journal* was sold in most major U.S. cities, but it was still a specialty paper without a broad-based national audience. The *Enquirer* made no attempt to cover breaking news; the highly respected *National Observer* was a perennial money loser that would soon cease publication, and the advent of *USA Today* was still far in the future.

Still, Murdoch had never been bound by conventional wisdom, and his previous experiences, first with the *Australian*, then with the *Sun* and *News of the World*, whetted his appetite for more. The overwhelming popularity of the British national press convinced him initially that the same approach could work in America. But over the next two or three years, Murdoch was to learn just how different working-class British readers' tastes were from those of their American counterparts, and how much more dependent the Brits were on print media.

It would be one of the most expensive lessons of his career, and it would turn the future thrust of his U.S. operations increasingly away from print and more and more toward film and television.

But as Murdoch plotted his American strategy in the early 1970s, he could see several ways of establishing a national presence in the United States. One was by acquiring a network of daily newspapers at various points around the country, making them dominant in their markets, and possibly using their printing facilities to produce regional editions of a national paper. Other possible routes included taking over an existing paper with nationwide circulation or starting a brand-new one from scratch.

A careful analysis of U.S. print media made one thing obvious right away: This wasn't a very opportune time to go shopping for American dailies. The U.S. newspaper industry was going through a period of painful contraction, with profits being pinched by high production costs and labor disputes, and dozens of papers from coast to coast were being merged or shut down. Generally, the ones that were prospering weren't for sale, and most of those headed down the drain weren't worth buying.

Across the country, Murdoch found only one place that offered a promising environment for testing American media waters in a sizable metropolitan area. That rather unlikely spot was San Antonio, Texas, where Hearst's nominally profitable *Light* was being challenged by the equally marginal *Express-News*, owned by the regional Harte-Hanks chain.

It was at least a starting place, and Murdoch was so eager to establish a foothold in the United States that he decided to take the plunge, although it was an exceedingly costly one. He shelled out nearly $20 million for the morning *San Antonio Express*, the afternoon *News*, and their combined Sunday edition—a stunningly high price, considering that the two papers' circulation combined was barely 20,000 ahead of the *Light*. The sellers undoubtedly laughed all the way to the bank.

As one observer of the Texas newspaper scene commented at the time: "Harte-Hanks is pretty good at running smaller dailies, but they were way over their heads in San Antonio. They would've been lucky to get two-thirds of what Murdoch paid from anybody else."

Obviously, amassing a string of U.S. dailies was going to be a long, expensive process. So Murdoch simultaneously pushed ahead with plans for a brand-new entry in the supermarket tabloid field.

But first he made a concerted effort to talk Pope into selling him the *Enquirer*.

＊   ＊   ＊

In the fall of 1971, Pope had bid a more or less permanent farewell to the teeming Greater New York area where he'd spent the first forty-two years of his life. He moved the *Enquirer* offices and staff—lock, stock, and barrel—to the nondescript seaside town of Lantana, Florida, about forty miles north of Fort Lauderdale, where he'd bought a large tract of undeveloped land two years earlier.

As with most Pope-orchestrated maneuvers, the entire relocation was meticulously planned and carried out like clockwork. As articles editor Bill Dick recalled to friends afterward: "It was all done with total precision. We left our desks and typewriters at the building in Englewood Cliffs at the end of one week, and the following Monday, they were waiting for us at the new place in Lantana. We were fifteen hundred miles away from where we'd been, but we walked in and picked up right where we'd left off."

By this time, the *Enquirer* editorial staff had swelled to nearly sixty employees—up from less than thirty a year earlier—but not everybody was invited along. The opportunity for one last "Friday afternoon massacre" in New Jersey was simply too much for Pope to pass up. In classic GP style, a half dozen unfortunates were told just before quitting time on the final day that they wouldn't be making the long-anticipated trip.

"The rest of us, though, he treated royally," recalled writer Bob Abborino. "The company paid all our personal moving expenses, of course, but Pope also picked up the tab for meals and lodging for the staff and their families until we could find someplace to live. A lot of the clerical help made the move, too, so it was a big expense."

By the time Murdoch began making overtures about buying the *Enquirer*, not quite three years later, Pope reigned as the unofficial "Lord of Lantana." His paper was by far the town's biggest employer, and its sprawling headquarters building and manicured grounds had become Lantana's chief claim to fame. In fact, the *Enquirer* headquarters was about the only thing there, except for a nice chunk of beach, the boats lining the Intercoastal, and a few down-at-the-heels motels along U.S. 1.

Pope wasn't actually a resident of Lantana. He lived in a seaside mansion several miles away, but he reveled in his role as the town's most prominent figure, and he quickly turned the place into his own personal fiefdom.

He enjoyed notoriety, but only at a distance. Consequently, Pope's local subjects sensed his august presence, but they didn't actually see much of him. He'd always had a shy manner around strangers and had never been much for public appearances. Now, if anything, he became even more reclusive. For the rest of his life he rarely ventured more than twenty miles from his house or office. It was as if he'd created his own little world exactly as he wanted it, and he had no need or desire to leave it.

Stories abound about him prowling the grounds outside the offices, measuring the grass with a ruler to make certain it was exactly four inches high. (If it wasn't, they say, heads were sure to roll.) If neighbors on the quiet residential street that passed in front of the *Enquirer* building saw him, they probably didn't recognize him anyway. In his open-necked shirts and cheap polyester slacks, he looked more like a gardener or deliveryman than one of the nation's wealthiest publishing tycoons.

During the first Christmas season after the relocation, Pope began a holiday tradition that would last the rest of his life. He decreed that a huge Christmas tree be erected in front of the *Enquirer* offices, festooned with elaborate decorations and lighted during a gala community-wide celebration. The *Enquirer's* annual Christmas tree, towering some fifty feet into the tropical Florida sky, attracted thousands of visitors each year from near and far. Reportedly, it also cost Pope Gene a cool million dollars a year, but he kept right on doing it for seventeen years without the slightest apparent qualm.

"That first year, Pope sent Dino Gallo, who'd been with him just about forever, and who he trusted implicitly, all the way to the wilds of Canada to personally pick out the first tree," Abborino recalled. "All the rest of us heaved a big sigh of relief that we hadn't gotten the job. God help anybody else if they'd come back with a tree Pope didn't like."

Unquestionably, the tree was an effective public-relations gimmick and goodwill builder for the paper, but it was also an extravagance that could never be justified in a purely business sense. Just as unquestionably, veteran Pope watchers say, GP did it for deeply personal reasons. It enhanced his aura and stature as the benevolent lord of the manor bestowing a lavish gift on his loyal subjects. Pope had all the money he'd ever need, and to him, it was an acceptable price to pay for a dose of public adulation.

When new ownership took over the company after Pope's death, the annual Christmas tree extravaganza was among the first things to go. American Media's chief concern was the bottom line, which is why it was able to increase the *Enquirer's* annual gross earnings nearly fivefold between 1989 and 1999, even as circulation was steadily declining.

The point of all this is that making money was no longer Pope's primary concern. Intangibles such as respect and positive recognition were now more important. He relished the idea that the Associated Press dispatched stories about his Christmas trees to newspapers across the country. He liked seeing his name in print when he gave another hefty donation to the nearby JFK Medical Center. He'd come to enjoy pampering certain employees almost as much as he enjoyed firing others.

But his greatest pleasure of all was the *Enquirer*—the paper he'd built from nothing into a national institution and one of the publishing phenomena of the century. He was utterly possessive of it, down to the last file folder and the last blade of grass. It had become almost an extension of himself.

And now a foreign publisher wanted to buy it? Fat chance!

When Murdoch sent his emissaries to south Florida to discuss a deal, Pope refused to meet with them personally, but he did send a small group of trusted associates, including Iain Calder, who was about to be named editor in chief of the *Enquirer*, to hear what they had to say.

The amount of Murdoch's offer—if, indeed, the discussions ever got that far—isn't known. But it seems safe to suppose that the $20 million he was in the process of paying for the *San Antonio Express-News* was a mere drop in the bucket compared to what he would've paid for the *Enquirer*. Negotiations probably would've started at $100 million, possibly more.

Not that it mattered.

As longtime *Enquirer* staffer Bill Bates, who watched the Murdoch-Pope scenario unfold at close range, put it years later: "Pope would've sold his soul before he'd sell the *Enquirer*. Murdoch could've offered him a billion dollars in cold cash, and he still would've turned him down flat."

*   *   *

And so the battle was on.

Murdoch demonstrated the seriousness of his challenge with a $5-million ad campaign on network TV to launch the *Star*. It was the first time any supermarket tabloid had used the electronic media to boost interest and sales, and it did much to establish the *Star* immediately in the minds of viewers as a paper of more substance and class than the other tabs.

It really wasn't, though. On the contrary, its content was considerably sexier and its layouts and headlines more garish than any of its homegrown frontline competitors. It also relied heavily on the self-consciously "working-class" approach that had worked so well for Murdoch in Britain. The prevalent sexual themes and steamy prose disturbed supermarket executives, who reacted coolly to the new paper, and the tone seemed foreign, even offensive, to many readers.

As *Esquire* writer Chris Welles explained in a 1979 article titled "The Americanization of Rupert Murdoch": "Most workers in the much more fluid and upwardly mobile American society do not like to think of themselves as part of the working class and tend to avoid publications designed specifically for a downscale, or working-class, audience."

The *Star*'s circulation quickly rose to a million copies a week, inching ahead of perennial runner-up *Midnight*. But then it hit a stone wall, resisted all efforts to boost it higher, and sent Murdoch & Co. scurrying back to the drawing board in an urgent search for answers. He was far less comfortable and experienced in creating a product from scratch than in taking over an existing one—and it showed.

The effort had already been extremely expensive, even by Murdoch's lofty standards. He'd spent around $12 million just to launch the *Star*, and now his financial gurus were advising him to stop the bleeding and shut the paper down. But Murdoch was determined to keep tinkering with it. He was convinced it was only a matter of time until he found the right formula.

"We have no intention of failing," he said. "The only question is how great a success we'll have."

For understandable reasons, the paper's first staff was heavily British, including a number of journalists recruited from Murdoch's London operations. Larry Lamb, editor of the *Sun*, was brought over to help orchestrate the start-up, and he brought Mike Nevard, the *Sun*'s features editor, with him. Lamb soon went back home, but Nevard stayed on to become a steadying force at the *Star* during the next few turbulent years, then left to become editor of *Globe*.

Graphics designer Vic Giles also came over from the *Sun* to produce a mock-up of the *Star* to be used as a publicity and advertising tool. It bombed big time with the ad agencies and distributors in New York, who hated it and said it wouldn't sell in the United States. At the last minute, the cover and many inside pages of the *Star*'s inaugural edition were changed— "watered down," according to the Brits—to appeal to American readers.

One of the few Americans on the original staff was Christina Kirk, an Indiana native who'd worked as a feature writer for the *New York Daily News* for ten years and various other daily papers and wire services before that. "Nothing worked out as we'd planned," Kirk said later. "It was planned and it was unplanned. When we first started, we looked like the London *Sun*."

Murdoch hoped to offset some of his huge start-up expenses by making the *Star* the first supermarket paper to attract major advertisers. When circulation stalled and advertisers failed to materialize, this ingrained Britishness was viewed as one of the primary problems with the paper, and Murdoch took decisive steps to try to Americanize it.

In early 1975, he hired Jim Donahue, former executive editor of the *Enquirer*, to take over as editor of the *Star*. He gave Donahue a free hand to do whatever it took to make the paper more attractive to a working-class American audience that thought of itself as middle class. The move may have helped where story selection and overall tone was concerned, but it played havoc with the staff and threw the whole editorial operation into chaos.

Donahue immediately started ousting Britishers and bringing in Americans to replace them. Among the new hires was former *Enquirer* chief writer Roger Langley and former *Tattler* assistant managing editor Ben Stevens. Bob Abborino, who'd worked in various capacities for both the *Enquirer* and *Tattler*, also came aboard.

"Everywhere else I've been, the Brits and Yanks worked together just fine," Abborino said. "Each side thought it did a better job than the other side, but there was never any friction like there was at the *Star* when I was there. Donahue's whole thrust seemed to be 'let's get rid of the Brits,' and it became a real us-versus-them situation. The whole thing got out of control."

Within a few months, Murdoch realized he'd merely traded one unworkable situation for another, and a second chaotic housecleaning took place. When the dust settled, Donahue and several of his recruits were themselves long gone, and Murdoch had installed Ian Rae, a trusted longtime associate from Australia, as publisher with yet another mandate to revamp the paper.

Murdoch also began to use the same hands-on style that had served him so well during his early empire-building days Down Under. And despite the turmoil and the *Star's* failure to live up to its owner's expectations, he won the respect—even admiration—of many who worked for him.

"Lots of times he'd pitch in and help with the copy and layout, and he did it like a real pro," said Abborino. "He also struck me as a very likeable guy—not the overbearing 'big boss' type at all. I admired him because he really knew what was going on, and you can't say the same for everybody who ran one of these papers."

Eventually, Murdoch's patience and professionalism paid off. In 1976, he dropped the word "National" from the paper's name and changed the entire format. He unashamedly imitated the layout, writing style and heavy celebrity emphasis used by the *Enquirer*, but he purposely adopted a more subdued, less aggressive tone in his celebrity coverage. He also heeded the objections he'd heard from the chain stores and made sure the new-look *Star* conformed to their tastes. Most importantly, the *Star* made the transition from a black-and-white newsprint product to a slick, stapled, full-color magazine look.

"It seemed to work wonders in distinguishing us from the competition," said Ian Rae, who was in direct charge of the changeover. It also allowed Murdoch to dodge direct comparisons to the *Enquirer* by saying it was like comparing apples and oranges: "We're a magazine; they're still a paper."

Circulation immediately took off. By 1979, sales had tripled, to 3 million a week, and the *Star* ranked as Murdoch's most lucrative U.S. property, netting a profit of $5 million annually.

That same year, though, the Lord of Lantana struck back with a vengeance, launching an all-out counteroffensive that would keep Murdoch from ever fulfilling his dream of having the number one tabloid in America. The *Enquirer* switched to a full-color format of its own and kicked off a $30-million advertising campaign on network TV built around the now-famous phrase, "Enquiring minds want to know."

By 1982, the *Enquirer's* sales had passed the 5-million mark—still roughly a million ahead of the *Star*—and its annual gross revenues had hit a staggering $140 million, up more than 50 percent from the previous year.

It was a situation in which both sides could, and did, claim victory. But it also marked the beginning of a long downhill slide for tabloids in general, marked by a slow decline in circulation and influence that continues to this day.

ELEVEN
A SLOW SLIDE TO SUDDEN DEATH IN CHICAGO

By the mid-1970s, Allied News Company's *National Tattler* was widely regarded as the most respectable and "legitimate" paper among the supermarket tabloids. In just over two years, its average paid circulation had more than doubled, to about 600,000, and sales occasionally bounced up around the 650,000 mark.

The paper contained more news of substance than its competitors, but its lurid name was still a drawback, and the persistent money crunch that had started the previous year was still limiting the company's ability to compete with the other tabs. Instead of improving along with the *Tattler*'s growth, as Allied's owners had hoped, the financial situation was actually getting worse.

When Rupert Murdoch's *National Star* made its appearance in mid-1974, the crunch intensified. Then, when the *Star*'s introductory ad campaign shot the new paper's circulation up to a million within a few weeks, the *Tattler* found itself running fourth in a four-paper market. To keep from becoming odd man out with the supermarkets, Allied had to adopt a marketing strategy emphasizing shoppers' "natural desire for a choice" of tabloid titles.

As one Allied ad in a leading trade magazine put it: "The need for selection is basic to the way consumers relate to all categories in all stores, and national weekly newspapers aren't any exception."

This strategy may have been sound in some ways, and the Allied pitch might have been fairly effective if it had been aimed at the tabloid-buying public, instead of at cynical, uninterested chain store executives. The company couldn't afford thirty-second spots on national TV or space in daily newspapers and slick magazines or even billboard advertising. It had to target supermarket management through convention brochures and trade publications instead. And at the core of Allied's argument lay a thinly disguised pleading note: "We know those other papers are outselling us, but please—pretty please—give us a chance to sell our paper, too."

It all smacked of growing desperation, and in desperate times, clear thinking and sound reasoning often go out the window.

By now, the *Tattler*'s editorial department had grown to over forty writers, editors, reporters, researchers, and full-time correspondents. A few of the seasoned veterans of major dailies who'd recently joined the staff included Cliff Linedecker, lately of the *Philadelphia Inquirer*; Ted Sell from the *Los Angeles Times*; Tony Gieske from the *Washington Post*; Ben Stevens and Tom Ayres from the *Dallas Times Herald*; Jeanne King from the *Newark Star-Ledger*; John Moulder from the *Fort Worth Press*; Bill Hendricks from the *Fort Worth Star-Telegram*; and Bob Abborino, an *Enquirer* expatriate who had formerly worked for the *Wall Street Journal*.

The *Tattler* was also by far the most "homegrown American" of any of the supermarket tabs. Overseas editor Sean Toolan, formerly of the *London Daily Mail*, was one of just four Brits on the staff.

The paper had been recognized for its "serious" journalism by *Editor & Publisher*, the ultraconservative *National Observer*, the *Chicago Tribune*, and other mainstream publications. Several of its reports on waste, corruption, and abuses in Washington had been read into the *Congressional Record*. And when journalism students at Southern Methodist University conducted a comparative study of the *Enquirer*, *Tattler*, and *Midnight*, they found the *Tattler* to be the best of the three in overall quality, variety of subject matter, quality of writing, and credibility. Only in its quality of printing and photo reproduction did they rate the *Tattler* "a poor third."

All this was heady stuff for a publication that had begun life as one of the lowliest bottom-feeders in the history of U.S. journalism. Allied's marketing department did its best to capitalize on the paper's newfound status and esteem in wooing the chain stores. But the brutal fact was that none of this progress made up for the company's glaring cash-flow problems or its wobbly financial state. The squeeze on Allied resources was already to the point of pain, and with the advent of the *Star*, and the intensified competition it brought to the marketplace, the jaws of the vice closed even tighter.

✳   ✳   ✳

All the tabs were now devoting an increasing percentage of their space and cover display to celebrities, and the *Tattler* was no exception. But the paper's staff made a concerted effort week after week to keep the content balanced and varied. The three-tabloid comparative study by university journalism students showed twenty-five stories on entertainers in a typical *Enquirer* issue, fourteen in a typical issue of *Midnight*, but only eight in a typical *Tattler*.

The study also found that nearly three-quarters of the *Tattler*'s content—72 percent—consisted of "human interest" stories. This was the highest percentage among the three papers.

The *Tattler*'s editors had compiled a list of some forty story categories, with a goal of having at least thirty-five of these represented in each issue. High priority was placed on medicine and science, unexplained phenomena, government scandal, consumerism, courage and heroism, self-help, and spiritual/religious themes.

Illustrating this balance and variety are the seven headlines appearing on the cover of the August 11, 1974, issue (listed in order, based on their size and the amount of space they consumed):

**Painless 5-Cent Home Cancer Test
Could Save 15,000 Women a Year**

**EXCLUSIVE INTERVIEW:
"How I've Tamed
Steve McQueen,"
By Ali MacGraw**

**"Get Ready to Greet Beings
From Space," Expert Warns**

**Howard Duff, 55, Finds New
Love With 28-Year-Old Girl**

**How Psychic Power
Can Save the World**

**He-Man George Kennedy:
"My Wife Is My Strength"**

**Tattler Test-Drives
"Car of the Future"**

In contrast to the dark, sadistic humor sprinkled through the pages of the gore-era *Enquirer*, many *Tattler* articles and headlines now had a perceptibly upbeat, positive tone that seemed to fly in the face of the long-standing tabloid tenet of "negativism sells." Some examples from inside that same August 11, 1974, issue: "GROWING FOOD BY INDOOR PROCESS WILL END HUNGER"; "GIRL, 16, WINS HER FIGHT AGAINST REYE'S SYNDROME"; "BLINDNESS REALLY IS BLESSING, SAYS JUDGE"; "SINGER TONY ORLANDO LEARNED TO ENJOY MUSIC BY ENTER-

TAINING RETARDED SISTER"; "NEW FAA RULES WILL MAKE IT SAFER FOR YOUR PETS TO FLY"; "TINY TOWN'S ONLY DOCTOR STILL FINDS TIME TO BE WIFE AND MOTHER TO HER 5 KIDS"; "MAN, 83, IS WORLD'S OLDEST HELICOPTER PILOT"; "HOMER KING HANK AARON GETS MORE FAN MAIL THAN ANY OTHER CELEBRITY." And so on.

Many of the *Tattler's* biggest-selling issues carried blockbuster cover headlines that had nothing to do with celebrities but focused on social, economic and political matters. One of the all-time classics, dated July 7, 1974, set new sales records with this dire warning in inch-and-a-half-tall type:

<u>International Monetary Expert Sounds Alarm</u>:
NO GOLD LEFT
IN FORT KNOX!

The gist of the story was that Dr. P. D. Beter, a former counsel for the U.S. Import-Export Bank, claimed America's gold reserves were being systematically spirited out of the country by wealthy foreign speculators. Beter had made his charges a short time earlier before a congressional subcommittee on international trade, naming the Federal Reserve System and David Rockefeller, president of Chase Manhattan Bank, as coconspirators in this scheme.

Judging from the reaction, the headline apparently struck a raw nerve with many people. It appeared not long after President Nixon had cut the U.S. dollar loose from the nation's gold reserves and allowed the price of gold to fluctuate freely for the first time. At the time, the economy was slumping, the country was still shaken from the ruinous energy crisis of the previous year, the Watergate scandal was at the boiling point, and Nixon's resignation to avoid impeachment was only weeks away. Just about everybody had a full-blown case of the jitters, and the headline triggered one of those ultimate "suspicions confirmed" reactions from the public.

The issue sold some 670,000 copies—a figure rarely equaled for a regular edition of the paper—and it might well have done even better if many outlets in major cities hadn't run out of copies.

The no-gold story drew a stinging retort from officials of the Federal Reserve and the U.S. Treasury, who called it a glittering example of irresponsible journalism. But the article's author, investigative reporter Tom Valentine, stood solidly behind the story, and so did his editors. They said they'd contacted various sources at Fort Knox, Kentucky, in search of information, and that, while the sources denied any of the reserves were missing, none had actually seen the gold within the past ten months.

"*Tattler* does not necessarily accept either Dr. Beter's allegations or the government's denial," commented publisher Bob Sorrentino in an editorial column. "We believe the whole issue could be resolved, one way or the other, if the government would hack through some of its red tape and let a responsible party confirm that all's well at Ft. Knox."

As far as anyone knows, the feds never followed up on this suggestion.

On the other hand, an even more explosive cover headline published a couple of months earlier had won the paper surprisingly vociferous praise from Washington. Topping the front page of the May 12, 1974, issue, it warned:

DEADLY "ATOMIC BOMBS"
HANG OVER U.S. TODAY

The story related how potentially dangerous radioactive cargoes were being routinely transported aboard U.S. passenger jets and how Department of Transportation officials had lied to cover up the practice. It also revealed that the FAA had failed to report or acknowledge numerous cases of radioactive leaks aboard airliners.

On the floor of the U.S. Senate a few weeks later, Indiana Senator Vance Hartke rose to applaud the *Tattler* for spilling the beans on what he called "a very real threat to the lives and health of Americans." Hartke, who served as chairman of the Senate Commerce Committee at the time and who'd been interviewed for the article by *Tattler* reporter Cliff Linedecker, spelled out the enormity of the problem to his fellow lawmakers.

"During the next twelve months," Hartke said, "commercial airlines in the United States will carry more than 900,000 shipments of radioactive materials in the cargo holds of passenger aircraft." He credited the *Tattler*'s independent investigation for alerting the public to this situation.

"Its well-researched and documented findings . . . revealed conditions which are outrageous," the senator continued. "The *Tattler* investigators wove a tale of conditions so dangerous to American airline passengers that I believe their investigation deserves the attention of my colleagues."

The merits of the *Tattler*'s investigation, he pointed out, had been emphasized just a few days before the story hit the stands when nearly 150 airline passengers were exposed to radiation from a leaking container being shipped from Washington, D.C., to Atlanta.

"The *National Tattler* deserves high praise for a good job of investigative reporting on a situation which has been hidden from the public eye by government officials," Hartke concluded.

The kind words were appreciated. So was the favorable recognition in high places. But during the same week the *Tattler* broke the "Atomic Bombs" story, the *Enquirer* ran a bold headline across the top of its cover, boasting of record circulation gains. "THE ENQUIRER TOPS 4,000,000," it gloated.

In spite of everything, the *Tattler* was fading farther and farther into the distance in Generoso Pope's rearview mirror.

＊   ＊   ＊

The sequence of events that took place between the early fall of 1974 and the spring of 1976, when the *Tattler, Insider,* and *News Extra* ceased publication and the company that published them closed its doors forever, still almost defies rational explanation.

Without a doubt, the final crisis was precipitated in part by a string of faulty business decisions stretching over many months. But it also included a family feud among the company's owners, the Sorrentinos' subsequent loss of the company to an outsider, the dissolution of Allied News as a national distributor and its replacement by a new firm, and what appeared to many to be the cold-blooded, systematic gutting of the company by its new ownership.

Through it all, the death throes were overshadowed by a chain of bad luck and strange occurrences that convinced some observers the whole place was bewitched or possessed by evil spirits. A few still think so.

Those who subscribe to this theory trace the beginnings of the trouble to Bob Sorrentino's spring 1974 decision to publish a special "Exorcism" edition of the *Tattler*. It was to be devoted entirely to the smash-hit movie *The Exorcist*, probably the most controversial film of the decade, plus the film's themes of satanism, demonic possession, and Christianity's age-old ways of combatting them. It was timed to hit the stands just as the movie was being released to take advantage of the firestorm of accompanying publicity.

Because of the tremendous response to earlier occasional *Tattler* specials on such topics as the JFK and RFK assassinations, UFOs, and suppressed inventions, Sorrentino saw them as a possible solution to Allied's thorny cash-flow problems. The specials sold for fifty cents a copy, twice the regular cover price, which was one big advantage. They could also be kept on the racks longer in some cases, and they could continue to be sold indefinitely as mail-order items. Sorrentino was determined to start producing specials on a regular schedule of at least one every three months.

The exorcism issue was to be the first of these regular specials, and Allied pulled out all the stops to make it an attention grabber. It had the first full-color cover ever to appear on a supermarket tab, with white headlines on a deep purple background simulating the look of posters and billboards advertising *The Exorcist*. It featured exclusive interviews with such luminaries as evangelist Billy Graham; psychic Jeane Dixon; and Father John J. Nicola, the Catholic Church's top expert on demonology and a principal consultant to the movie's producers. And when Warner Brothers refused to allow the use of actual scenes of young star Linda Blair's transformation from cherubic child to murderous demon, a professional model and makeup artist were hired to duplicate them.

The issue's centerfold was devoted to a lengthy article about the "bizarre accidents" that had plagued the set and delayed completion of the movie by more than three months. Members of the production company had suffered freak injuries, and one had even died suddenly. Mysterious "unplanned images" and distortions had shown up on the film, causing some scenes to have to be reshot. The obvious implication was that the spirits didn't like the way they were being portrayed, and they were retaliating.

As anticipated, the exorcism special did extremely well, selling more than 800,000 copies and netting the company around $200,000 during its month on the stands. But in the process, something about the filmmakers' unsettling "poltergeist" experiences may have somehow rubbed off on Sorrentino and his staff. Some observers who witnessed what happened over the next year and a half tend to think so, anyway.

In the months ahead, the owners and employees of Allied News were destined to learn firsthand what it felt like to encounter their own assault wave of peculiar disturbances, inexplicable "accidents," and assorted episodes of misfortune and catastrophe.

As one editor said: "It was as close as I ever want to come to working in a haunted house."

Among the first victims of the "curse" that now seemed to hang over the company was *Candid Viewer*, a paper specializing in daytime TV coverage that had been reincarnated from the hot-pink ashes of the late, libidinous porno sheet, *Candid Press*.

Actually, curse or no curse, the demise of *Candid Viewer* had been totally predictable for months. A brainchild of Bob Sorrentino, it had been launched in September 1973 with glowing predictions for the future and the only champagne party ever held in Allied's offices. It was billed as the first paper of its kind, and it was, in fact, one of the earliest national daytime TV publications to hit the market.

But for a number of reasons, the paper never came anywhere close to living up to Sorrentino's expectations for it. For one thing, it may have been a little ahead of its time. But there were other, more significant factors in its failure.

First off, although it ran many solid, original articles on daytime TV personalities, close to half of *Viewer*'s weekly editorial content consisted of recycled stories on other types of celebrities that had appeared previously in the *Tattler*. Clearly, this was a cost-cutting device from the start, and the more money the paper lost, the more the practice escalated. Readers weren't supposed to notice—but they did.

Secondly, *Viewer* suffered from the same printing and reproduction deficiencies that plagued Allied's other papers. Touches of color were used to try to dress up its covers, but it simply wasn't very appealing. And based on the format used by today's most successful daytime TV publications—

all of which are digest-size magazines with slick covers—a newsprint tabloid was less than an ideal vehicle for reaching the target audience.

A third liability was the very name of the paper. *Candid Viewer* was an awkward attempt to retain some vestige of the *Candid Press* title in order to hang onto *CP*'s second-class mailing privileges. But the name didn't "say anything" to identify the paper to its intended audience, and at a casual glance, it looked like just another tabloid. In retrospect, most observers agree, the words "Daytime TV," or at least just "TV," should've been included in the nameplate.

But the most important key to *Viewer*'s failure was lack of exposure and visibility. There was no money to get it into the chain stores—all the company's financial resources were being poured into the *Tattler* sales campaign—and outside the chains, the number of available outlets continued its steady shrinkage. To get around this problem, the company's circulation hopes rested heavily on mail subscriptions, but they never materialized.

"Hell, nobody on the old *CP* mailing list gave a damn about daytime TV," grumbled one writer. "What they wanted was porn, so there was zero holdover among old subscribers, and there was no budget for advertising to attract new ones. It was all a ridiculous waste of time, energy, and money."

In September 1974, just a year after the new paper's grand debut, Bob Sorrentino called his top editorial management people into his inner sanctum and confirmed what they'd been expecting for months. The decision had been made to pull the plug. As of that moment, *Candid Viewer* was history.

"The percentage of sale is so low it's not even paying the printing bill," Sorrentino said glumly. "It breaks my heart, but we can't keep throwing good money after bad." Latest complete figures showed sales averaging an abysmal 15 percent of the press run.

By rights, the long-overdue death of *Viewer* should have ended a severe financial drain for Allied—one that cost the company several hundred thousand dollars in losses over the life of the paper. But by the Sorrentinos' reckoning, it also meant there was one less paper to produce, which meant, in turn, that fewer people were needed in the editorial department.

Before that same week was out, Sorrentino called his executive editor and managing editor back to his office and told them the staff had to be cut.

"As of this Friday, six editorial jobs have got to go," he said. "It's up to you to decide which six it's going to be—and I warn you, we may have to lose more people before we're through."

Candid Viewer had gone to its grave unwept, unhonored, unsung, and largely unmissed, but its death had set off a grim "domino effect" at Allied News Company.

Before it ran its course, lots of people were going to be in deep mourning.

*   *   *

The staff cuts continued throughout the fall. Every two or three weeks, a few more jobs were eliminated, and not all the victims were rank-and-file peons. The goal of each reduction was to trim the payroll by a certain amount, and the target figure couldn't always be reached by sacking only $325-a-week writers and $200-a-week editorial assistants. With a shrinking staff, fewer subeditors and midmanagement people were needed, and eliminating their higher salaries meant fewer casualties overall.

By January 1975, there were fewer than half as many editorial employees at Allied than there'd been four months earlier, and an ominous trend had been established. Somehow, all three of the surviving papers continued to come out on time each week. Their quality suffered to some extent, but for the most part, the differences caused by fewer people churning out the same amount of work were small ones that probably went unnoticed by 99 percent of the readers. Far more damaging was a growing sense of fatalism, even hopelessness, that descended over the remaining staffers.

The longer the downward spiral continued, the higher the odds grew against reversing it, and without a reversal, the ultimate outcome was painfully obvious. It was no longer merely a matter of worrying about when and where the axe would fall next. Now the concern was how much longer the company itself could stay afloat.

"We were pleasantly surprised at how well everybody performed under the circumstances," one editorial executive recalled later. "We hadn't thought of ourselves as having any 'fat' in the department when we had forty-plus people on the staff, but after the first couple of cuts, we could see we'd been wrong. For a while, I think we were actually doing a better job with fewer people than we were before, but when the cuts continued, they started getting into muscle and bone. That's when it really started to hurt. It's also when we realized it wasn't going to get any better. After that, most of us were just waiting for the other shoe to drop."

Adding to the feelings of anguish and forboding, meanwhile, was a series of freakish, unnerving events that affected every Allied employee. The evil spirits seemed to be working overtime.

The most tragic of these calamities occurred late one night in October 1974. At the time, the only two people in the building were a contract maintenance worker, who was doing routine cleaning chores, and his young son.

A little after 10 P.M., the workman left the boy on the second floor while he went to do an errand in another part of the building. When he came back about thirty minutes later, the father made a horrifying discovery. He found the mangled and severed head of his son lying outside an unmanned freight elevator. The boy's decapitated body was discovered inside the elevator, which had descended to the first floor.

Police searched the premises thoroughly, on the theory that a prowler or burglar might have been responsible for the accident, but they found no evidence of forced entry or of anyone else being present in the building at the time. Investigators finally ruled the boy's death accidental, although no one could determine how the accident happened.

"The elevator had an allegedly fail-safe set of doors that closed about waist high," said *Tattler* executive editor Tom Lutz, one of several management people who were briefed in detail on the incident. "But somehow, the little boy got his head caught between the closing doors, and when the elevator moved down from the second floor to the first, it decapitated him."

A lawsuit grew out of the tragedy, according to Lutz, with both the Sorrentinos, as owners of the building, and the maintenance company that serviced the elevator named as defendants. A jury later held both parties responsible and awarded the father a settlement of "considerable size," which Lutz speculates may have been as much as $1 million.

Although the settlement was actually paid by the Sorrentinos' liability insurance carrier, there were significant legal fees involved. The tragedy also cast a pall of gloom over the company's leadership, and investigations and court appearances became a major distraction at a time when many crucial business decisions were having to be made.

Exactly why and how it happened remains a mystery, but a number of shaken employees came up with their own explanations.

"Crazy as it sounds, that darn *Exorcist* special may have had some bearing on all the bad stuff that happened later," said ex-*Tattler* writer Connie Powell, currently on the staff of radio station KFYI in Phoenix. "The spirits were definitely put out with us about something."

But the demonic trickery—if that's what it was—was far from over. A few weeks later, when the first winter storm of the season hit Chicago, employees reported for work on a Monday morning to find the heat off throughout the building and the temperature in their offices hovering in the midthirties. The furnace in the basement had simply stopped working. No one knew why.

Repairmen were called on an emergency basis, but the suddenness of the cold snap had left every heating and air conditioning mechanic in the city swamped, and the earliest any could promise to check out the situation was the next morning. Several large, portable heaters were moved in to try to remove enough of the chill for work to proceed, but it was a lost cause. Temperatures continued to fall throughout the day, and writers shivered in overcoats and parkas while their fingers practically froze to their typewriter keys. Around noon everyone was sent home for the day.

That night, the temperature plunged to near zero. When the mechanics arrived the following morning, the place felt like Antarctica, but they couldn't find anything wrong with the furnace except that the pilot light was out.

Could it have blown out accidentally? they were asked.

"Very unlikely," they said. "In fact, we never heard of it happening before."

"Welcome to the Twilight Zone," somebody said.

That wasn't the end of it, either. When the staff came back to work, they found there was no water in the restrooms. In the extreme cold, pipes in the basement had frozen. One of them had also burst, but no one realized it for about eighteen hours. By that time, the basement was flooded with three feet of water, which, in turn, shorted out the building's electrical system. The high water also put out the pilot light on the furnace again.

It was almost the end of the week by the time anything resembling order and productivity returned. Staffers labored through the weekend to meet the printing and shipping deadlines for the *Tattler*. The *Insider* and *News Extra* were thrown irrevocably behind schedule, but because of their far smaller circulations, these delays were less crucial.

When it rains, it pours, they say. At about this same time, more bad news came from Allied's lawyers, who'd been sparring for two years with attorneys for *Tonight Show* host Johnny Carson over a libel suit filed by the entertainer against the *Insider*.

Unless Allied was willing to pay a substantial out-of-court settlement, Carson was prepared to take the case to trial—and Allied to the cleaners—his lawyers warned. The advice of the company's own legal team had originally been to string things out as long as possible. Now they were suddenly urging the company to settle, saying if Allied went to court and fought the suit, its legal fees alone could run in excess of $100,000, and there was no telling what the price tag would be if the ruling came back in Carson's favor.

"Our story was basically accurate, and our lawyers have been telling us for months we've got a strong case," Bob Sorrentino fumed. "Now they're telling us to cave in and settle. It doesn't make any sense, but I guess we'll have to do what they say."

It was the first and only time Allied ever paid off in a libel action. Various reports placed the amount of the settlement at $100,000 to $125,000. It wasn't an exorbitant figure, but it also wasn't one the company could easily afford at this juncture. Saving money in the long run was rather pointless, after all, if there wasn't going to *be* any long run.

Around Christmastime 1974, Frank Sorrentino abruptly vanished from the company, and none of the employees ever saw him on the premises again. Many people were puzzled and curious, but the grim look on Bob Sorrentino's face served as a warning not to ask where Frank had gone.

And finally there came the day, in April 1975, when what was left of the staff reported for work one morning to find that Bob Sorrentino was gone, too, never to return.

They were informed that the new president of the company and publisher of the *Tattler* was former supermarket whiz kid Drew Herbert. They were also assured that the *Tattler, Insider,* and *News Extra* would be published as usual that week, and that—at least for the moment—they still had jobs.

No formal announcement was made about the fate of Allied News Company. Employees were left to figure it out for themselves, but this much was clear: Allied had been stripped of its role as national distributor for the papers it produced. The circulation and marketing departments had been scrapped, and, except for Herbert, all their employees had been terminated. These functions had been turned over to a new distributor on the West Coast.

What was left of Allied was a name and little else.

$$* \quad * \quad *$$

How Drew Herbert managed to wrest control and ownership of Allied News and its subsidiary corporations away from the Sorrentino family still remains anybody's guess. It constitutes one of the most incredible episodes in the history of the tabloid business. Only the principals themselves knew the full story, and none of them ever showed any inclination to talk about it—which only adds to the element of mystery.

At the time, Joseph Sorrentino and his sons had owned and operated the company for almost twenty years. Sometimes in spite of themselves, they'd built its papers during that period from nothing to a combined average weekly circulation approaching 800,000. Herbert, on the other hand, had been with Allied only a bit more than a year when he staged his remarkable takeover. He was, and had been for some time, a highly paid executive, but most observers agree that he had little, if any, investment capital of his own.

So how could he, almost overnight, assume total control of the operation and oust the original owners from their own company? And how could a company that, according to Tom Lutz, had an unencumbered $1 million in cash in the bank when Herbert came aboard, find itself operating in the red so quickly?

Except for Herbert and the Sorrentinos, the person closest to the situation at the time was Tom Ayres, who served as editor in chief of the Allied papers for most of the last year of their existence. During that hectic period, Ayres became Herbert's closest confidant and was, in fact, the last employee on the payroll when the ship finally sank.

"I still don't know what happened," said Ayres, who now lives in seclusion in northern Louisiana and writes books. "All I know is that one day Bob Sorrentino was gone and Drew was in charge of everything."

Ayres and others have speculated that Herbert was offered a sizeable share of the company and the title of CEO in return for agreeing to mastermind Allied's supermarket strategy. According to this line of thinking, the Sorrentinos—especially Bob—were now convinced that landing someone with Herbert's apparent expertise and connections was their only hope of hanging onto an acceptable share of the market. These extra incentives were offered in lieu of a salary comparable to what other major tabloids were paying their supermarket gurus. Unable to afford this type of financial outlay, Allied's owners resorted to "giving away the store," or at least part of it.

Then, dealing from a position of strength inside the company, the theory continues, Herbert pursued a divide-and-conquer strategy that effectively drove a wedge between Bob Sorrentino and other members of the family.

"I think he convinced Bob that only he—Drew Herbert—could save the company," said one former Allied executive. "I think he convinced him so totally of this that Bob sided with Drew against his brother and the old man and helped Drew get in the driver's seat. Then, once Drew had what he wanted, he eased Bob out. I don't think Bob ever knew what hit him until it was too late. It was like being run over by a damned train."

It wasn't as if Bob, Frank, and Papa Joe walked away empty-handed, however. Apparently, as part of a deal between Herbert and a new California-based national distributor, they received a sizeable lump-sum cash payment of at least $1.5 million. Given the company's precarious position at the time, this may have seemed adequate enough compensation for bowing out of the picture and leaving Herbert totally responsible for whatever happened next.

"I distinctly remember Tom Lutz coming back from a meeting in Bob Sorrentino's office and saying, 'I just saw a check for a million and a half dollars,' " Ayres said in an April 2000 interview.

Not long after that, Lutz himself was axed, after more than four years as one of the *Tattler's* chief editorial decision makers, and Ayres, who had been an assistant managing editor, was elevated to the editorship.

"It was my impression that Herbert let Lutz go mostly because of the high salary Lutz was drawing," Ayres said. "At this point, Drew was making all the major decisions—about editorial and everything else—anyway."

For the next ten or eleven months, Ayres and a skeleton staff worked sixty to seventy hours a week to keep the *Tattler* and its companion papers in business. Miraculously, they also managed to produce several more special editions during this period, and they even made one final trendsetting innovation.

"The *Tattler* was the first supermarket tabloid to go to a full-color cover," Ayres said. "We did it in the late summer of 1975 while the *Enquirer*, *Star*, and *Globe* were all still black-and-white. Under the circumstances, it still amazes me that we were able to do it. Of course, the *Star* followed suit within a few months, but it took a lot longer for the *Enquirer* and *Globe* to make the change."

The first full-color cover on any U.S. tabloid appeared on the *Tattler's* edition of September 14, 1975. "For a while, the color really set us apart in the marketplace," Ayres said, "and it definitely gave our sales a boost."

Even at this point, many observers contend, the *Tattler* could've been saved if that had truly been Herbert's intent. The deal he'd signed with a company called Independent News Distributors had allowed him to eliminate two dozen "road men" from Allied's payroll, and IND was doing a credible job of expanding the paper's exposure in the chain stores. After the color covers were introduced, a few issues may have sold in the 700,000 range.

Herbert had also bumped the cover price from twenty-five cents to forty cents and approximately doubled the amount of paid advertising, while cutting editorial and production expenses to the bare bone. There were also indications of a lengthening trail of unpaid bills.

"One of the main reasons he switched printers and went to color was because he owed a ton of money to the old printing plant, and they were ready to cut us off cold unless he paid up," said one member of the steadily dwindling staff.

Production chief Hal Burns, a five-year *Tattler* veteran who'd worked closely with the owner of the old plant, was so angered by Herbert's tactics that he wrote a long, heated letter of resignation. But when Herbert pleaded that better days lay just ahead when all past-due accounts would be squared, Burns—whose experience and skills made him as close to indispensible as anyone on the staff—finally agreed to stay on.

Strangely, though, despite all of Herbert's cost-cutting and forced economies, and with no appreciable decline in *Tattler* circulation, there never seemed to be any money. The editorial staff was now down to eleven people. Payments to freelancers were months in arrears. And still, Herbert had to resort to advances against future sales of *Tattler* special editions to meet the weekly payroll. So he claimed, at any rate.

For the remaining staffers, their jobs became a tenuous issue-to-issue question mark. "As soon as we'd get our checks on Friday, we'd rush over to Drew's bank to get them cashed for fear they'd bounce if we waited," said Connie Powell. "We'd go home at the end of each week, thinking we'd all be looking for work the following Monday. Then, on Sunday night, somebody'd call and tell us to come on in the next day, that we were going to put out another issue."

The suspense dragged on for weeks, but everybody could tell by now that the end was getting close.

In some people's opinion, it had been the exorcism special that started Allied on its long slide toward oblivion. And now, in one last bitter irony, it would be another special—this one on Elvis Presley—that plunged the company to its final demise.

Like Bob Sorrentino, Herbert had relied on the specials for quick, sorely needed infusions of cash. But unlike the old days under Sorrentino,

Herbert could now draw money out front from the distributor before the papers even appeared on the racks, based on projected sales of each special. There was one small catch, however.

"Before they'd grant the advance," Ayres explained, "the distributor had to review the issue's content and decide if it had enough sales potential to warrant putting up the money. But in the rush to get the Elvis special to press, Herbert never got around to telling the distributor what he was doing until it was already done, and when he did tell them, they turned him down.

"They refused to pay anything on the issue until the actual sales figures came in—which would take weeks. The Elvis thing had been done in an expensive magazine format and we'd had a massive press run, which we had no way to pay for. Without the advance money, there was nothing left to operate on. That was the end of everything. It'd been a long time coming, but in a way it seemed sudden, too."

The final issue of the *National Tattler*, dated May 16, 1976, featured a red-white-and-blue, stars-and-stripes cover logo commemorating America's Bicentennial. The front page was dominated by a bold headline that claimed "UTILITY RATES ARE A RIPOFF," a large color photo of Audrey Hepburn with the notation "Back From Her Self-Imposed Exile," and a smaller picture of Ted Kennedy with a headline reading "Chappaquiddick Revisited."

At the end, there were few traces of the old *Tattler* spark left. Mostly, the last of the paper's 586 consecutive regular weekly editions was a real yawner, heavy on bland celebrity handouts and threadbare recycled exposés.

The masthead on page two listed Drew Herbert as "President and Publisher"; his wife, Jean D. Herbert, as "Corporate V.P., Secretary and Treasurer"; Tom Ayres as "Editor"; and the following ten editorial staffers: Sandra Cawson, Cliff Linedecker, Marty Gunther, Constance Powell, Paul Reining, Barbara Weres, Hal Burns, Lou Marra, Jean Janson, and David Mendenhall.

No copies of the final issues of the *National Insider* and *National News Extra* are known to exist.

*   *   *

There are still conflicting opinions about whether Herbert intentionally drove Allied News to its death by siphoning off large chunks of its cash flow for other enterprises. Some who witnessed the company's collapse at close range say this is precisely what happened. Others suggest that Herbert was partially blinded to the realities of the situation by an oversized ego, then overwhelmed by events beyond his control.

"I think it was totally an ego thing," said Ayres. "He had promises of financing that didn't materialize, but he was so busy wheeling and dealing—and so sure he was going to succeed—that he got careless and didn't take care of business. He thought he could walk on water. That's what sank the ship."

Connie Powell and Cliff Linedecker were among those who took a much less charitable view.

"I always felt Drew was purposely gutting the company and diverting the money to other projects he had going," said Powell. "I just can't see any other explanation for what happened."

"It was a classic case of corporate rape," said Linedecker a few years later.

A former *Tattler* editor who resigned in February 1975 after he "saw big, ugly handwriting on the wall" offered this summation: "Herbert took a company that had a few problems but was basically sound and profitable in early 1974 and turned it into an empty shell two years later. He had some help along the way, but for the last fifteen months or so, he single-handedly destroyed the place."

From all indications, Herbert went about the destruction with a preset plan in mind. For weeks before the final plunge, he was already talking privately to Ayres about relocating the company to the Los Angeles area. He also outlined his idea for a new magazine-style tabloid to be called *Faces & Places*, and, in fact, the last few issues of the *Tattler* actually contained an eight-page insert that prototyped what Herbert had in mind. Herbert also discussed the possibility of other new publications and asked Ayres for ideas. Ayres responded with a memo outlining a tabloid-style news-magazine titled *Newsmakers*.

"I tried to tell him that moving to the West Coast would make distribution much more difficult, but he was really hung up on the Hollywood scene," Ayres recalled. "He'd rented a beach house at Malibu, right next to Dyan Cannon's place, and he'd set his sights on a posh suite of offices in Beverly Hills. He had visions of himself out there as a publishing magnate hobnobbing with the stars."

Herbert told Ayres he intended for *Faces & Places* to be a "spin-off" from the *Tattler*, but it seems just as likely that he was thinking of it as a total replacement. After bankrupting Allied, Herbert unquestionably believed he had enough accumulated capital to pay for the move to California and the start-up of a new publication. Ayres was promised its editorship and a handsome financial package.

"He sent me to L.A. twice to look for office space, contact printers, and generally check out the lay of the land," Ayres said. "He talked about taking three or four other people from the *Tattler* to form the nucleus of a new staff, but he also had me place ads for editorial personnel in the L.A. papers. In the final analysis, I think Drew had about 600,000 and he probably would've needed ten times that much."

Ayres returned from the second West Coast trip with serious second thoughts that quickly turned to deep misgivings.

"At first, I figured I didn't have anything to lose, and I needed a job just as much as anybody else," he said. "But then I started thinking about moving my wife and four kids halfway across the country into a situation that could blow up in my face at any minute. Finally, I decided I just couldn't do it."

After informing Herbert of his decision, Ayres said he never saw or heard from his former boss again. Neither, apparently, did anyone else in the publishing industry.

*　　*　　*

Whenever they get together, former Allied employees still wonder aloud about what happened. Was it really all Herbert's fault? Was the "curse of the *Exorcist*" truly to blame? Or had the seeds of Allied's destruction been planted long before, in the form of shoddy, skinflint business practices?

For several years, according to Tom Lutz, the Sorrentinos had a habit of firing large numbers of employees just before Christmas, purely as an expedient bookkeeping practice.

"It became sort of a tradition to clean house during the holiday season," Lutz said, "because that was when they started to balance their books for the year-end. They'd fire a bunch of people at Christmas, and then, about February, they'd be putting ads in the Chicago dailies for writers and copy editors."

On the day before Christmas in 1970, a young Hispanic layout artist was among those who abruptly received their pink slips. No one recalls his full name today, but Lutz and other staffers of the period clearly remember that his first name was Jesus (pronounced "Hay-sus" in Spanish).

With this in mind, one former *Tattler* staff writer, who now works for *Globe*, recently offered a final insight into the cause of Allied's downfall: "The way I figure it, if you're mean enough to fire Jesus on Christmas Eve you're flat-out begging for trouble—and you darn well deserve what you get!"

TWELVE
NEWS EXTRA'S LOONY LEGACY LIVES ON

Few Americans paid much attention, in the spring of 1976, when the *National News Extra* quietly passed from the scene, along with the other remnants of Allied News Company. It was, to put it mildly, an event of little note among media watchers. There were certainly no obituaries in *Time* or *Newsweek* for the obscure, outrageous little rag—or anywhere else for that matter.

Even most of the readers who regularly paid fifty cents for a weekly dose of *Extra*'s zany headlines, doctored photos, and preposterous stories undoubtedly shrugged off its passing and promptly forgot about it. To be brutally frank, many of them may have been too stoned or stupid even to notice it was gone.

But among some of Allied's former competitors, *Extra*'s maniacal excesses had left a lasting impression, and its death presented an intriguing opportunity to test the concepts it had pioneered in a much broader market than Allied had ever obtained for it.

Generoso Pope, in particular, was fascinated with the potential he saw in a *News Extra*-style paper that would appeal to a different audience than the *Enquirer*—fascinated enough to use *Extra* as a model when he launched his immensely successful *Weekly World News* in 1979.

Originally born in 1968 as the *National Exploiter*, a haphazard product of Joseph Sorrentino's "more papers equal more money" philosophy, *Extra* had gone through a gradual but dramatic evolution to become what it was at the time of its death.

165

It had started life as one of a genre of papers (including Vince Sorrentino's *National Informer* and Globe Communications' *National Examiner, National Bulletin,* and *National Close-Up*) that tried to fill the niche left behind when the old *Enquirer* cleaned up its act. For the most part, these papers had only limited success in this attempt because (a) the number of sales outlets available to them was shrinking, and (b) the gross-out gore on which the old *Enquirer* had prospered was getting harder and harder to find.

Even after undergoing a name change, *Extra* remained among the least successful of these papers. It leaned more heavily toward blood, brutality, and horror than blatant sex, but it never had nearly enough of the type of graphic photos that "gore freaks" relished. For several years, it floundered miserably in the marketplace as a tab with no established audience and not much identity.

Once in a blue moon, the paper managed a minor triumph with a cover display nobody else had done yet. An example from late 1972 was a completely authentic—and totally nauseating—photo of a man who weighed over thirteen hundred pounds and resembled a giant jellyfish. It was accompanied by a headline that read: "Drugs Made Me The . . . FATTEST MAN IN THE WORLD!"

At least 90 percent of the time, however, *Extra* existed almost entirely on recycled ghoulishness ("NECROPHILIAC PLAYS BASKETBALL WITH DEAD GIRL'S HEAD"; "MOM MAKES STEW OUT OF HER BABY SO HER OTHER KIDS WON'T STARVE"); brutal sex-torture crimes of the "He Rape, Kill Her" genre, often of foreign origin; and long, unearthly columns by self-styled satanist Anton LaVey and other quirky characters.

As Papa Joe's goofballs gave way to more knowledgeable editors and writers, a makeshift editorial formula emerged by which all three Allied papers could use the same story by playing off different angles. The *Tattler* would basically run the story straight; the *Insider* would sensationalize and exaggerate any sexual implications; and *Extra* would take a few of the facts and weave an outlandish fantasy around them.

Aided by desperation and the alcoholic inventiveness of their Wednesday night "cover conferences" at the Charm bar, Allied's staff devised a formula that gave America its first lunatic-fringe tabloid. It also gave *Extra* a unique ability to appeal to two totally different audiences. One was made up of hard-core nutcases who were convinced the end of the world was at hand and that science, politics, economics, and society in general were all part of a massive plot (yet, for some inexplicable reason, tended to accept as gospel anything they saw in print). The other included campy college kids and other irreverent fun lovers who got a kick out of all the nonsense.

In the process, the paper became the unofficial "Three Stooges of American Journalism," and many who followed its trail of inspired idiocy thought it kept getting nuttier right up to the end.

During the last eighteen to twenty months of its existence, when growing financial constraints left it with practically no budget in its own right, *Extra* became a veritable lampoon of its previous self. The lack of money inspired a frenetic creativity among the writers and layout artists who conspired each week to invent its entire content. Together, they turned it into a sort of *Mad* magazine in tabloid disguise.

From the summer of 1974 on, there was hardly ever a word of truth anywhere in the paper. The stories were concocted of booze, smoke, and whole cloth by a small corps of Allied writers who embraced them as comic relief from the rigors of serious *Tattler* articles. Replacing satanist LaVey and other bargain-basement columnists were a nonsensical staff-written "advice" column called "Dr. Know It All," a collection of freakish news briefs titled "This Mad World," and other tomfoolery.

Many stories were illustrated with any-occasion photos of anonymous people in Europe, South America, and the Far East that arrived in large batches each month. The pictures cost next to nothing, and nobody cared what alterations were made to them with an airbrush. Other photos were shamelessly stolen, faked, distorted, and taken out of context. How else could a blow-up of an ordinary housefly become the catalyst for a double-page spread headlined "9½-POUND FLY TERRORIZES MEXICAN VILLAGE"?

Many of *Extra*'s classic cover headlines reflect a special kind of twisted artistry among those who composed them—as the following examples attest:

Farmwife Licks Energy Crisis, Turns Plum Jelly into Gasoline

109-Year-Old Man Lives in Hollow Log With Pregnant Wife & 6 Kids

Innocent Little Girl Scalped By Berserk Tortilla-Making Machine

World's Shortest Bandit In World's Shortest Holdup: 3 1/2-FOOT DWARF ROBS BANK WITH BUTCHER KNIFE

Lonely Widow Tries to Marry Her Dog But Dies Before Wedding Takes Place

Be a B.O. Sniffer—For $1,000 a Week!

625-Pound Gospel Singer Marries 135-Pound Preacher —Crushing Details, Page 4

To produce copy that justified headlines like these, writers sometimes simply let their imaginations run wild. More often, though, they used widely reported current events as a starting point in order to lend authenticity, then added the liberal doses of pure fantasy that made the stories live up to their billing in the headlines.

One article from fall 1974, for example, was headed "SEX-CRAZED ROBOTS ATTACK CALIF. TOWN." The writer pulled background information from two real but unrelated wire service dispatches—one on new robotics experiments in Japan and one on a cargo ship that had run aground in a storm—then shifted into sci-fi gear to come up with a gem of unexcelled absurdity.

According to the story, a Japanese freighter carrying two dozen hybrid, life-size robots programmed with the sexual impulses of a twenty-year-old human male had crashed on the rocky coast of Baja California during shipment to a U.S. scientific lab. The impact had somehow activated the robots, most of which escaped and went on a rapine rampage in several coastal towns.

One section of the story described how the manager of a large service station had watched in horror as two of the overstimulated robots started making indecent advances to a row of self-serve gasoline pumps. It then offered the following "eyewitness" account of what happened:

> "So your name's Ethyl, huh?" the manager heard one of the robots say, as it circled the closest pump excitedly. "Well, you're kinda cute, Ethyl. I think we could have ourselves a real good time together."
>
> When the pump didn't respond, the robot's voice turned angry: "Dammit, take your finger out of your ear and pay attention to me when I'm talking to you. Otherwise, I'll burn this place to the ground."

"It's hard to understand how anybody could take this craziness seriously, but some people apparently did," said one editor who helped shape *Extra*'s new personality. "After we ran the robot story, a lady wrote in to ask if all the robots had been captured and if any of them were still in working order. If they were going to be for sale cheap, she said she might like to buy one."

When *Extra* ludicrously branded Altoona, Pennsylvania, as the "sin capital of America" in a spring 1975 issue, the manager of the town's only radio station called and demanded, in all seriousness, to know where the paper had gotten its information. "They wouldn't believe we were joking," said executive editor Tom Lutz.

In its very best weeks, sales of the old copycat blood-and-guts *Extra* rarely reached 30,000 copies out of a print run of about 100,000. But after the emphasis was changed to spoofs and slapstick satire, circulation more than doubled. By November 1975, the paper was regularly selling over 60,000 copies a week, and sales were still climbing, according to Tom Ayres, its last editor. For obvious reasons, the paper was never displayed in a single chain supermarket, and the number of small stores that stocked it was still declining. Nevertheless, it became one of the more eagerly sought publications among the "in crowd" at numerous colleges.

"We even had a few *News Extra* fan clubs springing up here and there," recalled Ayres. "The college kids ate it up, and as word spread, it really started taking off. If we could've found some way to get saturation distribution in areas around every major university in America, we might've sold ten times as many copies as we did."

Extra even captured attention in Britain, home of some of the world's most experienced and perceptive tabloid readers. In its issue of October 27, 1975, the *U.K. Press Gazette* (roughly the British equivalent of *Editor & Publisher*) took note of a series of stories in *Extra* about the fictional European kingdom of Miltar.

Miltar was one of a number of ongoing ruses that produced such headlines as "JACKIE BEING WOOED BY EUROPEAN EMPEROR" and, a little later, "JACKIE ENGAGED TO EUROPEAN KING—TO BE QUEEN OF TINY NATION OF MILTAR." Along the way, *Extra*'s writers also gave mythical Miltar a variety of other dubious claims to fame.

At one time, the *Gazette* article explained, *News Extra* had been like most of its competitors, endlessly exaggerating celebrity scandals with at least some basis in fact. But coming up with new material week after week was arduous, to say the least. "Finally, *News Extra* decided to go all the way and make up the stories completely," the article said, adding:

> In recent weeks, Miltar has been the scene of some fantastic scandals. For example, Miltar's national airline, Air Miltar, was under international investigation, according to *News Extra*, because it has the worst safety record of any airline in the world. One out of every three flights crash, the paper claimed.
>
> American tourists were also warned to steer clear of Air Miltar because, according to *News Extra*, it so overbooks its flights [that] many passengers have to strap-hang.
>
> And then there was the week the Miltar Navy took on the entire might of the Russian Fleet in the Mediterranean and sank the lot.
>
> *News Extra* is beginning to acquire a cult following, especially among American college students. Some think it's funnier than the *National Lampoon*.

The new satiric *Extra* never bothered to impugn any but the biggest names among the world's celebrities. Its perennial favorite targets were Jackie and Ari, but it also took frequent potshots at Liz Taylor, Richard Burton, Elvis Presley, and other members of the Kennedy clan. (A few of its more excessive celebrity coverlines are reprinted in chapter 7.) Some others included:

Liz Gets High on Cocaine
& Takes Up Bullfighting!

Caroline Crashes Her
Plane; Jackie is Hysterical

Liz' Heartbreaking Secret:
BURTON IS IMPOTENT!

Elvis Is in Love
With a Deaf-Mute

One of *Extra*'s more creative pieces of celebrity "coverage" appeared in the issue of November 14, 1975. It featured a large, liberally retouched front-page photo of Ted Kennedy, barefoot and wearing nothing but a wooden barrel, along with a massive headline that read:

They're Flat Broke
KENNEDY FAMILY
LOSES FORTUNE!

But it was a smaller headline on that same cover—"OATMEAL PLANT BLOWS UP; OMAHA BURIED IN ICKY GOO"—that caught the attention of *Omaha World-Herald* columnist Robert McMorris.

The story inside, under the byline of "Sinna Glutney, food editor," told the lamentable tale of how a night shift attendant at the "world's biggest oatmeal factory" had fallen asleep during a torrential rainstorm and allowed 195 billion tons of concentrated instant oatmeal to get soaking wet.

According to Ms. Glutney's account, the resulting oozy gray mass had "spewed out of the burst seams of the automated plant, and before it was over, most of the pleasant Nebraska city lay buried beneath sticky, smelly slop." The story was illustrated by another artistically airbrushed photo, allegedly showing an Omaha resident wading through thigh-deep torrents of oatmeal.

McMorris knew, of course, that none of this "ridiculous nonsense"—or anything remotely resembling it—had actually happened. His doubts about *News Extra*'s veracity were further aroused by other headlines in the issue ("AMAZING CHICKEN ACTUALLY LAYS EGGS THAT ARE SQUARE"; "BIGFOOT MONSTER ADOPTS HUMAN BRAT"; "THINKING ABOUT SEX WILL MAKE UGLY HAIR GROW ON YOUR BODY"). So he put in a call to long-distance information in search of a phone number for the publication. When he found it, he demanded an explanation.

A few days later, on November 24, 1975, McMorris reported to his readers what he'd learned about the story of "the breakfast that buried Omaha" and the paper that printed it. He wrote:

Listed as the editor of *News Extra* is "Bernard (Big Scoop) Pulitzer," who writes a column called "Scooping It Out."

By telephone, I tracked him to his lair in Chicago. He confirmed the suspicion that Pulitzer was a nom de plume. With some reluctance he confessed that his real name is Tom Ayres. But he insisted that the masthead listing of I. W. Harper as editorial assistant is legitimate.

Ayres, who practiced journalism in Texas and Canada before moving to Chicago, said *News Extra* entered the world in 1968 as a more or less "straight" news-feature publication. The present policy, which emphasizes what Ayres calls "bizarre stories, kinda clean fun," was introduced about a year ago.

Ayres has made the happy discovery that made-up stories are more popular than legitimate ones. . . . He says his staff has fun and enjoys writing stories that require no research. The writer of the Omaha oatmeal flood [story] was "quite proud of that," he said.

McMorris described *News Extra* as a "spoof on journalism" and a "non-newspaper [that] looks like a newspaper."

All in all, these were some of the kindest things ever said about the publication by a mainstream U.S. journalist.

*   *   *

In May 1979, three years after the death of Allied News Company, former *Tattler* assistant managing editor Ben Stevens, who'd been one of the architects of *Extra*'s redirection, was out of work and down on his luck in Corpus Christi, Texas. After leaving the *Tattler* during its final downward spiral, Stevens had put in a stint at the *National Star*, then served as managing editor of a country music publication. He'd come to the Gulf Coast in late 1977 at the invitation of Texas oilman/gambler Ed Driscoll, along with a handful of other former supermarket tabloid journalists, to help start a sensational new weekly tab called the *Corpus Christi Sun*. Driscoll, who was miffed at the local power structure, claimed he was willing to spend $5 million to launch an opposition paper. But within a few months, Driscoll developed severe health and legal problems. He also ran out of money, and the *Sun* folded, leaving Stevens high and dry.

Not eager to return to daily newspaper or wire service duty, where he'd previously spent a dozen years, Stevens was toying with the idea of going back to college in quest of a new career when he got an out-of-the-blue phone call from an acquaintance at *National Enquirer* headquarters in South Florida.

"Mr. Pope's planning to start a new tabloid within the next couple of months," the acquaintance said. "It's going to be a lot like the old *National News Extra*, and Mr. Pope thinks it'll sell like gangbusters. We could use a guy with your kind of experience and warped mind to help get it off the ground. You interested?"

It took Stevens less than an hour to pack his bag. By the next afternoon, he was in Lantana, Florida, where he was about to serve as one of a small group of midwives at the birth of yet another bastard offspring of U.S. journalism.

This time, they named the baby *Weekly World News*. He was quite a bit fatter, immeasurably wealthier, and even somewhat better looking than *News Extra*. But in many other respects, he was—and would remain—the "spittin' image" of his dearly departed cousin from Chicago.

✳   ✳   ✳

Pope was interested in starting a new paper primarily to make use of the well-equipped letterpress plant in Pompano Beach that had been printing the *Enquirer* for more than a decade. Now that the *Enquirer* was converting to offset color production, the Pompano plant would be left sitting idle unless GP found something to keep it occupied. The logical way to do that was to start a new black-and-white tabloid, but there were some serious questions about what editorial direction it should take.

"Some people thought Pope might go back to a format like the old, original *Enquirer*, but he wanted this one to be different," Stevens told friends later. "He wanted it to be utterly outlandish and kooky, but not quite so bloodthirsty. He wanted to appeal to readers at the bottom end of the cultural, economic, and intellectual scale—but he also didn't mind if a lot of other people bought the paper just to laugh at it. In fact, he was counting on it."

One major target audience was the subset of Americans who felt threatened or abandoned in an increasingly confounding world of high technology and low self-esteem: People who clung to simplistic, primitive, sometimes fanatical ideas about religion, politics, and society. People who were angry and confused at the uncontrollable changes taking place all around them. People who somehow managed to believe equally in space aliens and angels.

But another group that could prove just as important to the new paper's success was made up of those who got their kicks from ridiculing the first group and its silly, backward notions. *News Extra*'s demonstrated ability to connect with both groups, at least part of the time, was what made its example so intrguing.

"There's no question that Pope patterned the paper after *News Extra*," said Stevens. "The main difference was that we'd usually faked it all the way in Chicago, but at 'Wacky World News,' we had enough staff to start with the most oddball true stories we could find by combing eighty or ninety daily papers. Then we'd add whatever we could think of to spice 'em up."

Pope told the staff he was in no big hurry to find a perfect formula, and for quite a while he pretty much left them alone to figure out what worked and what didn't."

For nearly nine years, Stevens was a key part of the behind-the-scenes brain trust that helped editor Phil Bunton (later editor of the *Star*) shape the *Weekly World News* into a publishing phenomenon selling a million copies a week. Because of his background, Stevens clearly brought "something *Extra*" to the job.

Observers credit him with originating the idea for an ongoing series of biting sociopolitical commentaries—and outrageously nasty suggestions for dealing with gays, commies, foreigners, women, minorities, and other "undesirables"—that frustrated reactionaries could identify with. The idea evolved into the now-famous "Ed Anger" column, *WWN*'s most popular and most-vilified weekly feature.

Rolling Stone once called Anger the "most irresponsibly berserk columnist in America." One college radio station, meanwhile, read his column over the air each week with the Mormon Tabernacle Choir softly singing "God Bless America" in the background.

In reality, the column—which became a sort of Bible for rednecks everywhere while simultaneously developing a huge cult following on U.S. college campuses—was written by a former Chicago schoolteacher named Rafe Klinger.

As a big-city Jewish liberal, Klinger admitted often having trouble writing a column that was so flagrantly opposed to his personal beliefs. But Stevens was always there to inspire him with his own caustic philosophy and vicious, paint-peeling sense of humor.

Stevens' favorite expression, as remembered by longtime acquaintances, was: "Is there anyone here we haven't insulted?" And, according to Klinger, "The key to Ed Anger was to insult as many people as you could."

Klinger was fired in a wholesale housecleaning just after McFadden Enterprises bought the *Enquirer* and *WWN* from Pope's estate in 1989. Stevens died that same year of liver failure, and for a brief interlude, Ed Anger died, too.

But it's apparently hard to keep a raving bigot down. Within a few months, after a downturn in *WWN*'s circulation, Ed was resurrected. For a time, he was only a shadow of his former self, but as this is written, he's once again as obnoxiously rancorous as ever.

His March 28, 2000, column offers a typical example of his sledgehammer approach to sensitive issues. Ed's answer to the escalating violence in America's schools, as summed up in the accompanying headline: "Make EVERY kid pack a pistol!"

"Let's face it," the columnist wrote. "When the nice kids start shooting back, schoolyard gunplay will come to a screeching halt." He urged adoption of a new SHOTS FOR TOTS program that would supply .22-caliber pistols and shoulder holsters to every child in every public school in the country.

"Ben would've loved that one," said one of Stevens's longtime associates. "It was just like *News Extra* reincarnated."

The miracle of Ed Anger, as Klinger once summed it up, "was that a lot [of people] took him at face value, and others saw him as funny."

In essence, of course, that was the miracle of *News Extra*, too.

*   *   *

In 1983, a year after leaving Montreal and moving its headquarters to West Palm Beach, Florida, Globe Communications also got into the act by launching its own "outer limits" tabloid and calling it the *Sun*. Chosen to head the new publication was John Vader, tabloidism's established "old master" in the art of blending fact and fiction.

By this point in Vader's career, the industry he'd helped start from scratch almost thirty years earlier seemed to be leaving him behind. He'd created *Midnight* out of nothing in 1954, but now his handiwork had evolved into the relatively slick and truth-conscious *Globe*, and even before the paper's name change, Vader had been shunted aside as its editor.

"You could give Johnny the most dynamite factual story in the world, and he'd immediately start thinking of ways to make it better by adding a few wacky fabrications here and there," recalled one longtime associate. "Even when he had specific orders to keep the story as straight as an arrow, you could almost see the wheels turning in his head and sense how tempted he was to tweak it a little in spite of everything."

Although Vader's incessant "tweaking" had been instrumental in pushing *Midnight*'s average weekly sales to 1.4 million by 1977, his persistent tendency to play fast and loose with the facts eventually led to his removal as its editor. Former *Enquirer* chief articles editor Selig Adler was now editor in chief at Globe Communications, and he was stressing "credibility" and the taboo against sex and violence in *Midnight* more heavily than ever before.

Mike Rosenbloom refused to let Adler fire Vader, but he did approve what was, from all appearances, a serious demotion. He was relegated to the editorship of the *National Examiner*, a second-tier tab with limited supermarket exposure and little identity among tabloid buyers. Along with the job came the hot-seat responsibility of building up the *Examiner* and turning it into a solid money maker.

Vader proceeded to do with *Examiner* what he'd done with *Midnight* in the early 1970s, going back to a tried-and-true mix of celebrity, human-interest, and off-beat stories. He had to work within the same general restrictions on sex and violence that applied to *Midnight*, but at the same time, he had more freedom to do the kind of "tweaking" and fact stretching that was his forté.

Within a short time, the *Examiner* also went to a full-color cover, helping to set it apart from the "lowbrow" tabs. It joined the Audit Bureau of Circulations and picked up some key personnel, including former *Tattler* and *News Extra* staffer Cliff Linedecker and *Enquirer* ex Mike Irish. Britisher Mike Nevard replaced Adler as editorial director and helped focus on moving the *Examiner* solidly into the number four spot in the national tabloid market left vacant by the *Tattler*'s demise.

Despite all this sprucing-up, however, it retained that undeniable Vader touch with such cover headlines as "HITLER SEEN ALIVE IN U.S."; "VATICAN ASKED TO CONFIRM SAINT ELVIS"; "MY GRANDMA WAS A BIGFOOT"; and "Incredible report—confined for 22 years after fake death . . . MARILYN ESCAPES FROM GOV'T ASYLUM."

Although there were many other contributors besides Vader to the *Examiner*'s newfound success, circulation was near the 500,000 mark by 1983 and climbing steadily, enroute to an eventual high of 1.1 million. That same year, however, impressed with the hefty sales being racked up by Pope's *Weekly World News*, Rosenbloom decided to field *Globe*'s own entry in the "loony tunes" tabloid field.

The decision was made to name the new paper the *Sun*, after Rupert Murdoch's phenomenally profitable British tabloid, and almost no one was surprised when Vader was handed the job of making it go.

"We'd watched *News Extra* closely, and I was very much aware of what they were trying to do with it during the midseventies," Vader said in a recent interview. "It reminded me of some of the things we'd done in the early days at *Midnight*, but it carried them a step further, and I liked the idea of trying to appeal to two totally different levels of readers."

Out of the fertile ferment of Vader's imagination sprang a seemingly inexhaustible stream of invented classics that cost virtually nothing to produce. With his magic touch, a two-paragraph blurb translated from a remote foreign newspaper could mutate into a blockbuster cover story for the *Sun*. Photos were usually anonymous mug shots pulled from old files and airbrushed as necessary to illustrate such headlines as: "PLASTIC SURGEON'S GOOF GIVES MAN PELICAN BILL"; "GIRL, 15, HIT BY LIGHTNING TURNS INTO OLD WOMAN OVERNIGHT"; "MOM CLEANS KIDS BY PUTTING THEM IN CLOTHES WASHER"; and "WIFE TURNS INTO VAMPIRE & BITES HUSBAND TO DEATH."

Unlike the editors of *Extra* and *WWN*, Vader found it impossible to stay away from some of *Midnight*'s early-day standards—particularly themes that combined freakishness and sex. In the *Sun*'s July 3, 1990, issue, for example, a five hundred-pound sumo wrestler was pictured on the cover and billed as "THE MAN WITH 10,000 LOVERS." On the same cover, the main banner headline proclaimed: "She had baby at age 9, and now . . . GIRL, 16, BECOMES A GRANDMOTHER."

Vader's *Sun* was notably light on celebrity stories, however, and those it did run leaned heavily on bizarre elements: "PEE WEE HERMAN'S FACE FOUND ON PLANET MARS"; "LIZ TAYLOR'S DIAMOND IS CURSED—Million-dollar ring given to her by Richard Burton is dragging her to the grave"; "HEAD TRANSPLANTS OFFERED TO LIZ TAYLOR & 3 OTHERS" (the others being Bob Hope, James Stewart, and Ronald Reagan); and the like.

Fully 95 percent of the stories in Vader's *Sun* focused on unrecognizable "little people" doing extraordinary things and/or experiencing unheard-of problems. As one editor who worked closely with Vader on both the *Sun* and *Examiner* explained:

> When you mix a few isolated grains of fact with tons of imaginary hokum, like Johnny did so well, it's always easier and less risky to populate your stories with obscure nobodies. You hook together made-up names with generic pictures, and somewhere deep in the story, you mention it all happened in Turkistan or Outer Mongolia or someplace, and the odds are, no reader's going to say, "Hey, I know that guy!"

Once in a great while, though, as Vader candidly admits, this kind of subterfuge can blow up in your face.

"In my whole forty years as a tabloid editor," he recalled, "the only person who ever sued me was an old lady named Nellie Mitchell. We screwed up and used an old file picture of her in the *Sun* with a story about a ninety-year-old woman newspaper carrier who got pregnant on her route. Nellie wasn't that unhappy about it herself, but some lawyer contacted her family, and they talked her into filing suit. We paid her a little money and settled it out of court."

Under Vader's guidance, the *Sun* became yet another resounding success for Globe and Rosenbloom. By the early 1990s, its sales had skyrocketed from zero to nearly six hundred thousand a week.

Through it all, observers agree, Vader remained serenely imperturbable about what he was doing. For him, that razor-thin line that supposedly separates reality from make-believe—and legitimate journalism from illegitimate hucksterism—was as wide as an eight-lane superhighway.

A visitor to John's cluttered office once pointed out a particularly farfetched headline on one of the wild gallery of past *Sun* covers adorning the walls and wondered aloud how Vader justified running it.

The headline incorporated the strong spiritual overtones that were frequently seen in *News Extra* and later became something of a trademark for the *Sun* and *WWN*. "LUCY AND RICKY ARE REMARRIED IN HEAVEN," it read, "FAVORITE PAIR NOW TOGETHER FOR ALL ETERNITY."

Vader's response was a smile and a shrug. "Who's to say it's not true?" he said.

* * *

One final, backhanded tribute to *News Extra's* peculiar appeal came in the late 1980s when *Midnight* cofounder Joe Azaria's younger brother, Paul, picked up the name—now defunct for over a decade—and recycled it on a Montreal-based tabloid of his own.

By 1991, Paul (who spelled his last name with two z's instead of one) claimed to be circulating about 200,000 copies of his version of *News Extra*. This was probably a gross exaggeration, but the paper did attract considerable notice with a series of bombshell celebrity stories—resulting in a series of megalawsuits.

Sylvester Stallone sued over a story claiming that (1) he was left impotent by overuse of steroids, and (2) had had a penile implant performed to correct the problem. It was all a monstrous lie, Stallone said.

A few issues later, Azzaria's paper targeted Oprah Winfrey and her boyfriend, Stedman Graham, in a story alleging, among other things, that Graham had engaged in gay sex with a former male model.

Oprah and Stedman filed a $300-million lawsuit, and rather than go to court to defend a basically baseless story, Azzaria simply shut down *News Extra II* and went out of business.

If there's a lesson to be learned from this little footnote, it's probably that very few legal problems are caused by stories that only a lunatic could take seriously.

THIRTEEN
CHANGING THE GUARD
THE CAPTAINS AND KINGS DEPART

Almost without exception, the people who pioneered the concept of the supermarket tabloid in America—then battled and bamboozled their way to unprecedented wealth, influence, and readership—have now faded from the scene.

For more than three decades, the tabs represented one of the nation's most fertile fields for nervy risktakers, visionary mavericks, and defiers of the journalistic status quo. The original tabs were owned and guided by tough competitors, who were willing to go to virtually any extreme to best their rivals and boost their circulations.

But during the dozen years between the late 1980s and the dawn of the twenty-first century, each of the major national tabloids changed owners, some more than once. The corps of powerful leaders who built them from nothing to a peak weekly readership estimated at over 40 million either died, retired, or moved on.

Their departure set in motion a massive shift in both the philosophy and practice of the tabloid business. Within the space of just over ten years, it also turned the industry its originators left behind into what boils down to a one-horse race today.

As of late 1999, all six of the surviving supermarket tabloids—the *Enquirer*, *Star*, *Globe*, *Examiner*, *Weekly World News*, and *Sun*—came under the ownership of a single giant company, American Media, Inc. Centralized management, one-size-fits-all corporate policies, bean-counting mentali-

179

ties, and assembly-line methods have been in full sway ever since, according to disgruntled industry veterans.

Worse yet, critics contend, is that plans call for all six papers to be written and edited under the same roof in the near future, with an inevitable overlapping of staffs and homogenization of styles. (When the *Star* was critically shorthanded during a staff relocation in the spring of 2000, dozens of *Examiner* and *Sun* staffers were pressed into emergency service to get the paper out, and numerous other instances of cross-staffing and story shifting have since taken place.) In the view of many industry veterans, the free-wheeling, let's-see-you-top-this competitive spirit that kept the papers scrapping and scrambling in the old days simply can't exist in this new atmosphere.

"It may work with widgets, but not with tabloids," said longtime *Enquirer* hand Bill Bates. "Gene Pope would surely be turning over in his grave if he could see what's going on."

*   *   *

Death came suddenly and unexpectedly on October 2, 1988, for the man who'd founded the *Enquirer* thirty-six years earlier, personally molded it into a new definition of journalistic excess, and reaped hundreds of millions of dollars in profit from it. It was a warm, peaceful Sunday, and Generso Pope Jr. was relaxing at his home in West Palm Beach when the fatal heart attack struck.

Pope was sixty-one years old, almost exactly the same age as his father had been when a similar seizure claimed the elder Pope's life in 1950.

Considerable evidence suggests that Pope had had fears and concerns about his health for several years. Some said these fears were his main motivation for contributing a reported $5 million toward a new cardiac care unit at JFK Medical Center, which was located only three or four minutes from Pope's home.

"GP wasn't in the habit of tossing that kind of money around to charity," said Bates. "But he wanted to have the very best and latest in treatment options right there at his fingertips in case he did have a coronary. Unfortunately, though, he never got a chance to use them. He was DOA by the time they got him to the hospital."

Despite a seemingly clear-cut case of myocardial infarction and cardiac arrest—one of some 500,000 almost-identical deaths in the United States that same year—rumors still circulate today that the *Enquirer*'s creator was actually murdered. Suggestions as to motives, however, are vague and nebulous at best: An act of revenge by some scandal-scorched celebrity? An assassination aimed at avoiding some future exposé? Perhaps a long-delayed payoff for old, unfinished Mafia business? Even retaliation by a fired-and-forgotten former employee?

All are possibilities, of course, and the list of potential "suspects" who might fall into one category or another could easily run into the thousands. Despite suggestions that he'd mellowed somewhat with age, the callous, sadistic side of GP's personality remained very much in evidence in his latter years, and he continued to wreak havoc in the lives of people around him with whimsical abandon.

Former *Enquirer* reporter Byron Lutz, who can impersonate Pope's soft, insinuating voice with haunting accuracy, recently recounted the fate of one ambitious articles editor of the mid-1980s who sought to ingratiate himself with the boss and lived to regret it.

"The word was out that the quickest way to get fired was to let Pope know you were buying or building a house and trying to put down some roots," said Lutz. "He didn't like for people to start feeling too comfortable or secure. But this one guy had been there for a year or so, and he really wanted to get a place of his own. He thought he was already in pretty solid with Pope, and he figured if he told him about his plans and asked him for advice, everything'd be fine."

The articles editor approached Pope one day, showed him the architect's plans for the new house, tactfully referred to Pope's degree in engineering, and asked his opinion on whether the planned five tons of air conditioning was sufficient for a house that size.

"Pope looked the plans over and shook his head," Lutz recalled. "He said, 'Nah, nah, that's not nearly enough. You've got close to three thousand square feet there, and you'll never be able to cool that much space in this hot, humid climate with just five tons of air conditioning. You're gonna need at least fifteen tons to do the job right.'"

The articles editor thanked Pope profusely, and although it added considerably to the cost of the house, he dutifully followed the boss's advice to the letter and had the specified fifteen tons of air installed. When the house was finished, the articles editor proudly showed Pope a picture of it and told him: "I put in the fifteen tons of air, just like you said."

Moments after the happy new homeowner left, according to Lutz's account, Pope picked up the phone and growled to one of his underlings: "Get ridda that guy. Anybody stupid enough to put fifteen tons of air conditioning in a three-thousand-square-foot house doesn't deserve to work here."

By the time of his death, Pope had disposed of innumerable employees in similar fashion. It's reasonable to assume that at least a few of them would've killed him without remorse if they got the chance and thought they could get away with it. But it seems out of the question that such a person would've had the opportunity to go into Pope's secluded home and slip some deadly heart attack–mimicking drug into his orange juice. In fact, supporting evidence of any kind of plot or skulduggery is totally lacking.

Paul Pope, GP's thirty-three-year-old son, is among the more vocal proponents of the foul-play theories, however. The younger Pope has reportedly shelled out a small fortune and hired a small army of former *Enquirer* writers and reporters to gather information for a book he wants to publish on his father's life—and death.

In late 1999, Paul Pope told a writer for *Talk* magazine that he'd expected to inherit the *Enquirer* after his father's death and now felt "robbed of his birthright" by his mother and his father's disloyal friends. He echoed those sentiments in an April 2000 interview with Paul Reid of the *Palm Beach Post*, saying, "I was definitely screwed out of what was rightfully mine."

Paul Pope claimed his mother and father were on the verge of divorce at the time of Generoso's death. He also claimed the elder Pope was having a new will drawn, which would've left the entire paper to Paul. But an existing will, still in effect when GP died, stipulated that the *Enquirer* be sold to the highest bidder, and this had apparently been his well-thought-out plan for a long time. As early as 1974, GP was quoted as follows by the *Miami Herald*:

> Right now, my executives [the correct word probably should've been "executors," meaning those responsible for administering his will] are instructed that, if anything happens to me, they are to sell it [the *Enquirer*] and set up trust funds for my family. Of course, the employees would have first option to buy it, since nobody in the family could run it.

Paul Pope was, of course, only six years old at the time, and GP could easily have changed his mind—and the will—during the next fourteen years.

According to associates who helped young Pope collect some 10,000 pages of information on his father, one of Paul's three major objectives in pursuing the book project was to reveal evidence that the elder Pope was murdered. Reliable reports placed the project's out-of-pocket cost to Paul at more than $500,000, as of spring 2000.

Despite all this, virtually any cardiologist in America would agree that Gene Pope's risk-factor profile made him a prime candidate for a heart attack. The factors working against him included: (1) family history of coronary disease; (2) sedentary lifestyle with little physical activity; (3) moderately overweight; (4) heavy (three-pack-a-day) cigarette smoker.

"If he was concerned about his health, you'd never have known it from the way he chain smoked," said ex-*Enquirer* writer Bob Abborino. "I don't think I ever saw him without a Kent cigarette in his mouth or in his hand."

One thing seems certain: No one on Pope's editorial staff had the slightest inkling that the boss was seriously ill, much less about to drop dead. Even to Iain Calder, Pope's editor and trusted right-hand man, the news came as a devastating surprise.

"Pope had had some chest pains, but he shrugged them off, and his doctor apparently didn't think they were anything serious, either," said Calder in an interview eleven and a half years after that fateful Sunday. "When the call came in that weekend, it was a tremendous shock. I was stunned—just totally numb."

Paul Pope claims, however, that the doctors at JFK Medical Center were well aware of his father's heart condition but were afraid of offending GP by insisting he have bypass surgery. "My father's doctors didn't have the [guts] to tell him how sick he was," the *Palm Beach Post* quoted Paul as saying. "They were intimidated by my father."

Besides the genuine grief he felt, Calder said, he immediately sensed the broad implications of Pope's death and the vast repercussions it would touch off. He realized almost instantly that nothing would ever be the same again.

"It was like everything had exploded," he said. "One minute it was there, and the next minute, it was gone. Within the blink of an eye, the world as we knew it had ended."

$$* \quad * \quad *$$

Pope left a personal fortune estimated at $150 million, which doesn't include the additional $412 million received by his estate when the *Enquirer* and *Weekly World News* were sold at a "blind" auction in 1989. Under terms of the will, the auction was conducted by Peter Peterson, a former U.S. Secretary of Commerce, who was described as Pope's "closest friend" during his days at MIT. Each bid was held in strict confidence until all were opened, and the high bidder took everything, with no chance for counterbids by the losers.

Prior to the bidding, most financial experts were predicting a top sale price of no more than $250 million, but they grossly underestimated the level of interest among would-be buyers on both sides of the Atlantic.

To some media watchers, it seemed strangely ironic when the high bidder turned out to be a lightly regarded publishing entity known as Mac-Fadden Holdings, Inc. To gain control of Pope's publishing empire, Mac-Fadden had to fend off such formidable challengers as British media magnate Robert Maxwell, the French publishing cartel Hachette Filipacchi, and the giant German conglomerate Bertelsmann AG.

MacFadden reportedly beat out its nearest rival among these heavy hitters by a cool $50 million. But according to Paul Pope, he was also a serious bidder for the *Enquirer*—and was, in fact, the highest bidder among the losers. Paul told *Talk* magazine that, with the help of Shearson Lehman Brothers, he put together a management team and obtained enough financing to put up a $400-million bid, which he'd been assured no one else would match.

Word of Paul's intentions may have leaked out and caused other bidders to raise their ante. At any rate, young Pope's effort fell just $12 million short. Although he received a generous share of the money from the sale, along with his mother and siblings, Paul was crushed by the defeat.

"It was like my father dying all over again," he said.

In a 1996 interview with one of the researchers on Paul's book, his mother supposedly admitted she hadn't wanted her son to gain ownership of the company, but she claimed she was motivated only by motherly concern. "If he was the highest bidder, so be it," she was quoted as saying, "but the fact is, I was afraid those sharks would kill him."

MacFadden chairman Peter Callahan, who was written off by many at the time as a minor player, had swung the deal for the *Enquirer* by forming a partnership with the Boston Ventures investment group. The irony lay in the fact that Callahan had created MacFadden Holdings in 1975 out of the ailing remnants of the publishing dynasty built in the 1920s by Bernarr MacFadden, founder of the original *Midnight* and the scuzzy old *New York Evening Graphic*. What goes around comes around, it seems. MacFadden had lost his shirt on the *Graphic*, but now the organization bearing his name owned one of the most profitable media properties in the country.

Very soon it would own another. In 1990, in a major step in its evolution into what would become American Media, Inc., MacFadden Holdings also bought the *Star* from Rupert Murdoch for an additional $400 million. This gave the company control of America's two largest weekly tabs with a combined circulation at the time of about 7 million.

Murdoch's move was almost as shocking to the *Star*'s staff as Pope's death had been to *Enquirer* employees. After years of tooth-and-nail competion, the idea of the two papers becoming "siamese twins" under the same ownership was a bitter pill for "Rupe's troops" to swallow.

Murdoch's rationale for selling out to the enemy—or at least to the company that now owned the enemy—and for choosing this particular time to do it, is still open to question. Even many of those closest to the situation were left wondering about it. Had the excitement simply gone out of the fight now that Pope, his longtime adversary, was dead? Had bigger, more important enterprises relegated the *Star* to the back burner among Murdoch's interests? Did he sense that supermarket tabs had reached their zenith and were now sliding into a long, irreversible decline?

In retrospect, it was probably a combination of all these factors that motivated him. Murdoch had launched the Fox Television Network in 1986, and according to some critics, he'd discovered ways to make prime-time TV more vulgar, fetid, and tasteless than the lowest of the tabs—and reap even bigger profits by doing it.

By the early 1990s, Murdoch's U.S. interests had also expanded to include moviemaking (20th Century Fox), slick magazines (*TV Guide*), and major-market dailies (the *New York Post*). The *Star*'s relative importance in the overall scheme of things had definitely diminished.

Whatever Murdoch's reasons for abandoning the supermarket tabloid field, the *Enquirer*'s Calder quickly claimed victory in its fifteen-year battle with the *Star*.

"Murdoch ended up being number one in Australia and number one in Britain, but he had to settle for being number two in the United States," Calder said. "We're the only ones who stood in the way of his steamroller and came out on top."

*   *   *

For the last five years before his death, Pope had been making a tidy operating profit of up to $20 million a year on revenues of about $140 million. But the company's annual profit margin hadn't grown appreciably since the early 1980s, and new boss Peter Callahan was determined to change that.

Part of the reason profits had remained flat was a gradual shrinkage in circulation that was affecting all the tabs more or less equally. The *Enquirer*'s average weekly sales had peaked at 5.4 million in 1978, then drifted downward to around 4.7 million by 1981. Pope's "Enquiring minds" TV ad campaign had reversed the trend for a time, boosting *Enquirer* circulation back to almost 5.2 million and, in a spin-off effect, helping propel the *Star* and *Globe* to all-time highs of 3.9 million and 2.1 million, respectively. From that point on, though, it had been downhill all the way for all three papers, and not even Pope's alleged genius had been able to turn things around.

But a second key reason for the static profit margins was GP's notorious policy of sparing no expense where his "baby" was concerned. By the late 1980s, the *Enquirer*'s editorial staff had ballooned to almost four hundred—an exorbitant number by anyone's standards—and salaries remained the highest in American journalism. Productive reporters could easily earn $70,000 a year in salary while living, in large measure, on unlimited expense accounts. Many editors earned $150,000 a year or more. Reliable estimates placed Iain Calder's annual salary as editor in chief and president of the *Enquirer* at $865,000, plus stock options, profit sharing, and other perks.

Pope also devoted staggering sums of money to sheer whims, PR stunts, window dressing, and overkill. One oft-repeated story has him spending $150,000 to send a reporter on an around-the-world junket in search of Utopia, then trashing every story the reporter wrote. Another $150,000 was spent on massive coverage of the funeral of Princess Grace of Monaco. Even routine stories were often staffed by a dozen or more reporters and photographers. Then there was the $1-million-a-year Christmas tree and party each year for the citizens of Lantana.

"Mr. Pope was Santa Claus," Callahan told an interviewer, "and we can't afford to be." The days when the *Enquirer* was run like a rich man's hobby were over, he added.

Callahan lost no time showing he meant business, immediately instituting a series of drastic cost-cutting measures to improve the bottom line. He fired no fewer than forty-seven editorial staffers in a single mass bloodletting that made GP's old Friday afternoon massacres look like Sunday school picnics by comparison. Within a few weeks, the staff had been slashed by more than 15 percent, but the survivors continued to draw top salaries, and Calder remained the chief editorial decision maker with minimal interference from above.

Callahan cut the number of pages from sixty-four to fifty-six while simultaneously raising the cover price from seven-five cents to eighty-five cents, moves designed to increase revenues by $15 million a year. He also tried, with only limited success, to beef up national advertising lineage in both the *Enquirer* and *Star*.

And, as we know, Pope's Christmas trees got the axe, too.

"They ran a tight ship," said former *Star* editor Richard Kaplan, who also served a hitch as an *Enquirer* staffer, in describing the MacFadden operation. "Pope used to throw money around like they were minting it. I think that day and age is over."

Kaplan was right. Coming as they did within a period of about eighteen months of each other, Pope's death and Murdoch's departure signaled the end of a lot of things in the tabloid business. These two watershed events may one day be remembered, in fact, as the beginning of the end for the business itself.

*   *   *

As this is written, none of the major figures who helped shape and define America's supermarket tabs are still actively involved in producing them.

Like Pope, many have gone to their eternal reward—whatever it may be. Nat Chrzan and Carl Grothmann, who spent the better part of twenty years leapfrogging each other as editor and managing editor of the *Enquirer* before Iain Calder ascended to power, are both dead.

Also deceased is Selig Adler, who went from a position as the last managing editor of the *New York Mirror* to a job as chief articles editor of the *Enquirer* to the post of editor in chief at *Midnight/Globe*. Adler's legendary short temper and foul disposition once got him fired by Mike Rosenbloom after he referred to a secretary whom Rosenbloom was planning to marry as "that stupid cunt." But the marriage didn't last long, and after a costly divorce, Rosenbloom invited Adler back for another stint as editorial director, during which he persuaded Rosenbloom to shift his operation from Canada to the United States.

Calder himself was eased out as editor of the *Enquirer* in 1995—

although he continued to be listed on the masthead for a while as "Editor Emeritus"—and was replaced by Harvard-educated Steve Coz. He now lives in retirement in Boca Raton, where he spends most of his time playing tennis and attending to a variety of investments.

"I'm still under contract to the *Enquirer* as a consultant," Calder said recently, "but they never ask me to do anything. It suits me just as well. If they did, it might cut into my time on the tennis court."

Midnight cofounder John Vader also retired in 1995 after a forty-three-year tabloid career in which he directed the editorial fortunes of three of today's six surviving papers (*Globe, Examiner,* and *Sun*). He now lives quietly in South Florida, only a few miles from Calder.

Joe Azaria, Vader's original partner in *Midnight,* went on to found the *Sunday Express,* Canada's first Sunday newspaper, and own the *Police Gazette,* America's oldest magazine, after selling his tabloids to Rosenbloom. Azaria later bought a pepper plantation in the Costa Rican rain forest with part of the reported $8 million he made as a Montreal publisher. He moved to the Central American country with his wife in the late 1970s, and except for Vader, Jack Tabatch, and a handful of other old friends, no one in the States has heard from him since. At last report, according to Vader, Azaria was suffering from "several serious health problems."

After Allied News Company and its tabloids went out of business in 1976, former *Tattler* publisher Bob Sorrentino made one last grab for the brass ring. He teamed with Robert Preuss, one of Hugh Hefner's original associates in *Playboy,* who was retiring as treasurer of Hefner's company, to establish a tabloid-style country music weekly called *Country Rambler.*

Several Allied expatriates, including Tom Ayres, Ben Stevens, Bill Klasne, Bill Hendricks, and John Moulder, went to work for the new publication (described by one staffer as a "shitkicker's version of *Rolling Stone*"). The paper was one of the first weekly publications to concentrate on country music and its personalities, especially the so-called outlaw movement led by Willie Nelson and Waylon Jennings. It was enthusiastically received by fans and entertainers alike, and Preuss's contacts as a former *Playboy* circulation director helped it gain good exposure, but major national advertising accounts failed to materialize. By the time *Rambler* folded in February 1977, Sorrentino and Preuss had suffered personal financial losses of more than $300,000 each.

Sorrentino never surfaced in publishing circles again. He dropped out of sight, and none of his former associates knows his whereabouts today.

*   *   *

By the late 1990s, Mike Rosenbloom, the mild-mannered accountant whom skeptics had expected to have his company repossessed out from under him within a few months after he bought it from Joe Azaria, was the last of the old-line independent tabloid publishers left standing.

Of the small group of shoestring operations from which the supermarket tabloid industry had sprung, only Rosenbloom's Globe Communications was left. Everything else, representing well over three-quarters of all weekly tabloid sales in the country, belonged to American Media.

But being the underdog didn't bother Rosenbloom. In his almost thirty years as Globe's main man, he'd learned to thrive on that role. In his own way, he'd proved to be as tough, canny, and ruthless as either Pope or Murdoch—and some said he could be more unscrupulous than both of his old-time rivals put together.

"Rosie looked like a big, overgrown Pillsbury doughboy," said one of his top editors of the 1970s. "He always seemed nervous and shy, and he kind of lisped when he talked. He gave the impression that if you yelled at him, he'd run and hide under his desk. But as a lot of people found out the hard way, he could also be one mean, conniving son of a bitch."

Rosenbloom had a penchant for firing key people, then hiring them back in a lesser position at a lower salary. In 1971, he enticed a high-priced group of seasoned U.S. journalists to Montreal specifically to spruce up *Midnight* for the supermarkets. Less than six months later, when they'd done the job with far more speed and efficiency than Rosenbloom had ever expected, he decided he was paying them too much and sacked the lot of them. But a few days later, two members of the group were offered reinstatement—for about two-thirds of what they'd been paid originally.

Since both were stranded and jobless in a foreign country and had wives and children to support, they accepted the offer. One ended up staying at Globe for the next twenty-eight years—until the company was sold to American Media in 1999.

But this episode was strictly minor-league compared to the one, just over a decade later, in which Rosenbloom became tabloidland's undisputed champion of mass beheadings by dumping practically his whole editorial staff at once. It happened in April 1982, when a Montreal chapter of the Newspaper Guild organized Globe's newsroom with the support of at least 90 percent of its rank-and-file employees.

"It wasn't like the people supporting the guild didn't have fair warning," said John Vader. "Rosenbloom told them he'd never tolerate a union shop, but they went ahead with the thing, anyway. Selig [Adler] had already talked Rosie into opening an office in the United States, first in Greenwich, Connecticut, then in West Palm Beach, and when it became obvious the union was going to be approved, they started assembling a new staff in Florida."

On a Friday afternoon, no fewer than seventy Globe editorial staffers lost their jobs. The following Monday, when Adler, Vader, and a few other key editors arrived at the offices in West Palm Beach, they had a new staff waiting for them.

"Basically, Rosie just took the whole editorial operation to another country and left the union people behind," Vader said.

Three years later, Rosenbloom moved the company, now known as Globe International, into a modern new building in Boca Raton that was, in many respects, more opulent and impressive than the *Enquirer* headquarters in Lantana. In front of it towered a bronzed statue of Atlas holding a huge globe in his hands.

After American Media took over the *Enquirer* and *Star*, both papers strived, in the words of one observer, to "edit and market their way out of the tabloid category" in order to attract more national advertisers. They toned down their celebrity coverage and generally went back to a diet of less inflammatory stories similar to the mix they'd used to crack the supermarkets in the early 1970s.

As *Newsweek* of October 21, 1998, described the change: "[T]hey increasingly turned to SMERSH, a term coined years back by a *Washington Post* editor, which stood for Science, Medicine, Education, Religion and all that S—t."

Rosenbloom seized the initiative by taking the opposite tack. He purposely heated up the contents of his papers and showed no hesitation in claiming the "low road" his rivals were trying to rise above. For a while, it worked. *Globe* and *Examiner* both posted circulation gains in the early 1990s while sales of the *Star* and *Enquirer* were on a steady downward curve.

In late 1990, Rosenbloom was reportedly confident enough in his approach to turn down a $300-million offer for Globe International from British media czar Robert Maxwell.

But nine years later, after *Globe*'s circulation dipped below 750,000 for the first time in a quarter century and *Examiner* sales also plunged drastically, Rosenbloom sold out to American Media for $105 million, or slightly over one-third what Maxwell had offered.

Rosenbloom's last big adventure as a tabloid publisher had been the flagrant 1998 setup in which *Globe* paid a former airline stewardess $50,000 to lure former football star and sportscaster Frank Gifford to a hotel room for sex while the paper's operatives secretly recorded the encounter for "posterity."

One of the century's scurviest examples of "checkbook journalism," the story triggered an orgy of media coverage in which Gifford was repeatedly flogged and his wife, TV talk show host Kathie Lee Gifford, publicly pitied. It dragged on for the better part of two years, culminating in a joint interview of the couple by Diane Sawyer on *20/20* with Frank cowering in the background and mumbling apologies while Kathie Lee tearfully "forgave" the louse and pondered how to tell their children about his disgrace.

Next to the JonBenet Ramsey murder case, Frank and Kathie Lee were the longest-running tabloid story of the late 1990s—even longer than Monica and Bill. But when it did almost nothing to reverse the Globe papers' circulation eclipse, Rosenbloom found the American Media offer too tempting to pass up.

"From what I've heard, Rosie was already worth around $500 million," said John Vader a few weeks after hearing the news, "so he really wasn't hurting for money. He was pushing seventy, and I think he just decided it was time to go—so he did."

With that, the changing of the guard was complete.

FOURTEEN
FROM ELVIS TO O. J. TO PRINCESS DI
THE TABS AT HIGH TIDE

In the early 1970s, at a time when the *Enquirer*'s circulation was rising by the thousands each week, Gene Pope frequently predicted that his paper would one day sell 25 million copies. As it turned out, his goal was unrealistically high, but if he'd predicted instead that 25 million people would read the *Enquirer* in an average week, he wouldn't have been that far wrong.

At its high-water mark less than a decade later, the tabloid that boasted the "largest circulation of any weekly paper in America" was selling an average of 5.4 million copies per issue, according to official Audit Bureau of Circulations figures. At times, it flirted with the 6-million-copy mark (it topped it only once, though, with the Elvis-in-his-coffin issue in late 1978) and, with an estimated 3.5 readers per copy, it sometimes may have had a total readership of 20 million or even slightly more.

Editor Iain Calder once went so far as to estimate that one in every ten Americans read the *Enquirer* during its heyday, which, at the time, would've translated to around 28 million people. And Paul Levy, former *Enquirer* senior editor and former editor in chief of *Globe*, has been quoted as saying the combined readership of the six existing supermarket tabs, as of the early 1990s, could've run as high as one in every seven Americans.

Tabloid circulation in general peaked in 1982 when the *Enquirer*, *Star*, *Globe*, *Examiner*, *Weekly World News*, and the newly launched *Sun* had a combined average weekly sale of around 12.5 million copies. (According to a report by *Business Week* in early 1983, the top four supermarket tabs accounted for 11.4 million of these sales, making them the fastest-growing periodicals in the country.) If the figure of at least 3.5 readers per copy can be applied to all six papers, this means a total readership in excess of 43 million.

These numbers made the tabs a powerful sociopolitical force throughout the 1980s and most of the 1990s. They became such a strong cultural influence that even people who never picked up one of them— much less actually sat down to read one from cover to cover—were affected by them. The majority of Americans still thought of them as "rags" and smarmy scandal sheets, but their omnipresence in virtually every chain store made it impossible not to see their blaring headlines or hear shoppers asking each other, "Did you see what the *Enquirer* said about so-and-so?"

Those close to Pope knew he was fully aware of the growing power of his paper. They say he glimpsed an unprecedented potential for it to influence both broad U.S. social patterns and key initiatives by the federal government. In 1974, he confidently told a reporter for the *Miami Herald* that when the *Enquirer* reached 20 million in sales, it would have the ability to cut off the flow of illegal drugs into this country.

When the reporter asked how, he got quite an earful.

"How?" Pope responded. "Pressure. Enough pressure on Congress, plus our own good staff out in the field exposing it [the drug traffic]. It's almost an open secret how they smuggle the stuff, and there's a tremendous rivalry among law enforcement agencies. Instead of fighting crime, they're competing with one another."

If the *Enquirer* could marshal the support of enough ordinary citizens for this kind of antidrug campaign, Pope continued, government would have to go along with it. He also strongly indicated that he wanted his paper to move beyond the borders of the United States and become an international influence.

"If I can reach the common people . . . I don't care what kind of government is in a country, it has to respond to the wishes of the people, even if it's a totalitarian government," he said. "And you've got to force the governments to help. I guess I'm saying what we're trying to do is what the United Nations hasn't been able to [do]."

Maybe GP didn't realize how arrogant this sounded, or maybe he was feeling his oats at the time and simply didn't care. But those who observed him close-up over the years say such comments were totally in character for the Pope of Lantana.

As one former *Enquirer* editorial executive phrased it: "If we'd ever actually hit 20 million circulation, there's no telling what kind of egocentric crusades Pope would've gotten us involved in."

During those mid-1970s, the *Enquirer* drew a deafening chorus of hoots from "responsible" journalists for sending one of its reporters to dig through former Secretary of State Henry Kissinger's garbage. But within a decade or so, the mainstream media could no longer afford to take such a holier-than-thou attitude.

The "legitimate" press now began to find itself—at least occasionally—in the embarrassing position of playing follow-the-leader after being soundly scooped by the tabs. It was easy for "straight" papers to ignore stories about psychic predictions, space aliens, and two-headed babies, except to poke fun at them. But if they failed to report well-documented cases of misbehavior by prominent public officials that were first brought to light by the tabloids, it would be *their* credibility, rather than the tabs', that suffered.

A classic case in point was the *Enquirer*'s 1987 photo of Donna Rice sitting in the lap of U.S. Senator Gary Hart aboard a yacht appropriately named *Monkey Business*. At the time, many political observers thought the handsome, popular Hart was on his way to winning the Democratic Party's 1988 presidential nomination. Mainstream reporters had staked out Hart's house and reported on Rice's comings and goings there, but it was the photographic proof of Hart's marital infidelity splashed across the front page of the *Enquirer* that solidified his guilt in the public mind and deep-sixed his White House hopes forever.

"Most of the other papers would've given their eye teeth to have gotten one of those pictures," said Iain Calder.

*   *   *

Another long-overlooked fact about the tabs that was now being forcefully driven home to the mainstream media was simply this: Despite the scorn and ridicule heaped on them, tabloid journalists were among the most talented, most resourceful—and toughest—reporters in the world.

Paul Levy, who'd won a sackful of awards, including two Pulitzer Prize nominations; covered the White House, Supreme Court, and civil rights demonstrations for a major daily; and taught journalism at two major universities before joining the *Enquirer*, put it this way:

> The perception from outside was wrong. . . . I think tabloid reporters, by and large, are better than daily newspaper reporters. . . . They are, in fact, some of the top people in journalism, who just like the freedom to travel [and] the fact that they're going to work on interesting stories, not dull stories.

Calder firmly agrees. He points with considerable pride to the fact that he was recently named by the Freedom Forum, founders of the world-famous Newseum in Arlington, Virginia, as one of the nation's ten most influential foreign-born journalists of the twentieth century.

"This is a tremendous honor for me personally," Calder said, "but I think it also says a lot about the caliber of people we had at the *Enquirer* while I was editor. You can't bribe or frighten people into going out and getting stories. You've got to have people that get excited about what they're doing, people who'll do anything it takes to beat the competition. We had guys who'd run through brick walls if they had to, because, more than anything, they wanted to win."

By the 1990s, the tabloids were turning their resources more and more toward serious coverage of the kind of major ongoing stories that grabbed and held public attention—the Branch Davidian seige at Waco, Texas; the O. J. Simpson case; the Oklahoma City bombing; the Bill Clinton sex scandal(s); and so on. As they did, the rest of the media began to learn what tenacious competitors the tabs could be.

When the *Star* broke the Gennifer Flowers story in 1992, Clinton aides and scores of mainstream journalists tried to hide their red faces behind the same old bombast. "Clinton's people said, 'What do you expect from a paper that talks about two-headed space aliens?' " *Star* editor Phil Bunton told *Newsweek*.

The fact that the *Weekly World News* (owned by the same company that published the *Star*) had recently run a cover story and "exclusive photos" of a space alien endorsing Clinton for president may have given tabloid haters some ammunition. But the truth was, except for *WWN* and the *Sun*, tabloid coverage of space aliens was as much a part of ancient history as the "gore era." Intelligent people with no axes to grind could tell the difference, so the old put-downs weren't nearly as effective anymore.

As *Newsweek* noted: "Tab people point out indignantly that they haven't focused on space aliens for years, but no matter: they got their revenge. Their always-aggressive reporting and willingness to pay for news led them to break stories that swiftly bubbled up to the rest of the press."

Even in presenting the tabs' side of the story, so to speak, the magazine had touched on a sensitive point. The fact that tabloids do pay for some of their hottest stories is, inarguably, a key factor that sets them apart from the "legitimate" press. But this difference is probably more pronounced in the minds of mainstream journalists than among the public in general.

As an example of aggressive tabloid reporting, *Newsweek* pointed out another Star story headlined:

MONICA'S OWN STORY
"Affair started on day we met
— after I flashed my sexy underwear"

The story had appeared in the *Star* in February 1998, months before the mainstream media had belatedly rediscovered those very same notorious thong panties and made a big deal of them.

When the *Enquirer*, in particular, decided to chase a story, it did so with a vengeance, sending not just one or two of those "guys who'd run through a brick wall" to get the scoop, but a whole army of them. In the process, its smothering brand of blanket coverage became legendary.

"Whenever you went out on a major story in the '90s, you could always count on being outmanned and outmaneuvered by the reporters and photographers from the *Enquirer,*" said longtime *People Weekly* correspondent Carlton Stowers, who watched them in action at both Waco and Oklahoma City. "Time-Life would send maybe five or six of us, but the *Enquirer* would have twenty people there. And they weren't satisfied with just getting there first; they also tried to grab all the pictures and hide all the sources. They did their best to keep the rest of us from getting anything."

This, of course, is a standard part of the cutthroat brand of British journalism that Iain Calder practiced as a young reporter, then preached for twenty years to *Enquirer* staffers.

"You don't just take one or two pictures [of a deceased victim] from the family's collection, even if that's all you plan to use," Calder said. "You take the whole lot if you can, just to keep anybody else from getting them. And when you locate a valuable source, you try to persuade him to let you move him and his family out of their house and into a hotel, where none of the other reporters can find them."

* * *

In 1995, when Nicole Brown Simpson and her friend Ronald Goldman were found stabbed to death and former football star O. J. Simpson was charged with their murders, the case arguably became the biggest celebrity story in supermarket tabloid history. But it was big in ways that were much different from—and not nearly as profitable as—the ongoing saga of Jackie and Ari in the 1960s and 1970s.

The O. J. case was big because it won unprecedented respect from the mainstream media for the *Enquirer,* which scooped the daily newspaper and TV reporters time and again. By inference, it also won respect for tabloids in general.

The *Enquirer* ran a photo of a fifteen-inch-long knife identical to one Simpson was alleged to have bought shortly before the killings. It found and interviewed the clerks who claimed to have sold the knife to O. J. It unearthed another photo of Simpson wearing expensive Bruno Magli shoes that matched a bloody footprint found at the scene of the crime. It tracked down Nicole's harrowing diary. It obtained inside information—much of it bought and paid for in traditional tabloid style—from O. J.'s cook, Nicole's therapist, and other sources that the rest of the media missed. Some of the information turned up by the *Enquirer* may have been instrumental in the verdict of a civil court jury that found Simpson responsible for the "wrongful deaths" of Nicole and Goldman, even after O. J. had been acquitted in a criminal trial.

In the end, the *Los Angeles Times* ran a five-thousand-word tribute to the *Enquirer's* coverage of feminist issues relating to the case, and the *New York Times* itself bowed, more graciously than many other establishment papers, to the *Enquirer's* exceptional coverage. It called the tabloid's stories "required reading" for anyone seriously interested in the facts of the case.

The O. J. story was a watershed event and a portent of things to come. On the other hand, it was anything but a big success where sales figures were concerned. Stories on Jackie and Ari had once sent circulation soaring by as much as 30 percent on given issues, but the massive Simpson coverage—which, at one point, made the front page twenty-one times during a twenty-seven-week span—didn't cause so much as a blip in the steadily descending line on the *Enquirer's* sales graphs.

It was the same problem encountered by the *Star* with its Gennifer Flowers exposé and a subsequent story on Clinton campaign strategist Dick Morris letting a two hundred dollar-an-hour prostitute listen in on his conversations with the president. Both articles were well investigated and well-timed (the Morris story broke on the very eve of the 1996 Democratic National Convention), but saleswise, both were duds.

Plaudits and recognition are nice, but in the tabloid business, it's still profits that count most. And as the 1990s wore on, profits continued to slide.

✳   ✳   ✳

The *Enquirer's* enterprising O. J. Simpson coverage was directed by a thirty-five-year-old Harvard honor graduate named Steve Coz. Partly on the strength of the outstanding job he did, Coz would soon succeed Iain Calder as the paper's first new editor in two decades. During the late 1990s, he'd also become the foremost symbol and spokesman for a "new direction" in tabloidism.

When Coz took charge in 1995, he lost no time in outlining his vision for the *Enquirer* of the future. What he wanted, he said, was a kinder, gentler, more respectable, more honorable, more trustworthy version of sensationalism. He wanted a tabloid with a conscience—a sort of "Boy Scout of the scandal sheets," as it were—yet one that was still as bold, exciting, and hard-hitting as ever.

It wasn't a really a new concept. Joseph Pulitzer had used basically the same approach a hundred years earlier. Pope himself had taken the same tack during his sanitizing project of the late 1960s, and editors at the long-defunct *National Tattler* had often employed the term "responsible sensationalism" to describe what they were trying to do in the mid-1970s.

But the America of the 1990s wasn't the same place it had been a century before, or even twenty years before, for that matter. It was a place where gleeful character assassination, sadistic sucker punching, and unfettered explicitness were becoming the journalistic order of the day. The norm, rather than the exception. And not just for low-class "gutter" publications, but for the media at large.

Because of his determination to swim against the current in this shock-happy environment—and simultaneously defy the tides that traditionally bore tabloids into the darkest, most dreadful extremes of the human experience—Coz drew a lot of favorable attention from the mainstream. His preppy good looks, smooth manner, and Harvard cum laude background didn't hurt, either. They opened doors to him that had always been locked and barred to other tabloid editors.

Under Coz, the *Enquirer* continued its enterprising reporting. When Bill Cosby's son, Ennis, was brutally murdered, the *Enquirer* offered a $100,000 reward and established an information hotline that led to an arrest. But it also showed that it could still hurl brickbats with good-old-days impact. At the height of the 1996 presidential campaign, for example, it reported that GOP nominee Bob Dole had once had a mistress. To some degree, the story offset the allegations of sexual misconduct swirling around Clinton and may have helped him win reelection.

The *Enquirer* has also led the tabloid pack in covering the JonBenet Ramsey murder case (coverage that continues unabated as this is written), with its reporters displaying a dogged persistence sometimes approaching fanaticism. After a spate of early coverage of the December 1996 slaying of the exquisitely beautiful six-year-old child model, investigators couldn't come up with conclusive evidence or indictments, and the mainstream media was ready to let the story fade away.

But week after week, month after month—and eventually year after year—headlines and photos in the *Enquirer* and other tabs kept breathing new life into the JonBenet case. *Globe* offered a $500,000 reward for information leading to the arrest and conviction of the killer. Both papers kept reporters working full-time on the story for months, constantly developing new angles and revelations, most of which pointed the finger of guilt at the girl's parents, John and Patsy Ramsey. To date, the case has dragged on for nearly four years and may never be officially solved, but the tabs have singlehandedly made it one of the most-reported crimes in history.

Because of the new direction and growing reputation for serious reporting Coz brought to the *Enquirer*, he was named by *Time* magazine as one of America's twenty-five most influential people of 1997. *Newsweek* and *U.S. News & World Report* ran mostly complimentary profiles on him. *Meet the Press*–style TV talk shows started inviting him as a guest.

But despite such widespread acclaim, the *Enquirer*'s circulation has continued its downward drift under Coz's editorial direction. During most of the months when the O. J. case dominated the paper's cover, sales were flat. And even JonBenet at her peak sold barely a third as many copies as Elvis in his coffin had sold two decades earlier.

As Gene Pope well knew, it takes time and perseverance for a tabloid to reinvent itself. But when *Enquirer* circulation dipped below 2 million in 2000—down more than 60 percent from the early 1980s—suspicions grew that Coz's vision was an unworkable oxymoron.

"I think Steve Coz is a really good editor," said Iain Calder of the man who took his place, "and there are still lots of fine journalists at the *Enquirer*. But I'm not thrilled with everything they're doing editorially."

Today, after five years with Coz at its helm, there's still no indication that the *Enquirer* can sell greater respectability and more papers at the same time.

$$* \quad * \quad *$$

While Coz tested the "kinder, gentler" approach in Lantana, *Globe* editor in chief Tony Frost was doing just the opposite a few miles south in Boca Raton.

A Britisher who first came to the States to handle celebrity coverage for the *Enquirer* and later also worked for the *Star*, Frost earlier spent fourteen years on London's Fleet Street and won notoriety as its "highest-flying sleaze merchant" for stories milked from newly wed Princess Di's hairdresser. Hired by Mike Rosenbloom for the express purpose of heating up *Globe*, he's calculatedly taken it on a prolonged tour of the "low road" since taking over there in the fall of 1997. To date, it's been one helluva ride.

"Some tabloid editors sometimes appear to be ashamed or embarrassed that they're in the tabloid business at all," Frost told *US* magazine in 1998. "I'm not, and *Globe* isn't. We're rock-solid tabloid."

Tony's concept of "rock-solidness" has included, among other things: engineering the sex trap into which Frank Gifford strayed, then overseeing the relentlessly tasteless coverage of the ensuing fiasco; publishing the grisly photos of the JonBenet Ramsey murder scene; running a topless photo of Ryan O'Neal's girlfriend and another of Goldie Hawn's fifty-one-year-old rear end; and shelling out $210,000 for the first grainy photos of Princess Diana and Dodi Fayed all cozied up on a private yacht.

Of the big three national tabs, *Globe* had always run a distant third behind the *Enquirer* and *Star*, but for a long time, even before Frost's arrival, it had often won first place in the salaciousness category. It was unfondly remembered for its 1991 decision to publish the name of William Kennedy Smith's alleged rape victim, which subsequently "forced" the *New York Times* and other highly respected papers to follow suit. And, shades of the old *Enquirer*, it had even published autopsy photos of Nicole Brown Simpson.

Of all U.S. tabloid editors, Frost was the most avid pursuer of pirated paparazzi photos of Diana and her new flame. Just three weeks before Di and Dodi died in their Mercedes in a Paris tunnel in August 1997, the cover of *Globe* featured a photo of the princess in a bulging bathing suit. It was headlined "FAT DI!" and "Princess of Whales."

A bit on the pudgy side himself and once described as resembling a "slightly bewildered schoolteacher," Frost has freely admitted to his dislike for British royalty and other celebrities who demand royal treatment. "I'm very much against privilege and elitism," he told *US*. "I loathe it."

When Princess Di was killed, the loathing was returned in kind.

$$* \quad * \quad *$$

For reasons that are nose-on-your-face obvious, the relationship between the tabs and the celebrities they cover has long been a bitter, fractious one. In tabloid terminology, "celeb coverage" has often been synonymous with stalking, invasiveness, torment, ridicule, cheap shots, and cynical distortions.

Even so, most of the celebrity stories published by the tabs over the past thirty years have been based, at least in part, on factual information. Beneath the embroidery, exaggeration, and innuendo usually lies a kernel of truth—and true stories can be far more damaging than fabrications. Ask Pee-Wee Herman, Hugh Grant, Michael Jackson, Woody Allen, or Marv Albert.

In the early days of the national tabloids, however, many editors didn't give a particular damn whether a celebrity story had any basis in reality or not. They manufactured stories about big-name personalities with total impunity, and they really didn't have much choice, since no star in his/her right mind would spit on them, much less talk to them. For editors like John Vader, it was always easier, and often more effective, just to invent something that sounded like it could be true: Elvis caught with some bimbo in a cheap motel, Jackie's kids caught growing pot, and so on.

Top celebrities either ignored the scurrilous, made-up stories printed by tabs of that era and refused to "dignify" them with any kind of rebuttal, or they laughed them off like the pack of lies they were. One example was a totally absurd 1970 story in Globe Communications' *National Bulletin*, claiming that Robert Redford and Warren Beatty operated a "human stud farm," at which eager young women paid $10,000 each to be impregnated by one of the two popular stars.

"Why would they sue over something like that?" the editor shrugged. "All the story does is build up their image as superstuds."

In the old days, even stories that could clearly inflict severe personal or professional damage were usually considered safe by editors because of an "unwritten law" holding that major celebrities risked far more than they could hope to gain by filing libel suits. Once in court, the tabloid defendant is free to introduce any evidence of immorality or wrongdoing that might help substantiate the tab's published story—even if they aren't directly related to the story's allegations.

Back in the late 1960s, *Enquirer* managing editor Carl Grothmann used to call it the "Principle of Historic Precedent." It held that any celebrity who had the misfortune at any time in his career to be arrested for or charged with assault, drunkenness, drug possession, wifebeating, adultery, child abuse, or such, could have his name attached to similar misdeeds for the rest of his life without fear of a lawsuit.

"They wouldn't dare sue," Grothmann told *Enquirer* staffers of the period. "They know if they took us to court, even though we might not be able to prove the item in question, we could produce enough evidence, press cuttings, and so forth, to show they'd been in similar incidents before."

It apparently didn't bother Grothmann that such evidence might be ruled irrelevant or inadmissible.

"By this time, the guy would be getting so much negative publicity that he'd be wishing he'd never sued us in the first place," he said. "As far as the public's concerned, it's the charge against the guy that's important, not whether he's guilty or innocent."

Under historic precedent, for instance, if a certain star is known to have a habit of sleeping around, there's theoretically no way a story claiming an extramarital affair by this same star can be libelous. But if he goes to court, all his past indiscretions can be dredged up for public inspection. It's the old business of "once a thief, always a thief," and it's given many an angry celebrity reason to pause and reconsider.

"It's the scorpion defense," said Hollywood attorney Vincent Chieffo, who's often advised celebrity clients against suing the tabloids. "You don't attack a scorpion because you're going to get stung."

In clawing, scratching, and dealing their way to the top in the no-quarter arenas of politics and show biz, many successful people resort to tactics that are less than honorable, if not downright despicable. As Iain Calder has expressed it: "It's a dog-eat-dog world. To get to the top there, it takes a certain type of person. They're not all bad—some of them are terrific—but there's a share of the dregs . . . people who are desperate to become famous, and they'll do anything."

According to tabloidism's unwritten law, celebrities of this stripe are never eager to press a libel suit in open court where all their past sins could come back to haunt them.

As the tabloids grew immeasurably in wealth and influence, however, some stars decided to take the risk anyway. In 1981, comedian Carol Burnett filed a much-publicized libel action over an *Enquirer* story claiming Burnett had gotten drunk in a Washington restaurant and become embroiled in a loud argument with former Secretary of State Henry Kissinger.

Initially, a sympathetic jury awarded Burnett $1.6 million in damages, but the trial judge cut the amount to $800,000, and an appellate court reduced it to $200,000. After further appeals by the *Enquirer*, Burnett ended up settling for a much smaller sum, widely rumored to be $75,000 or less.

"We were wrong, and we apologized," said Calder, "but it wasn't like the story was some big cover exposé. It was only four or five lines in a gossip column, and there was nothing malicious about it. We really tried to get good sources on anything like that, and we fired the lawyers who said it was okay to run it. Still, we were wrong."

Although the financial settlement was insignificant, the Burnett suit became a watershed event. It was the first time the *Enquirer* had ever had to pay anything in a legal action, and the suit was hailed in Hollywood as a massive victory over the "sleaze merchants."

It also brought down orders from Pope to exercise the most extreme caution on celebrity material in the future. The fact that the Burnett suit is the only one the *Enquirer* ever lost at trial demonstrates just how religiously these orders were followed.

That doesn't mean, of course, that nobody else ever sued.

A couple of years earlier, Hollywood agent Marty Ingels, husband of actress Shirley Jones, had launched a crusade to crush the tabloids, placing special emphasis on the *Enquirer* and calling it "a newspaper in which careers are mutilated every week." In addition to filing a $20-million suit himself, Ingels also persuaded actor Steve McQueen to sue over an *Enquirer* story claiming McQueen had terminal cancer. Before the legal process ran its course, however, McQueen died of the cancer the paper had reported. In a closed-door settlement reached in 1984, the *Enquirer* reportedly agreed to pay Ingels's legal fees of $300,000 plus a small amount of cash.

A few years later, Carroll O'Connor, nettled by published rumors that he was trying to dump Howard Rollins as his costar in *In the Heat of the Night*, told reporters: "You know, at first I thought I might sue the *Enquirer* for $20 million. Now I think I'm going to sue for $100 million." When Rollins was fired a short time later, O'Connor apparently changed his mind.

In 1990, Roseanne Barr filed a $35-million lawsuit against the *Enquirer* in federal court, claiming the paper had violated the Racketeer Influenced and Corrupt Organizations Act (RICO) in publishing portions of four love letters Barr had written to Tom Arnold. When the case was thrown out, Iain Calder called it "just another pathetic publicity stunt by Roseanne." (Nine years later, both former adversaries benefited from another "publicity stunt" when Roseanne served a stint as guest editor of the *Enquirer*, then featured virtually its entire newsroom staff on her TV talk show. "At least this time I'm editing a magazine that real people actually read," she said, in an apparent dig at the *New Yorker*, where she'd previously served as a guest editor.)

Liz Taylor endured decades of fabrications, half-truths, and degrading headlines from the tabs. But when she finally sued the *Enquirer* in 1993 over a story that said her then-husband, Larry Fortensky, had threatened a neighbor in a real estate dispute, it proved to be a costly error. After nearly six years of litigation, a judge dismissed the case and ordered Taylor to pay the tabloid's $500,000 legal fees. *Enquirer* editor Steve Coz said part of the money would be given to AIDS charities, one of Taylor's favorite causes.

Cher, when she was trying to break away from Sonny Bono and establish a separate identity, deliberately planted stories in tabloids to promote her career, just as many other entertainers have done on the way up—or the way out. But after achieving stardom as an actress, she wanted nothing further to do with the tabs, and when the *Star* ran a less-than-flattering story on her, Cher sued for $30 million. At the first trial, she won a $400,000 judgment, but the case was tossed out on appeal, and she ended up getting *nada*.

Tom Cruise and Nicole Kidman came out a little better when they sued the *Star* over a March 1999 story alleging that the couple had to hire a sex therapist to help them overcome marital problems. The *Star* paid an undisclosed amount to a charity chosen by the pair and printed a retraction.

Even *Globe*, which has flirted with libel countless times in its forty-six-year history, has seldom been sued by a celebrity—and almost never successfully. Singer Dionne Warwick once demanded $30 million after the paper reported she had a disease of the jawbone that could affect her career, but she dropped the suit when *Globe* printed a retraction. A $12-million suit brought by one Scott Thorson, who claimed to have been the late Liberace's gay lover, was dismissed by a judge in Los Angeles.

Globe was, however, forced to pay an undisclosed amount to charity in settling a $50-million suit by Arnold Schwarzenegger over a 1998 story claiming the actor/musclebuilder was in ill health and in danger of a heart attack. Schwarzenegger had undergone successful heart valve surgery the year before, and doctors said afterward there was no reason he couldn't continue his active lifestyle.

In fact, the most significant monetary damage ever inflicted on Globe Communications in a court of law was the 1992 noncelebrity case involving elderly Arkansan Nellie Mitchell (see chapter 12). *Sun* editor John Vader mistakenly assumed Mitchell to be deceased when he ran her photo with a made-up story about a 101-year-old woman being impregnated in Australia. Dead people, of course, can't be libeled, but unfortunately for Vader, Mitchell was very much alive at age ninety-six. She also became very rich after a jury in Mountain Home, Arkansas, awarded her $1 million in damages.

All in all, the major tabs have fared incredibly well in fighting off libel suits. For years, the *Enquirer, Star,* and *Globe* have used batteries of high-priced lawyers to read and reread all celebrity copy before it goes to press. Truthfulness—always an effective defense against libel—has been the main criterion for deciding what makes headlines and what ends up in the wastebasket.

Meanwhile, an increasing percentage of their celebrity stories have taken an upbeat, positive note. Consequently, even if a story isn't totally accurate, it isn't defamatory. (Even so, actor Tom Selleck once threatened *Globe* with legal action over a story that was downright flattering.)

Historically, only the smaller papers have really been hurt by libel suits. Johnny Carson's victory in his suit against the *National Insider* was one of a series of financial blows that preceded the collapse of Allied News Company in the mid-1970s, and a barrage of celebrity lawsuits wiped out Paul Azzaria's reincarnation of *News Extra* in the early 1990s.

But not all the combined libel suits ever filed against the tabs in courts of law represented nearly as great a potential threat to their long-term future as what happened in the so-called court of public opinion after the horrendous accident that killed Princess Diana.

*   *   *

The happening in question has been described as "the most vociferous backlash" in the history of tabloidism. No pictures of mutilated corpses or "MOM BOILS BABY" headlines had ever generated such a firestorm of public outrage and disgust against the tabs as their supposed role in Princess Di's death.

At long last, it seemed, the tabs had finally committed the unpardonable sin.

By shelling out the megabucks that motivated the paparazzi to stalk, spy on, entrap, and even physically attack famous people around the world, strident voices shouted, the supermarket papers and their editors were nothing more than accessories to murder. As the outcry reached lynch-mob volume, some of Hollywood's biggest names eagerly joined in to feed the flames.

Film star George Clooney vowed to "spend every free moment" making it easier for celebrities to sue for libel. He compared the tabloids to drug pushers, demanded they be boycotted, and blasted the legal requirement that public figures who accuse the media of libel must prove "malicious intent."

"I wonder how you sleep at night," he railed at two hundred media representatives attending a news conference. "You should be ashamed."

Clooney was hardly alone. Tom Cruise, Sylvester Stallone, and Fran Drescher also launched bitter verbal attacks on the tabs. Nationally syndicated gossip columnist Liz Smith reported that "three of Hollywood's top stars" were spending "millions" to hire private investigators to dig out "every possible unsavory fact" about *Enquirer* editor Steve Coz, *Star* editor Phil Bunton, and *Globe* editor Tony Frost.

Coz, for one, was alarmed enough to hit the TV talk show circuit in an effort to defuse what he perceived to be a ticking bomb. He told viewers of NBC's *Meet the Press*, ABC's *This Week*, and CNN's *Reliable Sources* how the

Enquirer had been offered photos taken at the crash scene for $250,000 and turned them down. He talked about the paper's new "anti-stalkarazzi" policy of refusing to purchase any pictures obtained through physical harassment.

"There's a difference between observing celebrities and hunting them down," said Coz, who had written an Op-Ed piece for the *New York Times* a few months earlier deploring *Globe*'s "entrapment" of Frank Gifford. He worried aloud that the paparazzi's aggressive tactics would turn the reading public against the tabs. "We didn't want to be smeared in that backlash," he said, "and unfortunately, that's what's happening."

But his paper's recent behavior gave his claims of newfound respectability a hollow ring and made his pleas for understanding sound self-serving, if not cynical. On the very night Diana died, the *Enquirer* issue then on display in supermarkets across the country carried perhaps the most provocative cover headline any tab had ever run on her:

DI GOES SEX MAD
"I CAN'T GET ENOUGH!"

In response to widespread protests, the issue was quickly pulled from the racks after the fatal crash. Coz published an apology for the headline in the following week's paper, and all the major tabs offered lavish, laudatory tributes to the dead princess.

"We'll miss you!" said the cover of *Globe*'s sixty-four-page commemorative issue.

"A FAREWELL TO THE PRINCESS WE ALL LOVED," proclaimed the banner on the *Enquirer*'s cover.

Globe's Frost called Diana "a wonderful person."

It was all very sweet, but it also may have been too late for meaningful amends. George Clooney was unimpressed with what he labeled Coz's "scramble for high ground," and Frost got little or no sympathy when he complained: "The celebs are ganging up on us. They're trying to capitalize on Princess Diana's death for their own ends."

How long-lasting is the bad taste left by the tabs' duplicity in the Diana tragedy? How deep the distrust? How real the revulsion?

Nearly three years later, no one can say for sure. But talk of boycotts and retribution has died away. Tabloid circulation hasn't dropped sharply, yet it continues to decline—except when some new revelation about Diana emerges.

The greater impact on future tabloid sales may grow out of the void left behind by her death, rather than lingering resentment over the tactics used to get pictures of her and stories about her when she was alive.

From her virginal beginnings as Prince Charles's shy fiancée to her last wild flings with Dodi, Diana was ideal fodder for the tabs. No woman since

Jackie O better personified that almost-mystical heroine/fallen angel dichotomy that tabloid readers find so irresistible. None has been a more reliable meal ticket for tabloid editors.

Globe was right. They will sorely miss her.

FIFTEEN
HORRORS!
TABS OUTSLEAZED BY MAINSTREAM MEDIA

On the weekend in June 1969 when the death of Mary Jo Kopechne in Ted Kennedy's car touched off the second-biggest sex-related scandal of the century, the story was almost lost in the hoopla of what was deemed a far more noteworthy event. In virtually every daily newspaper in the country, the Ted and Mary Jo story was overshadowed by coverage of the first successful moon landing by U.S. astronauts.

It's utterly impossible to imagine the same thing happening today. Despite its massive historical significance, Neil Armstrong's "one giant leap for mankind" would now at least have to share top billing with Ted's calamitous misadventure and its steamy overtones. If you don't believe it, ask Bill Clinton.

When news of the tragedy at Chappaquiddick first broke, of course, almost no one realized its far-reaching implications. Only a handful of the toughest-minded observers grasped the future political impact of what had just happened. But the main reason the story wasn't covered more thoroughly, more aggressively—and more sensationally—was the prevailing mindset of the mainstream press of the period.

Any reporter with half a brain could sense something fishy going on, even before Ted started waffling and changing his story. But editors and publishers of the serious school of journalism shied away in droves from the broad evidence of scandal. After that initial weekend, the story got considerable front-page space and TV air time, but the media generally continued to treat its more explosive aspects with kid gloves.

Maybe they held back out of sympathy for a family that had already lost two sons to martyrdom. Maybe they thought digging into the "juicy details" was beneath their dignity as "family newspapers." Maybe they simply slipped into the same "let's act like we don't see it, and hope it'll go away" mode that had characterized the establishment press for three decades or more.

Whatever it was, it gave the sensationalists a golden opportunity for some gritty, gutsy reporting, and they jumped at it—especially the *Enquirer*.

Gene Pope immediately dispatched several staffers and freelancers to Chappaquiddick to dig into every facet of the story. Acting on direct orders from Pope, articles editor Joe Cassidy rented the very cottage where Senator Kennedy and his campaign workers had partied on the night of the fatal accident. Cassidy combed every inch of the place for clues, while a photographer shot pictures from every angle. Other reporters prowled around Martha's Vineyard, seeking out eyewitnesses and police investigators. Their numbers fell well short of the teams of fifteen to twenty people routinely sent out by the *Enquirer* on major stories later, but no other U.S. news-gathering organization was better represented at the time. One of their biggest finds was the scuba diver who pulled Mary Jo's body from Kennedy's submerged Oldsmobile and told of finding an air pocket inside the car that could have kept her alive for some time after the accident.

The next few issues of the *Enquirer* had the story splashed across their covers and featured a series of major articles and dozens of photos inside. One of the more provocative pieces was headlined: "I COULD HAVE SAVED MARY JO IF I HAD BEEN CALLED IMMEDIATELY, DIVER SAYS." Overall, it was the best, most resourceful job of reporting Pope's paper had done up to that point, and it set the stage for more to come.

In those pre-Watergate days, mainstream coverage of ugly stories involving high government officials ranged from bland to nonexistent. If readers wanted the real scoop on a would-be future president's peccadilloes with a moonstruck young female volunteer in his campaign, they had to get it from sources like the *Enquirer*. If they wanted to read suggestive speculation about who really killed JFK and what women he entertained on the sly in the White House while Jackie was away, they found it in the tabs, not the *New York Times*.

By the time of the Gary Hart–Donna Rice exposé, the mainstream had grown much bolder and more adversarial in its coverage of public officials. But even then, the dailies were reluctant to go for the jugular. Rice's visits to Hart's Washington apartment were documented by mainstream reporters, but it was the *Enquirer*'s sizzling *Monkey Business* photos that applied the coup de grâce.

"When it published the infamous photograph of . . . Hart with Donna Rice sitting on his lap," observed *Talk* magazine writer Jonathan Mahler, "the [*Enquirer*] not only ruined Hart's political career, it ensured that the competition for scandal reporting would be much stiffer."

By the time "Monicagate" erupted just over a decade later, the situation was vastly different. The dailies and network TV went after the story like starving dogs after raw meat. By the time they finished devouring it, smothering it, regurgitating it every day for weeks, and rolling in the kinkiest, most explicit details of it, the tabs were basically left with nothing to add.

Within the space of ten years, everything had changed. The hunger for dirt and the thirst for scandal that fueled the tabs' immense popularity in the 1970s and 1980s had spread like a virus through every level of "serious" journalism. Today's mainstream media revels in sex scandals, shamelessly employs innuendo and unnamed sources to create titillating "news," and eagerly presents explicit, detailed articles on oral sex and other timely topics.

The decidedly upscale magazine *Vanity Fair* ran a lengthy article in its February 1999 issue titled "The Tabloid Decade," examining the rise of vulgar, down-and-dirty journalism during the 1990s. In it, writer David Kamp referred to a comment by take-it-to-the-edge film director John Waters, who talked about how the tabloids have been outflanked for the first time by their "straight" competitors.

"My sense is that [the tabs] hate the Monica story because they've been robbed of it," Waters said. "They feel gypped. It should be theirs and it's everyone's."

In an August 1999 article on "Tabloid Law" in *Atlantic Monthly*, writer Alex Beam also referred to the "creeping tabloidism" affecting major dailies. "[A]s I wandered around Los Angeles interviewing lawyers," he wrote, "it was hard not to notice Monica Lewinsky's picture on the front page of the *Los Angeles Times* every day. . . . A few weeks before, the *New York Times* had printed a front-page story on Lewinsky's state of mind, attributed to 'a friend'—the classic tabloid formula."

In other words—horrors!—the tabs were being decisively beaten at their own game. They were being outsleazed by the mainstream media.

Why? Because the mainstreamers had finally figured out that's what the public wants.

As *Vanity Fair* summed it up: "The tabloidification of American life—of the news, of the culture, yea, of human behavior—is such a sweeping phenomenon that it can't be dismissed as merely a jokey footnote to the history of the 1990s. Rather, it's the very hallmark of our times . . . the years when America reveled . . . in 'going where the stink is.' "

* * *

Monicagate wasn't the first time the mainstreamers had invaded tabloid territory—far from it—but this time it was on a larger scale than ever before. And no other long-running scandal better illustrates the inherent weaknesses and built-in limitations of the supermarket papers in trying to cope with such invasions.

Obviously, since the tabs come out just once a week, they have trouble keeping pace with developing stories in which new revelations are constantly emerging. Dailies, on the other hand, have seven opportunities each week to hit the high spots. Meanwhile, TV networks can preempt regular programs with the latest snippets at any time, or simply suspend regular programming entirely; Internet news sites offer minute-by-minute updates; and, of course, the news is always on on CNN.

In an attempt to counteract the speed and omnipresence of the electronic media, daily newspapers have come to specialize in providing endless details. Instead of running a main article and a couple of sidebars as they once did, the dailies now routinely devote page after page to major stories, often with dozens of articles and photos covering every conceivable angle. Events like the slaughter at Columbine High School or the plane crash that killed JFK Jr. and his wife and sister-in-law often merit entire special sections. It's called overkill.

Even if the tabs could come up with enough material that wouldn't turn stale by the time it hit the stands, they don't have the space to do this. In their heyday, the *Enquirer* and *Star* frequently published sixty-four-page issues, but now they almost never contain more than forty-eight pages. Besides, concentrating on the kind of exhaustively detailed coverage served up by the dailies would violate two time-honored rules of tabloid editors: (1) Keep even the hottest stories short and snappy, and (2) offer a wide variety of subject matter in every regular issue. These are inescapable tenets of a tabloid philosophy that always places entertainment value ahead of pure information.

"For traditional tabloid readers, even a story about Monica threatening suicide gets too long after twelve hundred words or so," says one veteran of editing stints at the *Examiner*, *Sun*, and *Tattler*. "Our readers like to get in, get the dirt, and get on to something else."

Longtime *Enquirer* staffer and former *Examiner* editor Bill Burt once put it this way: "Tabloids are supposed to be for fun. They're supposed to be fascinating. Regular newspapers act like they've got a sacred duty to put people to sleep, but tabloids provide an alternative. When you don't want to be bored, you turn to a tabloid."

But during the late 1990s, the ability of mainstream papers to run column after column of congressional testimony, legal depositions, and taped interviews spiced with the juiciest, most sexually explicit details (and run them long before the tabloids could) sometimes left the tabs with nowhere to go.

Because of their esteemed position in society, respected papers like the *New York Times* could publish the grossest of four-letter words with no apparent concern about public reaction. In its September 12, 1998, edition, at the height of Monicagate, the *Times* ran the word "fuck" for the first time in its history in an excerpt from the transcript of the Linda Tripp tapes. A few weeks later, *Time*, the patriarch of U.S. newsmagazines, included an assortment of obscene slang in a Clinton-Lewinsky story about—what else?—oral sex.

These are words no supermarket tab would dare to print, even in today's libertine, anything-goes environment. Clearly, the risk of being tossed out by major chains, at least temporarily, is simply too great for low-brow publications already tainted by their real or imagined pasts.

"There's some stuff that's amazing in [the *Time* article]," said *Enquirer* editor Steve Coz. "Extremely racy stuff. Stuff you'd never find in a tabloid."

In other words, as *Globe* editor Tony Frost added, "We're being out-tabloided by the mainstream press."

*   *   *

Along with the logistics, practicalities, and lingering stigmas that handicap today's supermarket tabs, there are more subtle, less obvious reasons for their inability to capitalize on stories of the magnitude of Monicagate.

The fact that it involved a sitting president of the United States made the Clinton-Lewinsky affair unique from every other illicit celebrity romance in modern history. Other presidents had been tarnished by personal scandal, even accused of sexual improprieties. But always before, the charges had been delivered with winks and whispers. In Clinton's case, they were shouted from the rooftops, the halls of Congress, and every newsstand and TV set in the country. Make that the world.

Special prosecutor Kenneth Starr's investigation and the ensuing impeachment hearings in Congress legitimatized the whole mess as a news story in a way that such goings-on had never been legitimatized before. The tons of documents generated by the investigation and hearings also allowed the public to eavesdrop on the most wickedly intimate encounters between the president and the young White House intern.

The revelations were as raunchy as any of the free porn advertised on the Internet, but this was important stuff, history in the making. It was all legal and authentic—and oh, so *official*. People could almost con themselves into believing it was un-American *not* to read every engrossing detail.

In a very real sense, the Bill and Monica story was simply too all-encompassing and its implications too potentially earthshaking for the tabs to react adequately. And with the mainstream media beating the story to death day by day and hour by hour, it may actually have become a turnoff to the traditional tabloid audience.

"Ironically, when the mud really starts to fly," noted *Talk* magazine's

Mahler, "the *Enquirer* is limited by the demographics of its readership; the women in middle America who tend to buy the paper while grocery shopping don't necessarily want to read what President Bill Clinton did to his twenty-two-year-old mistress with his cigar."

One fact was certain. Bill and Monica did nothing to boost tabloid sales. In the six months after the scandal broke, the *Enquirer*, *Star*, and *Globe* all reported double-digit losses in circulation (18.8, 14.4, and 18.9 percent, respectively).

Early on, the tabs followed the saga closely and broke a number of major stories. Then, when it became apparent that readers weren't responding, they all backed off for a while. "People seemed a little tired of it," said *Enquirer* executive editor David Perel, adding that many tabloid readers were upset by what they considered "undue attacks" on the president.

"The tabloids are reflecting the ambivalence of their readers," media critic William Powers observed in the *National Journal*. "The tabs embody a rather traditional middle-class morality and hate nothing more than hypocrisy. This would seem to make Clinton-Lewinsky a ripe subject, but as long as a lot of Americans are unclear on the moral verdict in this case, the tabs will be testing the wind."

In the late summer of 1998, the wind shifted again. *Globe*'s covers stuck stubbornly to Hollywood fluff ("LEONARDO DECAPRIO'S SECRET LIFE"), "world exclusives" on the JonBenet case, and the latest trash on Frank and Kathie Lee. But the *Enquirer* and *Star* decided Bill and Monica was too big to ignore, and they started nipping at the fringes of it again.

As Perel explained: "As the story started to heat up before Clinton's nonapology, public interest grew, and we increased the scope of our coverage and the manpower we were putting on it."

But the unhappy truth was, political subjects didn't sell. Personal dirt on political figures sold just fine, but politics itself was an anathema to tabloid readers. Former *Enquirer* editor Iain Calder had hit the nail on the head several years earlier when he said: "If politics had sold, we would've broken more stories than the *Washington Post* and the *New York Times* combined."

The idea was to try to steer clear of the monstrous political implications on which the mainstream was now fixated in the Clinton crisis and do what the tabs had always done best—get personal. So, in its September 22, 1998, issue, the *Enquirer* zeroed in on Lewinsky's supposed guilt and heartbreak while scrupulously avoiding any mention of the impeachment trial then raging in the House of Representatives.

"MONICA SUICIDE DRAMA," screeched a headline spread across three-quarters of the cover. "'Tell Bill I'm sorry—I've destroyed the man I love.'"

The double-page story inside was a fanciful classic straight out of the old Jackie O mold. Its only sources were several unnamed "friends" and an anonymous "Washington insider," all of them eager to tell the world about

Lewinsky's humiliation, emotional torment, binge eating, and threats to kill herself.

"No question the story was concocted out of thin air to get some mileage out of a couple of unhappy-looking agency photos of Monica," said one longtime tabloid editor. "It was hokum from start to finish."

The only authentic statement in the whole piece was one sentence from Monica's father, Bernard Lewinsky, who was quoted as saying, "You go crazy sitting in a room, no matter how big the room is." The quote was buried near the end of the story—understandably so, since it had been published weeks earlier in the *Los Angeles Times*.

The results came nowhere near Jackie O proportions, however. Sales of the issue were flat. So were sales for the four out of six issues of the *Star* in August and September 1998 that featured cover stories on Monica and Bill. "We didn't get quite as many breaks [on the story] as we would've liked," admitted the *Star*'s Phil Bunton.

But if it was any consolation, the end of the shabbiest chapter in the history of U.S. politics was at least finally in sight. When the impeachment trial ended and the dust began to settle, tens of millions of Americans breathed a collective sigh of relief. But no one—except possibly Clinton himself—was happier than the supermarket sensationalists to lay the scandal of the century to rest.

It was time to get back to "business as usual." The problem was, nobody in tabloidland was quite sure what that meant anymore.

∗　　∗　　∗

Until the 1990s, the tabs seldom, if ever, had cause to worry about what the rest of the media was doing. They operated in what *Newsweek* has called "a kind of parallel universe" where mainstreamers never ventured, covering and creating stories that the mainstream wouldn't touch with a ten-foot pole—and amassing gargantuan profits in the process. There was no over-lapping of styles or subject matter. The tabs had the unspeakable, the unthinkable, the unimaginable, and the ultrabizarre all to themselves.

To a great extent, this is why the twenty years between the late 1960s and late 1980s represented a golden era for the supermarket papers. They snarled and bristled, leered and insinuated, lied and connived, raked muck and moralized—and, except for an occasional blast of derision, the main-stream basically pretended they didn't exist.

The rest of the media docilely accepted the pablum pumped out by the Hollywood publicity machines and left the scandal mongering exclusively to the tabs. Nobody else bothered digging out dirt (much less making it up) on who was sleeping with whom, which matinee idols were the sub-ject of gay rumors, what big-name stars were doping or boozing excessively, or which leading man had slugged his costar. Such stuff didn't qualify as legitimate news, and it was beneath mainstream dignity to pursue it.

Likewise, there was no room in the establishment press or on network TV for idiots who claimed they'd been kidnapped by space aliens or come back from the dead. Daily editors put no credence in psychic predictions, wacky inventions, or secret conspiracies to assassinate government leaders. They thought stories and pictures of deformed people were in hopelessly bad taste, even if the subject happened to be an armless artist who painted flawless portraits with his feet. And if they'd ever seen a two-headed baby, they would've screamed in unison and hidden under their desks.

Sex in all forms was taboo. One large afternoon daily in the Southwest maintained an absolute ban on the word "rape" and demanded that staffers substitute the term "criminal assault" in all references to forced sex. The ban lasted until the day a police reporter filed a rape story in which the victim was quoted as screaming, "Help! Help! I've been criminally assaulted!"

Even at the tail-end of the 1980s, there were no strong indications of what lay just ahead. President George Bush was talking about a "kinder, gentler" America. Historian Arthur Schlesinger Jr. sensed "a lot of pent-up idealism" lurking in the populace. Others looked ahead to the 1990s as a time when the "Me Generation" would clean up its act and discover it had a conscience, after all.

Then the Soviet Union collapsed, the threat of nuclear annihilation faded for the first time since the 1940s, and people started looking for other things to get excited about. Relieved of the great overriding concerns of two generations, the American public turned bloodthirsty, shock-happy, sex-crazed, and downright infantile in its approach to news. And suddenly, it seemed, the Tabloid Decade was changing everything. The taboos turned to dust. Nothing was sacrosanct anymore. The tabs' "parallel universe" vanished in the mainstream's mad stampede to embrace the sensational.

In the fall of 1998, *Newsweek* writer Richard Turner visited Tabloid Valley in south Florida and included the following vignette in an article titled "A Tabloid Shocker":

> Hanging on the wall of editor Steve Coz's office at the *National Enquirer* is a makeshift poster featuring four magazine covers. There's a recent *People* offering up "Men Behaving Badly," about celebrities who cheat on their wives; *Time's* "The Roswell Files," about UFOs; *Newsweek's* "We're Having a Baby," picturing gay musician Melissa Etheridge and her lover. And finally, the oft-scorned *Enquirer* itself, with Bill Cosby, JonBenet Ramsey, and other stories. Above all this is the headline WHICH ONE IS THE TABLOID?

To a great extent, they all are. No doubt *People*, *Time*, and *Newsweek* would vociferously disagree, but it's essentially true. The turf on which the tabs once frolicked, disdained but unchallenged, is now everybody's playing field.

As *U.S. News & World Report* columnist John Leo had noted about a year earlier: "[W]e live in a very competitive, tabloidy world now. Editors who used to look down their noses at the *National Enquirer* know that if they ignore some prurient story, their readers will see it on *Hard Copy* or *Dateline*, perhaps even on the network news, and once again think that the print media are hopelessly old fashioned."

As a result, the tabs' "parallel universe" is long gone—and the tabloids as we know them may not be far behind.

SIXTEEN
TABS IN THE TWENTY-FIRST CENTURY
CAN THE DINOSAUR BE SAVED?

During the long reign of Pope Gene I, *Enquirer* staffers used to joke (very surreptitiously) about some of their boss's more eccentric words and actions. Some of these legendary "Popeisms" have already been recounted in these pages, but none offers greater insight into the man's twisted thought patterns and unpredictable personality than one from early 1970.

Buoyed by Pope's oft-demonstrated fondness for animal stories and his approval of several recent pieces on man-made threats to wildlife, an articles editor suggested a story on efforts by preservationists to save the whooping crane and other endangered creatures. To the AE's surprise, Pope shot down the idea with far more vehemence than usual. On the bottom of the lead sheet accompanying the story material, next to his trademark turndown ("NG" for "no good") Pope had scrawled an angry red-ink notation: "What the hell do I care about whooping cranes? Who ever did anything to save the dinosaur?"

The articles editor blanched noticeably as he read the rejection, realizing from its tone just how close he might've come to being an extinct species himself. Plenty of people had been axed for offenses that were just as innocent and inadvertent, so the culprit quickly alerted his colleagues that, from now on, whooping crane stories should be considered a giant no-no.

In the months that followed, "Save the dinosaur" became a classic catchphrase in shrugging off Pope's weirdities and illogic. It was repeated hundreds of times when writers and editors congregated after work to unwind. It appeared in the form of occasional hand-lettered signs, anony-

217

mous bulletin board memos, and notes passed back and forth between office cubicles.

You had to actually know GP to fully appreciate this phenomenon, but to *Enquirer* staffers, those three little words captured the essence of the bizarre reasoning that each of them had to cope with—and try to survive—every day. They were the ultimate example of the incongruity, insecurity, and occasional insanity in which these people lived and worked.

Today, ironically, the paper to which Pope devoted his life and others of its genre are in danger of becoming dinosaurs themselves. During an age when the rest of the media may have cared too much about form and propriety, and when readers were less cynical and more easily shocked, the tabloids thrived like nothing else in print. But as a new century begins, they've begun to look more and more like hapless creatures from another time, threshing around desperately for attention, but sinking ever closer to extinction.

Herculean efforts are being made to save them, but unless something dramatic happens to alter their present course, the whooping cranes will probably still be happily nesting and laying their eggs long after the tabs are history.

As this is written, the supermarket papers have been losing circulation, profitability, and influence for the better part of two decades. Mostly, their year-to-year sales decline has been gradual, and on an issue-to-issue basis, it could even seem negligible and not worth worrying about. It's never been quite dramatic enough to set off hysteria among the executives who run the tabs or the several hundred editorial and production employees who continue to earn lavish salaries working for them. But the decline has also been dishearteningly steady and continuous, broken by only the briefest of upswings—an ominous sign that the trend may well be irreversible.

In terms of sheer size, the *Enquirer*'s loss has been the greatest by far—more than 3.4 million copies per week since its circulation peaked at around 5.4 million in the late 1970s. After a dip to 4.6 million in 1981, average weekly sales jumped back to 5.1 million in 1982, when Pope's paper ranked second in circulation only to *TV Guide* among U.S. weekly periodicals. But, as of mid-2000, sales had slipped to less than 2 million—a drop of more than 60 percent over an eighteen-year period.

Within that same time frame, the *Star*'s circulation fell from 3.9 million to 1.7 million—a loss of just over 55 percent. *Globe*, meanwhile, has suffered the smallest numerical decline but the greatest percentage loss among the top three tabs. Between 1982 and 2000, its sales fell by a full two-thirds, from 2.1 million copies to about 700,000.

Among the smaller papers, the story is much the same. *National Examiner* sales are also down more than 60 percent, from a high of 1.1 million to less than 400,000. *Weekly World News* once sold almost a million copies a week but has dropped to about 350,000, and the *Sun* has gone from about 500,000 sales at its apex to about 200,000 at present.

You don't have to be a mathematical genius to see where these figures are leading. If the trend continues at the same rate, the supermarket papers' circulation base—and the papers themselves—will have vanished totally by 2018, if not earlier.

As of late 1999, for the first time in their checkered history, the fate and future of all six existing tabs rested in the hands of one man. David Pecker, president, chief executive officer, and chief operating officer of American Media, Inc., is the man in the hot seat. For obvious reasons, he refuses to accept gloomy scenarios about the tabloids' future.

"There are 4,700 magazines published in the United States, and only 100 sell over 100,000 copies," Pecker said confidently. "We have six of them." His words came shortly after the new owners of American Media had spent $942 million to gain a tabloid monopoly in North America and put Pecker in charge of it.

What he didn't bother to point out was that, among them, these six publications had lost a total of close to 8 million in circulation since 1982. He also didn't mention that for eighteen years nobody had been able to stop their decline, much less turn them around.

Can David Pecker, a guy with a slick-magazine background and no previous tabloid experience, succeed in doing what Gene Pope, Rupert Murdoch, Mike Rosenbloom, Iain Calder, Steve Coz, Phil Bunton, Tony Frost, John Vader, and so many others couldn't?

Throughout south Florida's Tabloid Valley, inquiring minds want to know the answer to this all-important question, but most veteran media watchers and tabloid industry insiders say it's still too early to tell.

Meanwhile, for the tabs, it just keeps getting later.

＊　　＊　　＊

After MacFadden Holdings bought the *Enquirer* and *Star* in 1989, the new owners' first concern was improving the bottom line, and they were generally successful in accomplishing this. American Media, Inc., was soon established as a subsidiary of MacFadden Publishing, and according to published reports, the company's cash flow—defined as earnings before interest, taxes, depreciation, and amortization expenses—rose from $18 million in 1989 to $96 million in fiscal 1999.

Part of the improvement resulted from vigorous cost cutting, such as getting rid of Pope's annual Christmas tree and other expensive whims. Another major factor was a hefty increase in tabloid cover prices, from an average of 69 cents in 1989 to $1.49 in 1999. (They were raised again, to $1.69, in early 2000, and Pecker reportedly thinks they can go as high as

$1.99 without negatively impacting circulation.) Part of the gain also resulted from the introduction of new nontabloid titles including *Country Weekly* and *Soap Opera News*. Advertising revenues also showed a slight increase, although not nearly as much as American Media had hoped. Significantly, however, none of the cash-flow improvement resulted from increased tabloid sales.

After a largely unsuccessful ten-year struggle to sign up automakers, food manufacturers, and other mainstream national advertisers, coupled with a continuing decline in readership, the price of MacFadden's stock turned stagnant. The parent company decided it was time to cut its losses by bowing out of the tabloid business and putting American Media on the block.

The sale was announced in mid-February 1999 but not finalized until May. This time the buyer was a heavyweight investment group known as Evercore Partners, which paid a reported $832 million in cash and assumed debt to acquire American Media and the *Enquirer, Star, Weekly World News*, and *Country Weekly* (established in 1994).

It's worth noting that the price paid by Evercore Partners for four publications was barely $20 million more than the $812 million MacFadden had paid for just three publications a decade earlier. Allowing for inflation during that ten-year span, the 1999 price was actually lower, in terms of real dollars, than the 1989 price. At best, MacFadden hadn't even broken even on the deal, but at least it was out from under a massive debt load. It was also freed of the burden of three supermarket papers that appeared to be headed nowhere but down.

The sale involved several intriguing ironies. One of the two principals in Evercore Partners was investment banker Austin Beutner, who'd represented Pope's estate when MacFadden bought the *Enquirer* at auction. The other partner in Evercore was Roger Altman, husband of Lynda "Wonder Woman" Carter and a former deputy U.S. Treasury secretary, who'd been indicted and acquitted of criminal fraud in 1993 in connection with a major bank failure.

Then there was Pecker, who'd represented Hachette Filipacchi Magazines, one of the unsuccessful bidders at the *Enquirer* auction in 1989. On the day the Evercore deal was announced, Pecker quit his job as CEO of Hachette Filipacchi and signed on to be the new tabloid king of south Florida, motivated in part by an undisclosed equity stake in the new operation. Possibly in anticipation of the move, he and his wife had recently bought a house in Florida.

Pecker had already proved himself adept at garnering favorable publicity when he'd teamed with John F. Kennedy Jr. in 1994 to launch the sophisticated inside-Washington magazine *George*. The mainstream media quickly made *George* one of its darlings, but it's never come close to turning a profit, and following the death of JFK Jr. in 1999, speculation grew among media watchers that the magazine's days were numbered.

Almost immediately after assuming his new post, Pecker committed $50 million to an advertising campaign to beef up sales of the *Enquirer* and *Star* and carry out expensive makeovers of the two papers by a team of design experts, aimed at sharpening their images and nurturing separate identities for them. (At the time, it had been less than two years since another multimillion-dollar effort to create a "new look" for both papers.)

Later, Pecker boasted of "refocusing" the *Enquirer* newsroom and "repackaging" the *Star* as a people-oriented magazine. After years of blood-sport rivalry, even while they were under the same ownership, he persuaded the editors of the two papers to start sharing information with each other.

Meanwhile, though, the slide in sales continued. In its first quarter after its purchase by Evercore, American Media reported an 8 percent decrease in revenue and a $5.2 million loss.

Then, in November 1999—either to solidify its position or dig itself into a deeper hole, depending on your point of view—American Media announced a $105 million deal to buy *Globe, Examiner,* and *Sun* from Globe Communications, thus gaining control of every supermarket paper in the country.

"ALIENS TAKE OVER THE TABLOIDS," piped the headline in *Time*'s press section.

"A THREE-HEADED MONSTER IS BORN," added south Florida's *Sun-Sentinel* newspaper.

The most imperative question now was whether the monopolistic offspring of this unlikely union would gobble up new readers or merely feed on itself.

*   *   *

In media interviews following the Globe Communications buyout, Pecker claimed he had the logistics of the situation all worked out. Instead of competing head-to-head for the hottest stories—and sometimes running near-duplicate headlines—as they had in the past, each of the three frontline papers (the *Enquirer, Star,* and *Globe*) would focus on a different aspect of the story.

"If there's a Hollywood scandal, the investigative portion will be done by the *National Enquirer*," Pecker said. "The impact on celebrities, on their careers, that will be done by the *Star*."

As for *Globe*, which *Time* called "the naughtiest and most ethically challenged of the big three," Pecker promised it would "absolutely not" repeat a stunt like the Frank Gifford sex setup but would continue to emphasize "spice and controversy" in its coverage. "It's going to really be, shall I say, the unvarnished story [in *Globe*]," he explained.

He even outlined plans for the company's two bottom-rung tabs, although neither contained any actual reportage. *Weekly World News*, Pecker said, would be "all fictional" and "very, very funny," while the *Sun* would concentrate on stories of the paranormal and the supernatural. In other words, it was just more of the same. Only the *Examiner*, which had traditionally fallen somewhere in between the "big three" and the "bottom two," wasn't placed in a specific cubbyhole.

For the three top-selling tabs, this kind of positioning made sense because it aimed at eliminating duplication. But it had a definite downside, too, because it attempted to place a tight rein on the freewheeling, competitive pursuit of hot stories that had always characterized tabloid reporting.

In their assessments of how well such orchestration would work—especially with all six tabs to be produced under the same roof, as Pecker was planning—case-hardened old tabloidists ranged from dubious to cynical.

"You look at the covers of the tabs for any week this year [2000], and you'll see there's no overlapping of subjects and no two front pages have anything about the same people," said one veteran tabloid editor. "You can't tell your staffs, 'You guys over here are gonna work on this, and you guys over there are gonna ignore it and work on something else'—not if you expect them to use their initiative to go after the big stories. Pretty soon, everything starts getting stuck in little niches, and your coverage gets all ho-hum and predictable."

The temptation to dole out subjects and restrict competition between papers represented a "clear danger" in the tabloids' current environment, according to former *Enquirer* editor Iain Calder.

"There still should be guys kicking and fighting each other for the big stories," Calder said. "We kept that kind of rivalry going for years after the *Enquirer* and *Star* were under the same ownership. It's like two brothers playing tennis against each other when each one's determined to win. That competitive spirit doesn't have to be lost in this situation, but there's a definite risk that it could be."

The *Enquirer*, in particular, has already come under fire from critics for resorting to weak, watered-down celebrity stories instead of giving its readers the sharply barbed sensationalism of the old days. In a September 1999 commentary piece for the Internet's "MediAnatomy" Web site, writer G. Beato characterized the paper's celebrity coverage as "complacent" and "boring."

"These days . . . the *Enquirer* is more likely to be cross-promoting with the enemy than cross-examining it," Beato said. "In every issue now, B-list celebrities looking for a scandal-free plug are photographed holding a copy of the magazine while professing their love for the 'new' *Enquirer*."

Beato recalled an old story about how Generoso Pope used to keep a large chart in the newsroom showing how many stories each *Enquirer* reporter was filing each month, and how those in the bottom third of the rankings were often summarily fired. "It was a Draconian policy, but at least it gave the *Enquirer* a focus it seems to have since lost," he concluded.

In Pecker's view, as expressed in an interview with *Time*, the main reason tabloid sales took a 35 percent nosedive between 1994 and 1999 was that they were "competing against each other" and too often featuring the same stories. The question is, can noncompeting publications continue to have competitive, tough-minded, energetic reporters?

Some say yes. *Time* quoted one tab reporter as boasting: "We compete with everybody. The gap [between the tabs and the mainstream] has closed."

Others say no.

"You can't tie your reporters' hands and expect them to do their jobs," says a thirty-year veteran of the tabloid wars. "At some point, you've got to decide if you want to be a tabloid or a damned fan magazine. If you want to be a tabloid, you've got to find fresh, provocative material instead of just stretching out threadbare stories like Frank Gifford and the JonBenet Ramsey case to the point of nausea. You've also got to have people who are willing to get out and scrap for stuff that has sizzle."

At the moment, the jury's still out.

✳   ✳   ✳

On the surface, Pecker appears to have little in common with Pope and the other old-time tabloid czars he replaced. But from all reports, he *has* tried to emulate them in at least once respect—by ruling his new domain with an iron fist.

From the editors in chief of his three top publications on down, Pecker has made it abundantly clear that no one at any level in the organization— repeat, *no one*—speaks for American Media but David Pecker himself. Violators are subject to swift, no-quarter retribution. (For this reason, no current employees of American Media are quoted by name in this book concerning anything pertaining to current company matters or the status of any of its publications, although several such employees have granted interviews and supplied vital information to the author.)

Insiders say Pecker's "gag order" has made life especially difficult for Steve Coz, whose Harvard background and pronouncements about "respectability" have given him a high profile with the media since he took over the editorship of the *Enquirer* in 1995. In 1998, Coz's critical comments about *Globe's* flagrant Frank Gifford sex setup were widely quoted in the national press, and he even authored a *New York Times* Op-Ed piece on the subject.

In 1997, Coz was rumored to be a leading candidate for the editorship of the *New York Daily News*, the nation's oldest and largest daily tabloid, but he remained at the *Enquirer* (to the disappointment of his own mother, who stated publicly that her son "deserved better"). If his enforced silence has made Coz unhappy enough to consider leaving again, it's apparently also kept him from saying anything about it to his associates.

Globe's previously outspoken Tony Frost has also kept his lip tightly buttoned since becoming part of the American Media "family." Some colleagues think he may eventually return to London, where he was a tabloid fixture before coming to the States. But Frost's stock seemed to rise sharply in the spring of 2000, and the fact that he recently bought a $380,000 house in a gated upscale community indicate he plans to stay in Florida for a while.

To the dismay of many, it was the *Star*'s relatively low-key Phil Bunton who became the first top editorial executive to arouse Pecker to termination-level wrath. Some half-joking remarks Bunton made to reporters in February 2000, after learning the *Star*'s offices in Tarrytown, New York, would be closed and its staff moved to Tabloid Valley to be with everybody else, eventually cost him his job.

"It's going to be open warfare," Bunton quipped. "How we're all going to work together, I don't know. It's like putting the Bosnians, Croats, Jews, and Arabs all together in the same area. We've spent the last thirty years or more hating each other's guts, and now we're going to be sharing the same cafeteria and day-care center."

When he saw Bunton's comments in print, Pecker reportedly went ballistic. Some office rumors had him jerking up the phone and firing Bunton on the spot by long-distance, while other accounts had the crisis brewing for several weeks before it came to a head. At any rate, by late April 2000, Bunton's name had vanished from the *Star*'s masthead along with most of the rest of his New York staff.

Everyone in the *Star*'s seventy-member Tarrytown editorial department had supposedly been offered the opportunity to relocate to Florida with all moving expenses paid by American Media. But when the transfer came, in early April 2000, only ten people elected to make the move. Insiders say Pecker's anger and Bunton's shaky situation played a big part in many of the other sixty staffers' decision to stay behind.

"They knew Phil was in deep shit with Pecker, and nobody felt secure about coming down," said one insider. "Most of them felt like they'd be better off in the long run looking for jobs close to home than moving nearly two thousand miles away and then getting the sack."

It was a sobering moment for everyone in the organization and a stunning illustration of how mercurial Pecker's temper could be.

"Anyone who knew Bunton could tell he was just kidding around, and nothing he said really caused any harm," the insider said. "But I guess Pecker was looking for someone to make an example of, and Phil was it."

After Bunton's ouster, Frost assumed the title of editor in chief of the *Star*, in addition to holding the same position with *Globe* and *Examiner*. As of mid-2000, the Star was still operating with a skeleton editorial staff.

Meanwhile, by most accounts, Pecker's relationship with rank-and-file employees has also been less than cordial.

"David Pecker is set on making Boca Raton the scandal-sheet capital of the world—but he's rubbing workers the wrong way," wrote Jose Lambiet, a columnist for the daily *Sun-Sentinel* of south Florida, in February 2000. "Pecker, whose arrival as the head of *National Enquirer*, *Globe*, and *Star* is being accompanied by the firings or pending firings of 30 people, hit the roof recently after someone keyed the driver's door of his '99 black convertible Corvette."

Touching up the key scratch cost Pecker $110, but he wasn't without personal transportation, Lambiet noted, since he owned "a half-dozen other sets of wheels, including a Benz, Porsche, Bentley, and a Rolls."

Lambiet said Pecker thought the vandalism may have had something to do with his dismissal of eighteen *Globe* production employees. "We're doing our best to make this place better, but there are disgruntled people wherever you go," he quoted Pecker as saying.

Because of the incident, rank-and-filers were barred from the company parking garage and required to park outside. Pecker also revealed to Lambiet that one of the first things he'd done after arriving in Florida was to take out a concealed weapons permit. "I'm not carrying at work," he told the columnist, "but I've been an NRA member for twenty-five years."

Tabloid journalists have long been notorious for applying less-than-flattering nicknames to their superiors when they were sure the bosses weren't listening. "Pope Gene" and the "Pope of Lantana" come immediately to mind, but there were many others. Early-day *Enquirer* editor Nat Chrzan was often referred to derisively as "the Gnat." His successor, Iain Calder, was known as "the Ice Man" because of his cool demeanor. To many of his coworkers, John Vader was "Darth." *Globe* owner Mike Rosenbloom was invariably "Rosie"; the Sorrentinos of Allied News were "da Wops," and an eccentric editor at the *National Tattler* of the early 1970s was known so universally as "Colonel Crackers" that none of his former minions can remember his real name.

The new titan of the tabloids could hardly expect to be treated any differently—especially with a name like David Pecker.

"Sure, guys have been calling him 'Pecker Head' from day one," said a longtime *Globe* employee a few weeks after Pecker arrived. "He's got lots of people around here edgy as hell, if not downright scared, and calling him names behind his back is just a reflex action, a defense mechanism, I guess."

In fairness, however, many other employees have been supportive of Pecker—or at least of his efforts to reenergize the tired tabloids he commands. "Things are pretty chaotic at this point, and the whole organization's in a state of flux," said one. "But Pecker's doing everything he can to get it all straightened out, and I think we've got to give him a chance. I mean, face it, he's the best shot any of us has right now."

Pecker, who was forty-eight when he took charge at American Media, has frequently been described as "dapper." He's also been called egocentric, aloof, arrogant—and every bit as inaccessible as Pope Gene ever was.

"We almost never see him over here [at *Enquirer* headquarters in Lantana]," said one editor. "He spends all his time in the presidential suite over in Boca, playing big shot and listening to people tell him how great he is."

After the Globe Communications deal was consummated, Pecker reportedly offered Mike Rosenbloom continued use of a fancy office on the third floor of the old Globe Communications headquarters in Boca Raton. But when Rosenbloom actually started occupying the office, Pecker allegedly changed his mind and demanded the key back. As one source put it: "Pecker likes to be the only big cheese around, so he told Rosie to bug off."

"From everything I can tell, Pecker's pretty much of an egotist," observed John Vader, some four months after Pecker's ascension to the throne of tabloidland. "What else could you think of someone who runs a picture of himself with JFK Jr. after John-John was killed?"

Outwardly, Pecker appears undeterred by the sniping and name-calling. In his public appearances, he exudes confidence and seems fully focused on the mammoth tasks at hand. He talks matter-of-factly about spending up to $1 billion to turn his company into one of the giants of U.S. periodical publishing.

"American Media is not a large publishing company, compared with a Time-Warner," he said shortly after the Globe buyout. "To grow, we have to grow in categories."

He announced far-reaching plans to add a Spanish-language version of the *Enquirer*—tentatively titled *Mira!*—and a car magazine called *Auto World Weekly*. Other growth categories mentioned by Pecker include more online and e-commerce ventures and more one-shot special editions on top celebrities. He also promised further acquisitions of existing magazine titles.

"We're going to get on an acquisition binge," he said in February 2000. But by late in the year, there were no signs of that happening. On the contrary, several of *Globe*'s old titles had been dropped, including a long-running line of detective magazines and *Cracked*, a *Mad* magazine imitation.

Pecker emphatically denied persistent rumors that some of the existing tabs would be combined and that large-scale personnel cuts were in the offing. Instead, he announced plans to increase the overall number of employees by about one hundred. Approximately half the newcomers were designated as staff replacements for the *Star*, with the other half to fill specific needs on other publications.

In mid-January 2000, major daily newspapers around the country carried classified help-wanted ads headlined: "REPORTERS —The *National Enquirer* wants you!"

The body of the ads read, in part:

America's largest circulation paper is seeking hard-working, talented reporters. Daily newspaper or TV experience preferred. If you think we're reporting on two-headed babies and space aliens, don't bother applying! But if you've got what it takes to break the biggest stories in the entertainment industry and the world, send us your résumé and clips.

Indications are that Pecker hasn't fared very well in adding top-caliber journalists, however. To fill personnel gaps, a number of former *Enquirer* and *Globe* employees—some of them retired and some previously fired—have accepted temporary jobs at $200 per day, according to insiders.

"From what I hear, Pecker's squeezing everybody just about as hard as they can be squeezed, and close to 100 percent of his people are unhappy," said a former *Enquirer* writer who's stayed in close contact with more than a dozen current employees. "They aren't offering the high across-the-board salaries they used to offer, and working conditions are pretty miserable."

✳   ✳   ✳

Meanwhile, Pecker isn't likely to win any popularity contests among the citizens and community leaders of Lantana, Florida, either.

When Pope moved the *Enquirer* to Lantana in 1971, it was a nondescript hamlet of a few hundred people sandwiched between Lake Worth and Boynton Beach, and there was virtually nothing else there. Except for the *Enquirer's* foliage-shrouded headquarters and a row of upscale condominiums that have sprouted along the Intercoastal, the town remains a basically drab, uninteresting place. For thirty years, the presence of America's largest supermarket tabloid has given Lantana by far its biggest employer, as well as its solitary tourist attraction.

But hard on the heels of the *Globe* acquisition, Pecker announced his intention to move American Media's entire operation to Globe Communications' former headquarters in Boca Raton as soon as the 63,000-square-foot building could be expanded. The 7.5-acre *Enquirer* site, with its lush tropical gardens and campus-style office structure, was promptly put up for sale.

As this is written, one potential deal for the property has reportedly fallen through, and nothing else appears imminent. Because of its size and location, some observers feel it could be years before a buyer is found, but Pecker has shown no signs of backing off from his consolidation plans.

In the interim, the staffs of the *Enquirer, Weekly World News,* and *Sun*—comprising about half of American Media's total of approximately four hundred editorial and production employees—have continued to work at the Lantana site. *Globe* and *Examiner,* meanwhile, have remained in Boca Raton, where they've been joined by the relocated *Star.*

"Lantana will never be the same again when the *Enquirer's* gone," said a longtime staffer who lives in an oceanfront condo a few blocks from the old headquarters site. "And I'll never be the same, either. I won't be able to walk to work any more."

* * *

Where, then, do the supermarket papers go from here? Will the faltering dinosaur be able to survive in anything resembling its present form? Will it have to evolve into a different species to adapt to the demands of a new century? Or is it doomed to vanish into the mists of time, regardless of what it does?

In a physical sense, the tabloids have already become much more like magazines than papers over the past two decades. Their current page size ($9\frac{1}{2}$ by $11\frac{1}{2}$ inches) is only two-thirds what it was in the 1970s and just a tad larger than the most recent incarnation of *Life* magazine. The securely stapled pages are printed in full color on semislick paper that bears no resemblance to the dingy newsprint of the old days.

Cover up the nameplates of the *Enquirer* and *Star*, and it's next to impossible to tell them apart. Yet the *Enquirer* still refers to itself as a "paper" (as in its new cover slogan, "Find out why we're the best-selling paper in America!"), while the *Star* consistently calls itself a "magazine."

So what are they—"papers" or "magazines"? Fish or fowl? On the surface, the answer may not seem to matter much. But within the whole context of the tabloids' growing identity crisis, it *does* matter. It matters a lot. If you're unsure yourself about who or what you are, how can you recognize your audience—much less reach out to it?

The traditional readership that powered the rise of the supermarket tabs is dying off. Demographic studies conducted during the 1970s showed the typical tabloid buyer to be a moderate-income woman between the ages of forty-five and fifty-five. Assuming she's still alive, that same woman is in her seventies or eighties today. There's a good chance she doesn't do her own grocery shopping anymore, and she may also be living on old-age benefits and not have $1.69 to spare most weeks. Most importantly, though, she's probably not nearly as interested in Kevin Spacey as she was in Richard Burton or in Vince Gill as she was in Elvis Presley.

Many of those stereotypical readers of the 1970s now have daughters roughly the same age as their mothers were then, but the daughters aren't nearly as likely to buy a supermarket tabloid. Fewer women in their forties today are regular consumers of any kind of print media, studies show, and are far more likely to turn to electronic sources for their entertainment (cable TV was a rarity in the 1970s, and the Internet was unknown).

To compound the tabs' identity crisis, the defining lines between "mainstream" and "tabloid" have become blurred as never before in journalistic history. "Mainstream" once meant legitimate news, and "tabloid" once meant sensationalism, but today these definitions no longer work.

Joseph Angotti, former senior vice president of NBC News and currently a journalism professor at the University of Miami, summed it up this way: "It used to be that news organizations wanted to keep those [identifying] lines very defined. But now, as the result of entertainment values entering the news business, and a critical attention to ratings, there's little difference between the local news, network news, and *Entertainment Tonight*. News media of all sorts are sliding toward infotainment."

In the morally constrained atmosphere of thirty or forty years ago, the tabs were seductive, romantic, and packed with implied cheap thrills. But in today's media market, other formats ranging from Jerry Springer to *Cosmopolitan* leave nothing to the imagination. If it has anything to do with sex, it's totally explicit, and everything has a name.

And now, with the mainstream media invading the tabloids' once-separate universe, people like Pecker and Coz are doggedly steering the tabloids closer and closer to the mainstream. They preach reform and respectability. They say they want to erase the old stigmas and change the public's perception of their publications. They court powerful national advertisers whose influence could further impede the tabs' ability to deal with unsavory subjects. In the process, they further blur the lines that separate them from the rest of the media. They erode—and risk losing—their own identity.

"The twain has met," said Bob Abborino, who worked for all the major tabloid organizations in their heydays, "and when the other guys make up their minds to go after a story, there's no way the tabs can keep up with them."

*   *   *

As media watchers have often pointed out in recent years, the tabloids are the only class of periodicals that make their money almost entirely from individual copy sales. At last count, advertising revenues accounted for only about 8 percent of their income. For most magazines, that's barely a drop in the bucket.

In order to sell, a tabloid first has to turn a preoccupied shopper standing in a checkout line into a "looker." This is the whole point of screaming headlines, arresting photos, and provocative themes. But then—and this is the crucial part—the tab has to transform the "looker" into a buyer willing to pay $1.69 plus tax to find out more about what's on the cover.

Statistics show this is where today's tabloids are failing. Only one out of every eight people who pick up a tabloid to look at it ends up taking it home. If that figure could be increased to one in four, circulation would be right back where it was in the first half of the 1980s.

Otherwise, some attrition in the tabloid ranks is almost certain in the near future. "Despite Pecker's assurances to the contrary, a lot of people think at least one of the titles is going to have to go," said an American Media insider, "and it could just as easily be one of the 'big three' as one of the second-tier papers."

If the tabs as a genre are to survive much beyond the next decade, many observers agree, they have to find a way to redistance themselves from the mainstream, reclaim their separate universe, and reinvent themselves one more time.

"I'm not thrilled with the direction they're taking, and I doubt if they'll ever be as big as they once were, but tabloids will be around in some form for a long time," said Iain Calder. "They need to quit relying so heavily on celebrities and take a more varied and balanced approach. They need to make people say 'gee whiz' more often."

"Just going back to some of the things the old *Enquirer* used to do in the '70s would be a step in the right direction," said Bob Abborino. "That stuff really sold, and nobody else in the country's doing it today."

"Satisfying people's curiosity is what the tabloids have been all about," said John Vader. "If they die off, some other form of voyeuristic journalism will take their place. But maybe when Clinton's out of the spotlight, the mainstream will go back to more serious stuff and leave the voyeurism to the tabs again."

"Letting you get away from the pressures and problems of your own personal rat race," added another old-timer, "that's what the tabloids used to do for their readers. If they can find a way to do it again, they'll be okay."

From this perspective, space aliens and two-headed babies—possibly even an occasional grave robbing or Bigfoot sighting—may not be such a bad idea, after all. The market for such stuff is still there, but the message is missing the mark. Of late, the tabloid message has gotten so off-target, in fact, that it's become an integral part of the problem. Instead of giving readers a respite from reality, the tabs too often join the rest of the media in rubbing their noses in it.

Lois Pope, the philanthropic widow of the founder of the *Enquirer*, was once asked by an interviewer if she thought her husband would be proud of the influence his tabloid had had on modern news reporting. With a note of sorrow in her voice, she replied:

> This was never his intention. He just wanted to make people happy and provide escapism for about forty-five minutes. Now we watch twenty-four hours a day of the O. J. Simpson trial and . . . the Princess Diana tragedy. It becomes part of our everyday lives, and there's no difference between what we're reading and what we're living. Art is imitating life, and life is imitating art. We are living in a tabloid world.

Paradoxically, we may also soon be living in a world without tabloids.

But even if the supermarket papers as we know them go the way of the Tyrannosaurus rex, the breed of sensationalists that spawned them and made them a cultural force in twentieth century America will likely live on.

Both society and the media have changed immeasurably since the days of Hearst and Pulitzer. Yet the shadowy underside of journalism, where fact and fantasy mingle and mate, where nothing is forbidden, and where thrills and shudders are the only measure of success, has been around even longer. Chances are, it will always be there, waiting for another opportunity to weave its seductive spell, whether its medium of the moment is newsprint or cyberspace.

And there'll always be a subset of readers or viewers eager to respond— if the message is right.

APPENDIX
CHRONOLOGY OF TABLOIDS

1919
America's first successful daily tabloid, the *New York Daily News*, is founded by Joseph M. Patterson and Col. Robert R. McCormick and immediately begins breaking all previous newspaper circulation records.

1924
William Randolph Hearst launches the tabloid *New York Mirror* and Bernarr MacFadden establishes the *New York Evening Graphic* to try to capitalize on the runaway success of the *Daily News*.

1926
Hearst bankrolls a new weekly paper called the *New York Enquirer*, which he uses primarily to test new ideas for his dailies.

1952
The struggling *New York Enquirer*, long since abandoned by Hearst and with a circulation of just 17,000, is purchased for a reputed $75,000 by Generoso Pope Jr.

1954
Pope changes the name of his paper to the *National Enquirer*, converts it from a broadsheet to a tabloid, and makes gruesome, gory crime stories its number one specialty.

Joe Azaria and John Vader publish the first issue of a sensational local tabloid in Montreal, naming their paper *Midnight*.

1957–1960   The *Enquirer* gradually widens its circulation territory outside the New York area, as Pope strives to make it a true "national" publication. Sales of the paper soar to around 250,000 weekly. Meanwhile, *Midnight* expands from its base in Montreal to other Canadian cities and picks up its first U.S. distributors.

1961   *Midnight* cofounder Joe Azaria, now its sole owner, buys the name rights to three defunct Boston-based tabloids—*Spotlight, Close-Up,* and *Examiner.* The first two are published off and on with little success, but Azaria adds the word "National" to the *Examiner's* name, and it evolves into a major moneymaker.

1962   Joseph Sorrentino, owner of Allied News Company, a Chicago periodical distributor, begins publishing the *National Insider,* a shoddy imitation of the *Enquirer.*

1963   Vince Sorrentino, Joseph's nephew, starts a rival sheet called the *National Informer;* instead of gore, it concentrates on kinky sexual themes.

1964   Allied News launches the *National Tattler,* an almost-identical copy of its *National Insider.*

1966   Joseph Sorrentino adds a third tabloid, the sexually charged *Candid Press,* to his growing stable of tabloids.

1967–1968   With the *Enquirer's* circulation now approaching a million copies per week, Generoso Pope issues a stunning edict to his staff that will profoundly change the paper's image: No more gore! Pope's goal: To gain entry into the nation's supermarket for a new, "squeaky clean" *Enquirer.*

1969   Continuing to exercise his "more is better" philosophy, Joseph Sorrentino starts yet another Allied News tabloid and christens it the *National Exploiter.*

1970   Joe Azaria sells Globe Communications, publisher of *Midnight* and the *National Examiner,* to company accountant Michael Rosenbloom for a reported $4 million. Rosenbloom takes immediate steps to tone down *Midnight* to make it "supermarketable." John Vader remains as *Midnight's* editor.

1971   Joseph Sorrentino retires, turning over the management of Allied News to his sons, Robert and Frank. Robert assumes the titles of editor and publisher of the *National Tattler* and begins a campaign to clean up the paper and get it into the chain stores.

Pope relocates the *Enquirer* from New Jersey to the small town of Lantana in South Florida, setting the stage for what will become known as "Tabloid Valley."

1972   Robert Sorrentino upgrades the *Tattler's* editorial staff and changes the name of the *National Exploiter* to *National News Extra*.

1973   Allied News shuts down its scurrilous *Candid Press*, changes its name to *Candid Viewer*, and turns it into a daytime TV paper. In less than a year, *Candid Viewer* is also scrapped.

1974   After a massive TV ad campaign, Rupert Murdoch's *National Star* makes its debut as the most formidable rival yet to the *Enquirer's* dominance in the supermarket tabloid field.

Vince Sorrentino of Chicago begins publishing a clean "family" tabloid called *Modern People*. In striving to gain supermarket acceptance for the new paper, he is soon forced to discontinue his oversexed *National Informer*.

1974–1975   Allied's *National News Extra* evolves into the first of a new breed of satirically outlandish tabloids aimed at appealing to young, campy readers in addition to a traditional "lunatic fringe" audience.

1975   After a decade as an *Enquirer* staffer, Scotsman Iain Calder is named by Pope as editor in chief of the 5-million-circulation tabloid and president of its parent company.

Drew Herbert wrests control of Allied News Company from the Sorrentino family. Allied's *Tattler* becomes the first supermarket tab to feature a full-color cover.

1976   Allied News declares bankruptcy and permanently closes its doors. The *National Tattler, National Insider,* and *National News Extra* cease publication.

1977–1978   All three top-of-the-line tabs—the *Enquirer, Star,* and *Midnight*—go to a full-color format. *Modern People* ceases publication.

1978   *Midnight's* name is changed by Mike Rosenbloom, first to *Midnight Globe*, then simply to *Globe*.

A cover photo of Elvis in his coffin sends the sale of that *Enquirer* issue to an all-time high of nearly 7 million copies —a figure that no supermarket paper will ever duplicate.

1979 Drawing liberally from the format of the now-deceased *National News Extra*, Pope launches *Weekly World News* as a companion publication to the *Enquirer*.

1982 Fueled by the *Enquirer's* "Enquiring minds" ad campaign, total combined weekly circulation of the supermarket tabs hits a peak of about 12.5 million, with total readership calculated as high as 43 million per week.

1982 Globe Communications joins the *Enquirer* in Florida's Tabloid Valley, moving its headquarters from Montreal to Boca Raton—and firing virtually its entire Montreal editorial staff in the process.

1983 The *Sun*, another *News Extra* knock-off, is introduced by Globe Communications. John Vader becomes its editor.

1988 Generoso Pope dies of a sudden heart attack. His will specifies that the *Enquirer* be sold to the highest bidder in a "blind" auction.

1989 The *Enquirer* is purchased for $412 million by MacFadden Holdings, which, almost simultaneously, also acquires Murdoch's *Star* for another $400 million. MacFadden establishes American Media, Inc., as a subsidiary to manage its new acquisitions.

1993 Mike Rosenbloom rejects a vigorous bid by British media magnate Robert Maxwell to buy *Globe*, *Examiner*, and the *Sun* for a reported $300 million.

1995 Harvard-educated Steve Coz succeeds Iain Calder as editor of the *Enquirer*. The paper gains widespread recognition for its "serious" coverage of the O. J. Simpson trial. Globe's John Vader also retires.

1997 Princess Diana dies in an auto crash in Paris while being pursued by a small army of tabloid journalists. An international backlash against the tabs accelerates the supermarket papers' downward circulation spiral.

1999 American Media, Inc., along with the *Enquirer*, *Star*, *Weekly World News*, and other properties, is sold by MacFadden to an investment group known as Evercore Partners for a reported $832 million. David Pecker becomes president and CEO of American Media.

American Media also acquires *Globe, Examiner,* and the *Sun* from Mike Rosenbloom's Globe Communications for an additional $105 million, bringing all six of the surviving tabs under a single ownership.

SELECTED BIBLIOGRAPHY

BOOKS

Bernard, George. *Inside the National Enquirer: Confessions of an Undercover Reporter*. Port Washington, N.Y.: Ashley Books, 1977.

Bird, S. Elizabeth. *For Enquiring Minds: A Cultural Study of Supermarket Tabloids*. Knoxville: University of Tennessee Press, 1992.

Emery, Edwin, and Michael Emery. *The Press and America: An Interpretative History of the Mass Media*. 4th edition. Englewood Cliffs, N.J.: Prentice-Hall, 1978.

Hogshire, Jim. *Grossed-Out Surgeon Vomits Inside Patient! An Insider's Look at Supermarket Tabloids*. Venice, Calif.: Feral House, 1997.

Katz, Leonard. *Uncle Frank*. New York: Pocket Books, 1975.

MacFadden, Mary, and Emile Gauvreau. *Dumbbells and Carrot Strips, The Story of Bernarr MacFadden*. New York: Henry Holt, 1953.

Shawcross, William. *Murdoch*. New York: Simon & Schuster, 1993.

Swanberg, W. A. *Citizen Hearst*. New York: Charles Scribner's Sons, 1961.

——— . *Pulitzer*. New York: Charles Scribner's Sons, 1967.

Taylor, S. J. *Shock! Horror! The Tabloids in Action*. London: Transworld Publishers, 1991.

Tuccille, Jerome. *Rupert Murdoch*. New York: Donald I. Fine, 1989.

PERIODICALS

Alter, Jonathan. "In The Time Of The Tabs." *Newsweek*. June 2, 1997.

Blackburn, Tom. "Murdoch: The Man with the Worldwide Audience." *Palm Beach Post*. May 16, 1993.

Colford, Paul D. "Times Are Juicy, but Not for Tabloids." *Newsday*. September 21, 1998.

Coz, Steve. "When Tabloids Cross the Line." *New York Times*. May 29, 1997.

Engstrom, John. "Tabloid Fever!!" *Chicago Tribune Magazine*. June 3, 1984.

Finotti, John. "Secrets of the Tabloid King." *Florida Trend, The Magazine of Florida Business*. March 2000.

Fisk, Margaret Cronin. " 'People to People' Journalism Promoted by Tabloid." *Editor & Publisher*. September 15, 1973.

"From Worse to Bad." *Newsweek*. September 8, 1969.

Fulbright, Newton H. "Sex on Shelf, *National Enquirer* Goes after Supermarket Shoppers." *Editor & Publisher*. August 23, 1969.

"Generoso P. Pope Jr. Dead at 61; *The National Enquirer*'s Publisher." *New York Times*. October 3, 1988.

"Goodbye to Gore." *Time*. February 21, 1972.

Jones, Tim. "Inquiring Inside." *Chicago Tribune*. June 28, 1998.

Kamp, David. "The Tabloid Decade." *Vanity Fair*. February 1999.

Kelly, Keith J. "Checkout Champs; Investors Buy Enquirer, Star for $767M." *New York Post*. February 17, 1999.

Lanouette, William J. "Tabs Cut Out Gore and Stomp on It." *National Observer*. June 9, 1973.

Leiby, Richard. "Aliens Invade West Palm Beach." *Sunshine, The Magazine of South Florida*. November 27, 1983.

Mahler, Jonathan. "The *National Enquirer*'s Thwarted Heir Lashes Out." *Talk*. December 1999/January 2000.

McGrory, Brian. "Tabloid Power! Simpson Case a Turning Point for the Papers." *Boston Globe*. November 15, 1995.

Noah, Timothy, Elise Ackerman, and Jason Vest. "All Steve Coz Wants Is a Little R-E-S-P-E-C-T." *U.S. News & World Report*. September 15, 1997.

Peer, Elizabeth, and William Schmidt. "The *Enquirer*: Up from Smut." *Newsweek*. April 21, 1975.

Potterton, Reginald. "I Cut Out Her Heart & Stomped on It." *Playboy*. April 1969.

Reid, Paul. " 'Enquirer' Heir Forced Off Father's Path?" *Palm Beach Post*. May 14, 2000.

Schardt, Arlie. "Hollywood's Stars vs. the *Enquirer*." *Newsweek*. December 8, 1980.

Smilgis, Martha. "In Florida: The Rogues of Tabloid Valley." *Time*. August 15, 1988.

Smith, Stephanie. "American Media Aims to be Major Force." *Palm Beach Post.* February 17, 2000.

———. " 'Star' to Share Boca Building with 'Enquirer,' 'Globe.' " *Palm Beach Post.* March 15, 2000.

Turner, Richard. "A Tabloid Shocker." *Newsweek.* October 12, 1998.

Wilkinson, Peter. "The Trash Man." *US.* February 1998.

AUTHOR INTERVIEWS

Abborino, Robert, former *Enquirer, Globe, Examiner,* and *Star* staff writer and former *Tattler* articles editor. March 2000.

Ayres, Tom, former *Midnight* staff writer and former assistant managing editor and editor at Allied News Company. February 2000.

Bates, William, former *Enquirer* photo editor. February, March 2000.

Calder, Iain, former *Enquirer* articles editor, editor, and president. March 2000.

Giambalvo, Barney, former *Enquirer* production employee. February 2000.

Merle, Dominick, former *Enquirer* and *Midnight* staff writer. May 1999.

Lutz, Byron, former *Enquirer* reporter. March 2000.

Lutz, Tom, former Allied News Company executive editor. June 2000.

Powell, Constance, former *Tattler* staff writer. June 2000.

Stowers, Carlton, *People Weekly* correspondent. April 1999.

Tabatch, Jack, former Globe Communications circulation director. April 2000.

Vader, John, former editor and cofounder of *Midnight* and former *Examiner* and *Sun* editor. March 2000.

INDEX